'Terri has an encyclopaedic knowledge of fo[...]
for skin is palpable. In *Skinformation* she dem[...]
of cosmetics while providing clear and un[...]
gorgeous skin.'

**Sigourney Cantelo, founder of Beauticate and
former beauty and health director of *Vogue Australia*.**

'Terri Vinson has a rich history in skin care. In this book her knowledge as a cosmetic chemist of ingredients and skin science shines through, offering the reader a very readable and well illustrated guide, full of insightful information and interesting fun facts. I found the use of product labeling as a consumer guide particularly ingenious. Potentially difficult subjects for the consumers such as epigenetics, skin anatomy, sustainability, debunking myths and extolling strengths were elegantly simplified and explained. I have had a long and imbibing history in skin care for many decades but still found myself learning.'

**Associate Professor Greg Goodman, renowned dermatologist,
director of Script Skin Care technologies**

A CLEAN SCIENCE
GUIDE TO BEAUTIFUL SKIN

skinformation

TERRI VINSON
COSMETIC CHEMIST

WILEY

First published in 2021 by John Wiley & Sons Australia, Ltd
42 McDougall St, Milton Qld 4064

Office also in Melbourne

Typeset in Utopia Std Regular 9.5/15pt

ISBN: 978-0-730-38522-6

A catalogue record for this book is available from the National Library of Australia

Cover design by Wiley

Cover and internal images: © artcasta/Shutterstock, Prostock-studio/Shutterstock

Printed in Singapore by Markono Print Media Pte Ltd

10 9 8 7 6 5 4 3 2 1

Disclaimer
The material in this publication is of the nature of general comment only, and does not represent professional advice. It is not intended to provide specific guidance for particular circumstances and it should not be relied on as the basis for any decision to take action or not take action on any matter which it covers. Readers should obtain professional advice where appropriate, before making any such decision. To the maximum extent permitted by law, the author and publisher disclaim all responsibility and liability to any person, arising directly or indirectly from any person taking or not taking action based on the information in this publication.

Contents

About the author

Terri Vinson is a renowned Australian cosmetic chemist committed to educating men and women about the 'what' and 'why' of skin care ingredients so they can be empowered to make the best choices when it comes to their products.

She formulates only in accordance with her trademarked 'Clean Science' philosophy and is dedicated to creating safe and ethical cosmeceuticals aimed at protecting, changing, and nurturing the skin for long-term and optimal health.

Terri is considered an international expert in the aesthetics and beauty industry. She holds a Bachelor of Science, majoring in immunology and microbiology, a post-graduate Diploma of Formulating Chemistry, and a specialist Diploma of Education in biology and senior science. She is a world-recognised cosmeceutical formulator, lecturer, and medical conference speaker, making her highly sought after as an editorial writer in the cosmetic science field for numerous beauty publications. Terri is known for her ability to explain complex concepts in a simple and often entertaining manner. Her passion for ingredient technology is infectious and there is nothing she likes more than getting her audience excited about science!

When she hangs up her lab coat, you will find her painting oils on canvas, spending time with her partner and two adult kids, or in the kitchen concocting healthy recipes. As a self-confessed binge-watcher, she can always find a couple of hours to snuggle up in front of the latest streamed doco.

'As a woman in the second half of my life (eek), I believe in ageing with vitality, elegance and a great attitude. Ageing is a privilege, and with it comes wisdom and an inner confidence that should be embraced! In fact, we all have the right to look and feel our best at *every* age. So, let's get skin savvy, cut through the white noise and love our skin from the outside in!' – Terri

Acknowledgements

Writing this book was one of the biggest challenges and greatest joys of my life. It takes a village to write a book and that is certainly the case for me. So here is a big shout-out to those I love, respect and am so grateful to.

To my wonderful children James and Georgie: It has been my privilege to watch you both grow into adults who I both respect and often defer to. You have inspired me in so many ways to become a better version of myself. You also keep it real and still laugh at my over the top healthy recipes and tragic mum puns.

To my life partner Alan: Thank you for accepting my crazy quirks and nerdy rants, and for allowing me to be just Terri. Oh, and thanks for always making sure my glass was topped up while I was furiously working on my manuscript during our long-haul plane trips. You love and support me in all my endeavors, and I am so proud to have you by my side.

To my work family – and that is exactly what you are: Thank you for giving me those two-and-a-half hours every morning to work on this book without any interruptions. We all have our moments, but I know that you are always in my corner. A special thanks to P, my little buddy and general manager, who has seen me through both challenging times and incredible highs. You have been a great leader who continues to challenge my thinking in the best way possible. Most importantly, you are a loyal friend who gives the best hugs!

To my adoptive dad, Frank, who passed when I was just 22 but who I think of every day: You told me that women can be scientists and you gave me the confidence to pursue it. I hope I have made you proud.

Finally, to all those women and men whose lives I have touched with my formulations, it has been a privilege. We all have our calling in life, and helping people find their inner confidence through having healthy skin is mine. This book has been parked in my head for years and driving it to completion has given me such a sense of purpose knowing that if just one person benefits from reading it, then it was entirely worth it.

Preface: my story

It's funny—I'm so confident writing about almost anything in this book: skin, science, ingredients. But the 'why' of writing the book, and why I feel so passionate about what I do… that's the hard bit. It feels so intensely personal to me, so it's quite scary thinking of people reading about my journey in such detail. But I'm proud of how I got here… so here goes!

Discovering my inner confidence

My early years were filled with low self-esteem. I never quite felt like I fit in—a common story, but it impacted me significantly as a child. When I was 12 I discovered I was adopted. I don't remember being shocked or upset at the time. What I do remember is the feeling that my past now just had a black space… and that when I looked forward, there was a big spotlight that I could choose to step into. I knew with every fibre of my being that I was here to make a difference. I had no idea when, or how, but I knew that I would.

Despite the difficulties this reality presented for me growing up, I was given a lot of opportunity. I came from a lower middle-class home and my parents spent all their earnings ensuring I had a good education. My dad was a distinct source of support, always encouraging me to reach for anything I wanted. He was an incredible early feminist role model for me, which was rare to find in a male at that time. My mum did the best parenting she could at the time, but unfortunately she had no idea about nutrition. My diet consisted of processed food, refined sugar and coke. Fast-forward to the end of Year 8 and I was totally lacking confidence and straddling the awkward line between childhood and adolescence.

That summer holiday I began poring over *Dolly* magazines and applying makeup to my dolls. I convinced Mum to buy me a jar of Oil of Ulan and let me get my hair permed … eeek! But very '70s! I soon retired my doll to the cupboard and started using the makeup skills I had practised on my own face.

I was addicted to Monte Carlo biscuits and could down a whole packet along with a can of coke. I was looking decidedly 'pasty' and my congested skin was a good barometer of my overall health, so I decided to reduce my sugar intake.

In hindsight, I had so much to learn about nutrition. I came across a crazy diet called the Israeli Army Diet, and I spent just over two weeks eating apples, chicken, salad and cheese. OMG! My digestive system was in total distress and I would *never* recommend this diet, but I got over my addiction to sugar. I wish I had had access to the educational and professional advice available today. We're lucky there are so many great resources available for young girls to embark on healthy eating without crash dieting. To me it's about building a good relationship with food to create the healthiest version of you.

After finishing this horrendous 16 days of torture, I decided to look at food as my new friend and seek fresher options. My mum even stopped spending so much time in the sweet aisle.

When I returned to school in Year 9, one of the 'it' girls did a double take and exclaimed, 'Theresa, is that you?' (Theresa is my actual name but I was only ever called Theresa at school or when my mum was mad at me!) I was the same girl, but my skin was clearer, I looked healthy, my shoulders were back and I stood taller. I was wearing a new uniform: inner confidence! And everything changed from there.

I became more confident with my studies too. My dad believed in me and I was determined to make him proud. He was never one to say, 'only boys do science', so I focused on science and soon the results matched my passion. I remember drifting off to sleep in my final year of high school with the voice of my biology teacher in my ears, reciting notes on a cassette tape.

I had found my passion, and it didn't waver from then on.

Nurturing a love for teaching

I completed my science degree at Monash University, majoring in immunology and microbiology. I loved the learning environment and felt I was finally free to explore my love of science and the human body. I considered pursuing a research career when I came top of the class in my final-year immunology exam (yes, it sometimes pays to be a nerd), but I couldn't shake my second passion: people! I could never see myself in a research lab, poring over test tubes for the rest of my career life. I was 20 years old and needed a way to combine my love for science with my passion for people.

I decided to do a post-graduate diploma in teaching secondary school science. Following graduation, I taught at a Catholic girls' school for two years. Being in a school reminded me of the lack of self-confidence I'd experienced, and with a goal of helping the girls find inner confidence I started an after-school skincare and makeup course. A few months in, I mentioned to the principal that I had made a few hundred dollars from the course. I was told to stop the course immediately because the church had no place for entrepreneurs like me! A very different time! Disappointed that I had to stop, I began looking for a new career, but I never forgot how it felt to make a difference in those girls' lives. In the late '80s I began working for Colgate-Palmolive, where I gained a huge amount of business knowledge and really learned how to negotiate. After coming out of two almost entire female environments, it also taught me some valuable life lessons in discovering myself as a proud feminist in the early 90s.

Becoming a formulator

Getting married and starting a family meant putting my career on pause. But my entrepreneurial spirit remained strong!

At home I created essential oil-scented moisturisers and body oils and sold them at local fetes. When my friends at the gym vented to me about their dry skin, I would turn my kitchen into a 'mini lab' and create lotions for them. If I didn't have the ingredients, I would go to my local chemist and have them made up.

When my children started school I began working part-time for a skincare company and later gained a post-graduate qualification in formulating chemistry. Sometimes the greatest challenges present the biggest opportunities: my husband was retrenched twice in a short time frame and it hit the family hard. I knew it was my time to step up. I had saved some money from my part-time work over the years and decided to take a deep breath and open a skincare clinic at the age of 40.

I remember sitting in a café at Chadstone shopping centre waiting for my daughter to come out of a movie, as I wrote a list of what I could offer women. I was disillusioned that I couldn't find skincare products that actually worked, and frustrated with the white noise and false claims that so many skincare companies were making. There was no range that contained the ingredients at the dosage I wanted, and I couldn't find any products that had evidence-based science behind them! There were many ingredients in products I wanted to source for my own needs (in my case, anti-ageing) but reading the ingredient labels literally made me cringe. Plus it was a real challenge to find clean products for my kids' young skin. Even when it came to basic sun protection, the choices were limited. I decided the only way to find products that I'd be comfortable putting on their skin and mine was to make them myself.

I knew that skin was a highly absorbent surface but wasn't aware that the average woman absorbs over two kilograms of questionable and potentially toxic ingredients through her skin each year! After reading about the toxic load of personal care products on our bodies, I became determined to minimise my personal toxic load and pledged that what I didn't put in my products would be as important as what I did.

So I created products that used ingredients with a scientific basis, coupled with botanicals that really create change. I also created my list of 'no-no's': ingredients that I believed were questionable and could potentially cause harm. I hate fear mongering, so I didn't say these no-no's would cause instant harm to your body, but I was (and still am!) concerned about the ingredients that may accumulate in the body's tissues over time, and how this toxic build-up may negatively impact our bodies.

Opening Skinformation

There are very few female cosmetic chemists who truly understand the skincare needs of women, and I felt I knew what women like me needed. I'm also passionately Australian and was determined to make all my products on my own turf. Outsourcing to other countries took away both Aussie jobs and my quality control. Yes, I'm a control freak, and I'm constantly trying to keep that under control. Hah!… I just realised what I wrote!

I spent my savings renovating a little shop in Camberwell, Melbourne, that would become my clinic. I decided to call my clinic Skinformation, which is kind of a morph of 'transforming' the skin and 'informing' women about how to make their skin healthier. My book title is paying homage to where it all began.

I remember sitting at the bay window, overlooking the train station and praying for commuters to venture into my little clinic. In the first week of opening, waiting for a client to walk in the door, I thought, 'Whoa Terri. What were you thinking?' But soon, clients began to walk through my doors.

One morning a few weeks after opening, a woman walked in and quietly looked around reception, picking up makeup and skincare testers. She was very shy, and her shoulders were slumped. She was about to leave when I asked if I could help her. She said she didn't wear much makeup but was looking for something that would even out her skin and define her eyebrows. I looked closer and realised she had no eyebrows or lashes and was wearing a wig. This beautiful lady was suffering from a disorder called alopecia: she had lost all her hair. I asked her if she would let me give her a mini lesson on mineral makeup, and she nodded appreciatively. My clinic wasn't busy (I had so few clients in the beginning), so I spent over an hour showing her how to apply a natural foundation and blush, give her beautiful eyes more definition and create natural-looking brows with a taupe eye shadow and fine angle brush. I then gave her some samples so she could try the makeup at home.

I was a little anxious about her reaction to the final reveal, as not everyone is open to changing their look. She studied herself in the mirror for almost five minutes, then turned around, gave me a shy smile, politely said thank you and left. She stayed in my thoughts for the rest of the day. I kept wondering if she was happy with my advice and hoped I had been able to made a small difference to her day.

The following afternoon she returned looking like a different woman. She'd done a great job with the samples—but it was more than that. Her shoulders were back, her head was straight and she was beaming with confidence. She told me that yesterday had been her birthday and for the first time in years she felt so happy that she dressed up and went out with a friend to celebrate. All I had done was show her how to enhance her already beautiful features, but that inner surge of self-confidence really made a difference.

I knew I had found my calling.

A skincare range is born

In 2005 my clinic was going strong. I had formulated three products within the first six months of opening and then averaged a new product every three months. I employed a nurse to perform treatments while I worked on my formulations and did consultations with clients. These wonderful women provided me with opinions, feedback and inspiration that I still draw upon today for my products.

My skincare line grew a bit of a cult following in Camberwell, and soon one of my close friends asked if she could retail the small range in her clinic in Cairns. I had no idea about wholesaling and only felt comfortable selling at my clinic, but something inside me said, 'Let's do it!' Incidentally, she is still my dear friend and is my biggest account in North Queensland to this day! Thanks, Lisa P. ☺

When the GFC hit, many customers stopped coming to my clinic for treatments, but they would email me saying they couldn't afford *not* to have my products. This was truly my 'aha!' moment. Why was I running a skin clinic when I wasn't a beauty therapist or nurse? I was a scientist and I needed to channel my energy into what I was good at: creating skincare products that made a difference. It was then that I decided to close shop. I gave my client database away to a local skin clinic and my nurse set up her own skin therapy practice, which is still going strong today. I searched for a manufacturing facility where I could focus all of my energy on developing my own skincare and makeup products.

I found an empty warehouse in Burwood, Melbourne, and set out to transform the empty shell into a lab and space for invention. I took my loyal team of three with me: a bookkeeper, my warehouse supervisor and my operations manager. Two of these incredible women, Jess and Zoe, I'm proud to say, are still putting up with me to this day! From that moment everything started heading north. I knew I was doing what made my heart sing.

The beginning of Clean Science

Soon after this, I was in Vegas to present to cosmetic surgeons on skincare ingredients. I was standing in a corridor chatting to a colleague about my fundamental belief in skincare. 'What I do is just clean science,' I said. 'Wow, you should own that phrase!' she replied. Taking her advice, I emailed my IP lawyer asking if the phrase 'Clean Science' was available. The next morning she responded that, to her own surprise, it was. Bingo! I owned Clean Science, and from then on could use my Clean Science mantra for everything I created!

I went on to define Clean Science in more detail. To me, Clean Science is taking the best of laboratory science, and the best of 'natural' ingredients, and harnessing them together in synergy to create amazingly effective products without using anything that can potentially harm the skin or body.

Some people would ask, why aren't your products all natural? I would explain that, as a scientist, I believe that limiting your ingredient library to 100 per cent natural is not the best choice for getting the best results. Laboratory made and tested synthetic ingredients that are backed by science can really pack a punch when it comes to results. Yes, some synthetic ingredients can be toxic. But we need to remember that natural can also be harmful! Arsenic and lead are both natural, but high levels are fatal.

Clean Science means finding the best of both worlds. Formulating with the highest safety and ethical profile of each has always made the most sense to me!

Creating a vertically integrated business

My client base continued to grow from my production warehouse in Burwood, and I developed great relationships with some of the best cosmetic physicians, dermatologists, therapists and plastic surgeons in Australia. I also started growing my business overseas with a savvy and passionate client (and now dear friend) in Hong Kong. By listening to these people, I was able to understand what women wanted out of skincare and makeup. I also realised that my products and business needed to align with my values of transparency, communication, education and caring for our world.

One warehouse became two within the first three years. I said, 'Okay team, we'll be fine for another five years'. But warehouse number three opened two years later! Everything from product inception, sampling, full-scale manufacturing, filling, labelling, marketing and despatch was (and still is!) happening from that one location in Melbourne. I'm so proud of that. And last year I purchased a new larger scale manufacturing space in Melbourne, which my son describes as 'the aircraft hanger'. My team are so excited for our next chapter, which gives us so much room to grow.

I have a wonderful team who are dedicated to their roles; they truly are 'all in'. They take ownership and share my vision of making a difference in our own way. When I'm not feeling my best self I know that a few hours with my work family will get me back to a better place. We make each other laugh and feel safe together. They laugh when I say that hanging out at our team meetings is the highlight of my week! Tragic, but true!

I am so grateful that I can love what I do so much. I was a late bloomer at 40, but deep down I knew that one day I'd find what makes every cell in my body say *yes*!

Introduction

Strap in…You're about to go on a journey of skin discovery unlike any other. If you're serious about being armed with the facts about your skin health and vitality, then this book is for you.

I've become increasingly frustrated with the misinformation disseminated about instant skin fixes, companies that care about profit more than results and those ridiculous buzzwords created by marketing wordsmiths that sound oh so very sciency and convincing. And the word 'natural' in skincare—don't even get me started!

I think it's time to get the lowdown from a real scientist, and a proud female one at that.

I wrote *Skinformation* to be the go-to book for anyone who really wants to go 'skin deeper'.

If this book makes it to your bedside table, I'll be beside myself with joy! I really want this to be your bible for getting beyond the hype and looking at what really works. I want you to make informed choices about your skin with information provided by a cosmetic chemist with a true passion for skin.

The book is divided into two parts. Part I is for everyone. It's designed to give you all the facts and information you need to learn about your skin and its needs. This section is brimming with myth busts, geeky nerd-outs and plain, simple facts about skin, written in a straightforward and quirky manner—with the odd cheeky mum-pun ☺. I recommend you read this section from start to finish.

Part II is the 'dip-in' part of the book. It's where you'll find the answers to questions about any personal skin conditions or concerns you may have. It covers skincare from teens to menopause and beyond and looks at all those common areas that so many of us need more factual education on, such as cellulite, stretch marks and scarring.

I know for sure that you're never too old to make life-changing discoveries about yourself and what your true calling in life is. I was in my forties when a new journey began, and I gained a whole new level of identity and self-confidence that came from deep in my soul. To me, inner confidence will always be what makes us truly radiant. My aim in writing this book is to help to grow your inner confidence. I'm no psychologist, but I'm on a mission to teach women how to nurture themselves from the inside out and outside in. I hope that after reading *Skinformation* you'll feel truly confident in the skin you're in!

part I

Loving the skin you're in

Part I of this book should be read from start to finish to discover the truth about skin. You'll learn to familiarise yourself with how your skin functions, debunk common myths, understand the ingredient must-haves that we all need for skin health, demystify sunscreen facts and understand how to decode your skincare products.

My advice is not to skip a single page of part I. Our journey will take you so much further than what's offered by departments stores, hyped-up beauty blogs and unqualified opinion-givers. So buckle in for a ride of skin discovery!

chapter 1

What's the deal with skin?

What really blows me away about the skin is that, apart from being the largest organ of our body, it's constantly dealing with all the stuff that goes on both inside and out.

Internal factors include our blood (we have almost 18 kilometres of blood vessels), nutrients, hormones and chemical messengers, microorganisms, oxygen and waste products.

External or environmental factors include sunlight, pollution, heat, microbes, chemicals in the air, drugs, skincare products and oxygen.

Isn't our skin clever? It can deal with all this stuff at once plus keep us waterproof, protected and insulated. I have so much respect for this magical organ, which houses over 300 million skin cells and completely regenerates its surface roughly every four weeks. Amazing!

So here's what goes on inside our skin. For those of you who didn't get excited about biology at school (why?), please indulge me and check out this cool diagram: it's a cross-section of skin, showing how our skin is made of layers.

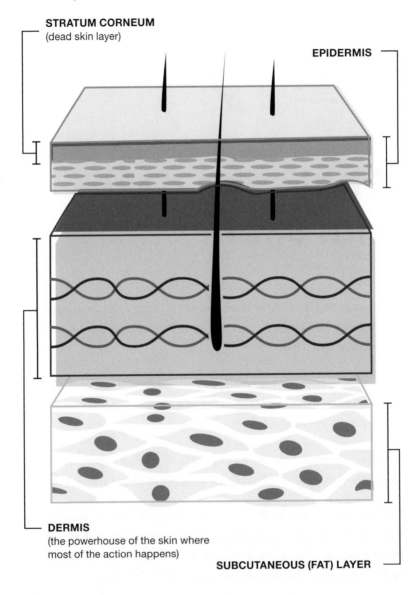

STRATUM CORNEUM
(dead skin layer)

EPIDERMIS

DERMIS
(the powerhouse of the skin where most of the action happens)

SUBCUTANEOUS (FAT) LAYER

The epidermis

This is the outer, visible layer. The surface of the skin (the fancy term is stratum corneum) is actually dead, but it's still very important because it's tough and keeps us protected from the outside nasties. It also keeps us waterproof so we don't turn into a swelled-up soggy mess in the shower! Plus it stops microbes from infecting our bodies. Think of the epidermis as the raincoat of the body, keeping the inside protected from outside aggressors.

It's important to mention that this protective layer makes it tricky for most ingredients, including many active cosmeceuticals (or ingredients), to enter the deeper layers of our skin where the magic happens.

The outside of our skin is slightly acidic (pH of 5 to 6.5) and this is called the 'acid mantle' of the skin. (All chemicals under pH 7 are acidic and over 7 are basic or alkaline). Our skin is very clever at keeping this level just right, but some highly acidic or highly alkaline chemicals can strip our skin and make it vulnerable to infection, outside attack and loss of water. That's why it's important to use products that are 'pH friendly' to your skin, unless you're being treated for a specific concern.

Our skin is also home to over one million bacteria per square centimetre. There are actually more bacteria on our skin than skin cells themselves! Not all bacteria are bad; if kept in balance they're essential for healthy skin because they help us defend against infection and irritation.

The time it takes our skin to completely regenerate itself is called the epidermal cell cycle. This cycle takes longer as we get older and is shorter when you're young, and shorter still if you have skin concerns like acne, eczema or psoriasis. You could say that we recreate ourselves every few weeks... I wish it were that simple.

The basal layer of the epidermis

So where do these new skin cells start from? There's a layer at the very base of the epidermis called the basal layer which is alive and produces new skin cells constantly. These baby cells migrate to the top of the skin and change as they travel. By the time they reach the top, they're dead and very protective. After they have served their purpose they shed and new cells replace them.

Fun fact

Over half the contents of your vacuum cleaner is dead skin cells. Gross but true!

The basal layer is also where the pigment-producing cells are made that give our skin colour: they're called melanocytes. These cells make a pigment called melanin, and this pigment is vital for protecting our skin from dangerous UV and blue light solar radiation, giving us light protection from solar radiation by stopping it from reaching the living cells deeper in the skin. It's like your own natural sunscreen, but don't get too excited: if you're fair skinned it only provides an SPF of around 2! Melanocyte cells look like an octopus under the microscope. They inject the melanin pigment through their tentacles into the epidermal cells above, and as the cells move to the top of the skin they carry this protective melanin with them.

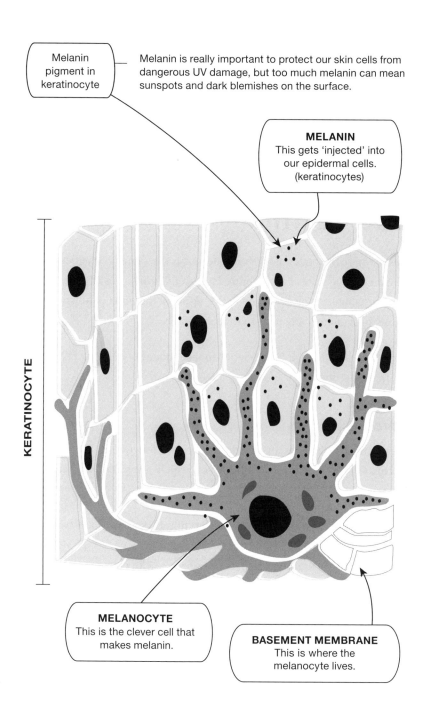

Melanin pigment in keratinocyte

Melanin is really important to protect our skin cells from dangerous UV damage, but too much melanin can mean sunspots and dark blemishes on the surface.

MELANIN
This gets 'injected' into our epidermal cells.
(keratinocytes)

KERATINOCYTE

MELANOCYTE
This is the clever cell that makes melanin.

BASEMENT MEMBRANE
This is where the melanocyte lives.

The dermal/epidermal junction

As the name implies, this is the area that joins the lower dermis to the upper epidermis; it looks like peaks and troughs under the microscope. The ridges form tiny 'pegs' that connect the epidermis to the dermis — if the pegs weren't there these two layers would literally slide off each other! The more ridges, the healthier the skin. These ridges flatten as we age, causing less oxygen and nutrients to reach the epidermis.

The dermis

This is where the action is. If the epidermis is the raincoat, the dermis is the brain of the skin. It sits right under the epidermis. This is the layer of the skin where I want all of my active skincare ingredients to work. It's where most of the living parts of the skin reside.

Sorry, but I need to get a bit sciency to talk about the amazing cells that live in the dermis.

Fibroblasts

These are special cells in the dermis whose function is to basically make the scaffolding and elastic tissue which gives the skin support and rebound.

The two main types of proteins that the fibroblasts make are collagen and elastin. Many people get confused about exactly what collagen and elastin do, so I like to use the mattress analogy. The collagen is like the stuffing that makes our skin firm and supported, while the elastin fibres are the springs in our skin that help it go back to its original position when stretched or pulled. Collagen and elastin work in synergy to form the connective tissue in our skin.

In young skin, just about the right amount of collagen and elastin are constantly being made so young people's skin looks youthful, but as we get older we lose collagen and elastin and our skin begins to sag and lose its elasticity. On my 45th birthday I realised I was getting older when I pulled at the skin on the back of my hand and let go and it didn't spring back instantly like when I was in my twenties. Happy birthday to me. ☺

Collagen: the mattress stuffing

Collagen is a big and complex protein that gives our skin structure and scaffolding. It is in fact the most abundant protein in the human body and makes up about 80 per cent of the dry weight of our skin! This clever molecule provides the structural support for the skin, making it firm and keeping those wrinkles at bay. Our skin would literally collapse without collagen. The collagen fibres are really well organised when we're young, like a piece of gauze, but over the years the fibres become tangled, brittle and disorganised and our collagen production slows down while the chemicals that destroy our precious collagen increase. Sunlight, smoking and pollution also speed this up — and taking a collagen supplement won't help (I explain this on page 138).

We need vitamin C and iron in our cells to help our bodies make collagen. This is another reason that vitamin C is very important in skin care products.

Elastin: the springs in the mattress

Elastin is also a protein, but it's very different from collagen. The elastin protein makes up only about 2 per cent of the weight of our skin, and it stretches and bounces back like a rubber band. It's the reason our skin returns to normal after we smile or crinkle our eyes.

GAGs: glycosaminoglycans

Fibroblast cells also make a very special sugar-protein complex called GAGs (glycosaminoglycans). The GAGs combine with water in the dermis and fill the space between the collagen and the elastin. The most important thing to know about GAGs is that they act like a giant sponge, taking water from the bloodstream as it travels through the skin. They're responsible for keeping the inside of the skin hydrated. You may have heard of the cosmeceutical hyaluronic acid, which is like the boss of all sponges and can hold 1000 times its weight in water. Well, this is actually one of the most common GAGs made by the fibroblasts. As we age, the amount of hyaluronic acid we produce reduces and our dermis becomes more dehydrated, which makes older skin look more saggy.

Pores

These are simply the hair and oil houses of the skin... and the source of angst for 85 per cent of teenagers! The base of the pore is deep in the dermis, and every pore contains a tiny oil gland (sebaceous gland) where all the sebum is made. The job of this waxy substance is to lubricate, balance and protect the skin.

Fun facts about pores

1. We have over 20 000 pores on our face.

2. Pores do not magically open and close; they can become larger if they're damaged or clogged with oil and debris.

3. The size of our pores is partly determined by our genes and skin type. Fair-skinned people often have smaller pores than darker-skinned people.

4. One of the main reasons our pores look larger as we get older is because of the loss of elasticity and support around them.

5. Sun damage can make our pores bigger because it damages the collagen around the pores and the tissue becomes 'slack'.

This phenomenal organ called skin isn't just designed to cover our bodies. It's a powerhouse of cells and processes perfectly equipped to protect, hydrate, restore and balance the surface and what lies beneath. And how cool is it that these cells and molecules all work together in perfect harmony to keep our skin as healthy as possible!

chapter 2

What's a cosmeceutical?

The term 'cosmeceutical' is often misused and misunderstood, yet it describes the most important active skin ingredients currently available. 'Cosmeceutical' was originally coined by Raymond Reed but popularised in the 1980s by Dr Albert Kligman. It's defined as an ingredient applied to the skin which is sold without a prescription but has properties that are able to change through the functions and processes of our skin cells. Cosmeceuticals are often called 'active ingredients' because they're biologically active.

Cosmeceutical products have a scientific basis in their formulations. I like to use the analogy of an iceberg, where we only really see the top 10 per cent; the exciting stuff all happens below the surface. It's the same with our skin. 'Fluffy' skincare products only affect the top layer of the skin — which is mainly dead — and don't have an impact on the health and appearance of our skin. I call these 'passive products'. They include cleansers, body wash and scrubs. These products don't affect the deeper layers of the skin where the living cells are; they simply clean the top with a mild detergent or scrub the surface to remove dead cells.

Many natural products are passive; they're nurturing and gentle, but may not create a biological benefit to skin cells in the deeper layers.

Cosmeceuticals, on the other hand, are 'active' and get beneath the skin surface to where most of the iceberg lives. This is the part of the skin where all the action takes place — including collagen production, deep hydration, elastin production, oil production, pigment production — and where the immune system acts on skin invaders and damaging microbes. Sure, luxe oils and glycerin are natural and gentle, but if you really want to get to the base of the iceberg, you need to call on the good stuff: the actives!

My SEED principle of formulating products

STABILITY

EFFECTIVENESS

ELEGANCE

DELIVERY

I love a good acronym. When I formulate my products I always make sure they tick off each box of my SEED principle: Stability, Effectiveness, Elegance and Delivery.

Stability

Many active ingredients behave perfectly in a test tube, but when you add them to a product in real life, they're unstable and break down, rendering them useless for the skin. To be effective, active ingredients need to be stable in the air, in normal light conditions (unless they're stored in a dark bottle) and in the presence of water (which most skincare products contain).

I also look at the stability of the formula as a whole. I test my products for months to make sure they don't separate, change colour, oxidise or grow microbes. I test in different temperatures; spin them in a centrifuge; test for bacteria, mould and fungus in incubators; and test over specific time frames to make sure the product can perform over the shelf life period. If any of my formulas shows signs of being unstable, it's back to the lab!

Effectiveness

A skincare manufacturer should only make products that do what they say they do. Cleansers should clean, serums should contain active ingredients for their purpose and moisturisers should perfectly suit the skin type they're created for. Too many cosmetic companies add an active ingredient just to boast about it on the jar, but with dosages too low to be effective. I always base my formulas on the dosage guidelines for effectiveness, so if 1 per cent of the active ingredient works for reducing the appearance of sunspots, then that's the minimum I'll use in my formula. I certainly wouldn't add half that just to say it's in the product. If the product isn't effective, what's the point?

Elegance

I learned this one through getting it wrong. Over 10 years ago I created a calming serum for irritated and sensitive skin that was packed with actives at the recommended dosage. It was effective at reducing redness and itchiness on my test subjects, but when I released it the clients simply stopped using it.

I have to tell you that initially a formulation failure really hurts. It's like someone is stabbing your stomach from the inside. So I took a gulp and I asked them to tell me what I did wrong. One lady vividly explained that while it did what it was meant to do, it looked like pale baby poo and wasn't pleasant to apply. Lightbulb moment... it doesn't matter how effective the product is, it must be great to use as well.

Since then, when we're doing the final testing on a new product, the first thing my team *always* does is look at it (to make sure it doesn't look like baby poo), gently massage it into their hands to get the sensory effect, and then smell it. If it doesn't pass the elegance test, it won't make it to the shelves.

Delivery

There are so many different results we can experience with active ingredients because the ingredients act on different types of skin cells. Sometimes an active ingredient helps collagen production, making our skin more firm and youthful; sometimes it helps the cells that make our dark melanin pigment, so we have a more even skin tone; and sometimes it may be an ingredient which protects our skin cells from free radical attack by sunlight or pollution. Each ingredient has a target cell. If the active cosmeceutical can't physically reach its target cell to create the change we want, then the product won't work.

Delivery of active ingredients is crucial, and this comes down to a number of 'sciency' characteristics:

1. Are the ingredients small enough to get through the outer surface of the skin? Ingredients like vitamin B3 (niacinamide) are tiny and penetrate the skin easily, whereas great big protein molecules are just too big to get into the target cell.

2. Can the pH (acidity or alkalinity) of the product help it get through to the target cells? For example, vitamin C in the form of L-ascorbic acid penetrates at below a pH of 3.5, whereas other ingredients may need a more alkaline pH to act on the target cells.

3. Can a protective coating around the ingredient help it get to the target cell before it's destroyed or changed on its journey?

4. Is the ingredient soluble in oil or water? This can affect the way the ingredient gets through the skin surface. Oil-soluble ingredients travel between the cells on the skin surface to go deeper, whereas water-soluble ingredients go through the cells.

As a formulator I really need to have an understanding of not only the ingredients (both the active cosmeceuticals and important ingredients such as thickeners, preservatives and emollient oils) and how they behave together, but how they interact with the biology of human skin cells. This is why I coined my SEED principle and use it every time I create something new.

chapter 3

Skincare essentials

The massive choice of skincare products available is nothing short of mind boggling! There are products for specific skin types, and the essentials that *everyone* can and should consider as part of their daily skincare routine.

Let's think of the ingredients in the products in your bathroom cabinet as a basketball team. We have the star players, which should always be on the court: the cosmeceutical vitamins A, B and C, along with the essential sunscreen for solar protection. Then we have the 'reserve team' products, which are important for particular skin concerns but are not as vital as the essentials. To create your ideal bathroom cabinet you need to start with A, B, C and sunscreen and then add your recommended sideliners.

We all need to look at two major areas to take the best care of our skin:

- protection
- active ingredients (cosmeceuticals).

Protecting our skin with the essentials

Sun protection is the number one area to focus on. Sun protection is like your skin's insurance policy! Protection is more than UV light. There are other types of harmful light, such as infrared light and blue light, that also wreak havoc on our skin. Yes, skin cancer is the worst-case scenario, but solar radiation and pollution also cause sun spots, redness and premature ageing. In chapter 4 I discuss protecting yourself from solar damage in detail.

The must-have cosmeceuticals

Now that we've identified sun protection as the number one essential (don't even consider cosmeceuticals unless you're using sunscreen), let's look at the three major categories of essential cosmeceuticals that *everyone* (from 20 to 120!) should use in their daily routine. They're the ABC vitamins of skincare.

Back in the '90s I was working for an Australian skincare company as a scientist and educator. It was there that I realised the importance of these skin vitamins and created educational modules for the therapists and skin specialists. I coined the phrase 'The ABC of Skincare' back then, and it's still used in many areas of Australian skincare education to this day.

I'm going to spend time focusing on these important skin vitamins because I really want you to appreciate the power they have to give you your best skin:

- vitamin A (retinoids)

- vitamin B3 (niacinamide)

- vitamin C.

There may be a little overlap with the exact skin functions of these three musketeers of vitamins, but they perform in very different ways and often work in perfect synergy to create the best results. These are my skincare staples. Quite simply, they work!

Vitamin A: 'the regulator'

This little cosmeceutical gem is part of a big family called retinoids. The power of vitamin A was first discovered in the '70s by famous dermatologist Dr Albert Kligman. He found that an ingredient called retinoic acid was helping acne sufferers and as a happy side-effect it was also reducing age spots, sun spots and wrinkles on his patients. Albert was onto something... complexion perfection!

Fast-forward: today retinoids are considered the gold standard in cosmeceuticals. I like to think of vitamin A as the great 'regulator' of our skin cells. When the skin is out of balance — too much oil, not enough collagen, too much pigment, too slow or fast cell production — vitamin A recognises there's something unbalanced in the cells and sends out messages to put the skin back into balance. It's like the skin's own internal thermostat.

A deeper dive into vitamin A

Dermatologists use vitamin A to treat so many skin conditions because it's able to interact with our skin's DNA and literally reprogram the cells to behave better. That blows my geeky mind! Here's what that means for you:

- *It regulates new cell production for glowing skin.* Remember how cells start off at the bottom of the epidermis as living cells, then travel to the skin surface and are shed as our own natural exfoliation? Well, vitamin A makes this process very organised so our skin cells constantly create healthy new cells and shed the old ones.

- *It helps make collagen for firmer skin and fewer wrinkles.* What's not to love about that? The fibroblast cells in our dermis make collagen, and vitamin A gives them a nudge to help them make more. Vitamin A also puts the brakes on natural skin chemicals that break down our precious collagen.

- *It evens out your skin tone and reduces dark spots and patches.* Vitamin A is a champion at reducing hyperpigmentation, which is a fancy word for darkened areas of the skin. Hyperpigmentation happens when our melanin misbehaves and overproduces the melanin pigment, causing freckles, spots and patches.

  Vitamin A works on many levels to make our melanin tow the line again. Because your skin cells are turning over more efficiently, the old cells with the excess melanin on the top of the skin are naturally shed, getting rid of the darkened skin. Vitamin A also sends a signal to a natural chemical in our skin (called tyrosinase) that makes melanin. If this chemical is hyperactive, vitamin A calms it down and stops it overproducing the pigment and uneven spots. Using vitamin A for a few weeks can result in fewer sunspots, the lightening of patches and a more even skin tone.

- *It helps to balance oil production.* Oil is vital to keep our skin moisturised and working properly. The oil glands (aka sebaceous glands) make our natural skin oils, called sebum, and this is the skin's natural lubricant. Vitamin A recognises when our skin is over-producing oil and lowers oil production, which is great news for oily skin and acne sufferers.

- *It can help restore cells that have been damaged by UV light.* If cells have been sunburned, vitamin A can actually reverse the damage. Wow!

- *It makes our skin's blood vessels really healthy.* It's our blood that brings the good stuff to our cells and removes toxins and waste, so healthier blood vessels means healthier skin.

So ... who doesn't need vitamin A?

Trick question: *everyone* needs it!

Sorting out the different vitamin A ingredients

There are many different types of vitamin A. This retinoid minefield can be very confusing, so let's try and sort it out.

Retinoic acid

This is the form of vitamin A that works directly on the living skin cells. It's the strongest form of vitamin A for the skin but it's also known to irritate the skin. It's only available through a doctor's prescription. The results are great, but you have to ease yourself into usage and even then you may find flaking and irritated skin around the mouth and corners of the nose. These side-effects usually aren't worth the results so people tend to stop using prescription forms of vitamin A.

In the end, all of the different forms of vitamin A must end up as retinoic acid in the target cells so you can get the great results that vitamin A offers.

Retinyl palmitate

This is old-school vitamin A. It was really popular in the '90s but we've come a long way since then. It's a very large molecule so it's difficult for it to penetrate into the target cells and create any real benefit to the skin.

Retinyl palmitate is the stored form of vitamin A in our cells, and there are three steps that occur before it's converted to the active form of retinoic acid.

These steps are:

RETINYL PALMITATE	RETINOL	RETINAL (aka retinaldehyde)	RETINOIC ACID
Storage form and not as effective as other forms.	Most popular cosmeceutical form of Vitamin A.	Often used, but not very stable.	Active form for cells to recognise. Prescription form and can be irritating.

Retinal (retinaldehyde)

I remember getting really excited about this ingredient about 10 years ago, because it's only one step away from the final active form of retinoic acid in the skin cells. I placed my order with the supplier and eagerly awaited its arrival so I could start formulating. After a few weeks I became impatient and rang my supplier and he told me that it had to be delivered under strict storage conditions because of its instability. Red flag!

The 'test tube science' said it had great promise, but the ingredient doesn't have the shelf life needed, so I passed on this one.

Retinol

Retinol still remains one of my favourite forms of vitamin A to formulate with. It's only two steps away from converting to the final retinoic acid, and it's a very small molecule that can penetrate the skin relatively easily. Unfortunately 'raw' retinol itself is unstable and tends to break down in air and light, plus it has a reputation for being a little irritating for sensitive skin.

I love how my industry is constantly evolving and taking good ingredients to the next level. A few years ago some clever chemists created more stable forms of retinol that have a protective capsule (a liposome) around them to protect them from breaking down and that helps them reach those elusive target cells. This was a great leap forward!

Retinol is one of the most popular forms of vitamin A used by today's cosmetic chemists. Look for products that use the stabilised forms and don't mix them with acidic products containing AHAs, BHAs and ascorbic acid because they make retinol less active in the skin.

Hydroxypinacolone retinoate (HPR)

It's a pity the name is so complicated — let's call it HPR. This is the latest addition to the royal family of vitamin A, and is being touted as the rising star in the vitamin A family for very good reasons.

The standout benefit of HPR is that it directly interacts with receptors in the skin cells and doesn't need to be converted to retinoic acid like the other retinoids.

According to a 2018 study in the *Journal of the American Academy of Dermatology*, HPR is seen as an effective alternative to prescription retinoic acid without the detrimental side-effects. It's also been found to be more stable than other forms of vitamin A, and the small molecule easily penetrates the skin. I think we'll be seeing many more vitamin A formulations in the future using HPR. Remember my SEED principle? This ingredient ticks *all* the boxes!

Table 3.1: types of vitamin A

Vitamin A specifications	Types of vitamin A				
	Retinyl palmitate	Retinol	Retinaldehyde	Hydroxy pinacolone retinoate (HPR)	Retinoic acid
Size of molecule for penetration	High	Low	Low	Low	Low
Stability	High	Low (unless encapsulated)	Low	High	Low
Effectiveness	Low	Medium	Medium	High	High
Skin irritation	Low	Medium	Low	Very low	High
Doctor's prescription needed?	No	No	No	No	Yes

Vitamin B3: 'the multitasker'

If there's one skincare ingredient I can't personally live without it's Vitamin B3, also known as niacinamide. It's known as the great multitasker of the skin. When I started formulating in my Melbourne clinic, vitamin B3 serum literally had a cult following (in a good way) in Camberwell. I remember one of my regular clients emailing me from England asking me to express ship her a bottle of my vitamin B3 serum! I knew this ingredient was pretty special.

What's so great about vitamin B3?

Where do I start? Apart from the wonderful skin benefits, it's a formulator's dream to work with. It's stable, it penetrates the skin easily to reach those targets, it's gentle on almost every skin type and it has many wonderful benefits for improving the health and strength of our skin surface, such as:

- *It reduces uneven skin tone and pigmentation.* It does this in a totally different way from vitamin A. This is why vitamin A and vitamin B3 are the 'soul mates' of cosmeceuticals: they totally complement each other. When the dark melanin pigment is transferred from the melanin factory cells (the melanocytes) to the cells in the epidermis, vitamin B3 acts as a gatekeeper. It can block this step if the melanin is clumping and forming dark hyperpigmented spots.

- *It increases collagen production for reducing wrinkles and increasing firmness.* Vitamin B3 is an essential part of the pathway to collagen production in cells, and B3 in skincare is a great way to deliver it directly to the cells that need it.

- *It helps reduce oily skin and is great for acne.* Vitamin B is a champion for acne sufferers. It can reduce the oil production in the skin, and may be a viable alternative to antibiotic creams for acne. This is great news for me as an immunology major as I'm totally opposed to the overuse of antibiotics in our community. Overuse of antibacterial drugs breeds resistant bacteria, which means that when we really need the drugs to work for us they're often useless! Excuse my rant …

- *It increases our skin's ability to fight foreign invaders.* Niacinamide is able to boost our own immune system. A 2017 study concluded that niacinamide boosts the production of natural peptides in our skin and protects us from bacterial infection. I'm seriously in awe of this ingredient.

- *It reduces skin redness and irritation.* Vitamin B is known to be a powerful anti-inflammatory, which is great news for sufferers of redness, rosacea, eczema and irritated skin.

- *It makes skin look luminous.* Niacinamide increases the levels of a natural oil in our epidermis called ceramides. Ceramides help keep the moisture levels in our skin high so we look dewy.
  Ever noticed how pregnant women have a 'glow' to their skin? In the first three months of pregnancy, women produce more ceramides, so their skin is naturally more hydrated. When I started formulating vitamin B products, my clients got very excited about their new glow within the first few weeks. No baby bump required!

See why I love vitamin B so much? SEED: tick … tick … tick … tick! But note that niacinamide doesn't like being mixed with acidic products. If you have a product containing high levels of lactic acid, glycolic acid, salicylic acid or L-ascorbic acid, keep it away from niacinamide because this can change its chemical structure and make it less effective. As a general rule, use your vitamin B serum at night with your vitamin A serum. They're a power couple.

Vitamin C: 'the fortifier'

We've all heard about how important antioxidants are in our diet. Well, antioxidants are just as vital for our skin. Every day we're literally bombarded with an aggressive army of damaging free radicals, solar radiation (UV, infrared and blue light) and pollution. Vitamin C (aka L-ascorbic acid) is the great fortifier. It creates a fortress around the cells to protect them from damage and destruction.

Vitamin C is the most abundant antioxidant in our bodies, but we can't produce it. We need to take it in the form of food, supplements and skincare, and our skin absolutely loves it.

Because it has a protective effect from environmental free radical assault, it's best to use this essential in the morning before you go outside and those perky UV rays try to attack your skin cells. Get your skincare army mobilised and start your day with vitamin C.

What exactly does vitamin C do for your skin?

As the ultimate fortress for your skin cells, vitamin C is incredible at doing the following:

- *squelching those free radical gremlins.* Vitamin C makes free radicals stable so they don't damage the outside of the skin cells or our DNA. Without vitamin C, free radicals (from pollution, sunlight and toxins) can penetrate the cells and attack our precious DNA inside. DNA damage is serious. It blows me away that vitamin C can neutralise the free radicals created by UV radiation, and it's why I recommend using it in the morning as the perfect partner with your sunscreen. (For further explanation on free radicals and antioxidants, see chapter 8.)

(A note about UV light) —————————————

Exposure to UV light reduces our natural reserves of vitamin C, so regular top-ups are needed, especially because our bodies can't actually make this skin vitamin!

- *making us look more youthful by helping with collagen production.* If vitamin C isn't around we can't make collagen, plus it helps silence the natural chemicals in our skin that break down our valuable collagen.

- *helping to reduce redness and inflammation in our cells.* Vitamin C helps with redness and inflammation including wound healing, acne and skin sensitivity. It's also great for reducing those red marks that persist for months after a pimple heals. Inflammation is one of the key contributors to ageing so this gem is important.

- *helping to lighten pigmentation and reduce uneven skin tone.* Vitamin C brightens sun-damaged skin and reduces pigmentation. It appears to only target the areas that are dark and patchy and leaves the 'normal' skin alone. How clever is that?

Different types of vitamin C

Newsflash...not all vitamin C is created equal. Just like vitamin A exists in different forms, so does vitamin C. Dr Sheldon Pinnell discovered all the amazing benefits of vitamin C as an antioxidant in the early '90s and concluded that all forms of vitamin C must be converted to L-ascorbic acid for the skin cells to use them.

Fun fact

When Dr Sheldon Pinnell was at medical school at Yale he got severely sunburned. He had already twigged that vitamin C can help with inflammation so he rubbed oranges all over his back and went to bed. He woke up the next morning and almost all the redness had disappeared! This was a lightbulb moment for Sheldon and he upped the ante on his research.

Here are the most popular forms of vitamin C you'll find in most skincare products.

Pure L-ascorbic acid powder

This is the original and purest form of vitamin C. It's a tiny molecule and is water soluble so it can easily penetrate the skin and reach those elusive target cells.

The challenge for formulators is that although L-ascorbic acid is very effective, it's very unstable as soon as water is added because it starts to oxidise, which eventually renders it useless for the skin. Because of this I always create my L-ascorbic acid formulas in dry powder or crystal form, which means the water base or serum is only added at the moment of use so it's still really active. The other challenge is that when you make up the vitamin C serum at the right 1:4 proportions (1 part L-ascorbic acid powder to 4 parts water-based serum) it's very acidic (around pH 3), and that's not great if you have sensitive skin.

Beware: most pre-made serums that contain L-ascorbic acid and water will be pretty much ineffective in a couple of weeks!

Magnesium ascorbyl phosphate (MAP)

This is a relatively popular form of vitamin C. It's fairly stable in a serum compared to L-ascorbic acid serum, but it doesn't penetrate the skin as effectively and is not as good at free radical attack as the original ascorbic acid. It's also very difficult to convert into L-ascorbic acid in the skin so very high doses are needed to create the desired results.

Ascorbyl palmitate

This is a fat soluble form of vitamin C. It's also not as effective as L-ascorbic acid because it doesn't penetrate the skin as effectively and it's less biologically active than L-ascorbic acid, and just like MAP it's difficult to convert to the active L-ascorbic acid.

Ascorbyl glucoside

This is another stable form of vitamin C, but my concern is that it produces glucose when it's converted to the active form of L-ascorbic acid in the skin. I have reservations about glucose molecules floating about in the dermis and ageing the skin cells (I discuss glycation in skin cells later). For this reason it's not my preferred vitamin C derivative.

Ethyl ascorbic acid

This is the new kid on the block and the best performer for those who find pure L-ascorbic acid too acidic. This little gem enables formulators like me to create a stable vitamin C serum at a skin-friendly pH. In fact, this type of vitamin C is the most stable form that I've researched so far, and I've been on the hunt for something like this for over 15 years.

Ethyl ascorbic acid is a tiny water-soluble molecule so it reaches those target cells and gets converted to L-ascorbic acid very easily compared to the other derivatives, and has tested to be superior to MAP and ascorbyl glucoside in reducing the formation of melanin.

Note: Some new ingredients derived from L-ascorbic acid can occasionally cause skin irritation, so it always advisable to test it on a small patch of skin for a few days before launching into daily use.

The bottom line about vitamin C

I still believe that L-ascorbic acid at 20 per cent (1 part to 4 parts) mixed with a compatible serum to a pH of around 3 is the best way of delivering the benefits of vitamin C to the skin, if your skin can tolerate it.

In short: L-ascorbic acid is the most active form of vitamin C as long as it's in powder form and mixed at the right proportions at the time of use or chemically stabilised. If you prefer the convenience of a ready-to-use serum or you have sensitive skin, I think ethyl ascorbic acid is the best option at this time.

How to use these skincare essentials

It really is as easy as ABC!

In the morning, use vitamin C and sunscreen (preferably physical or mineral). Both of these protect the skin from solar damage, but note that vitamin C is not an actual sunscreen.

In the evening, use vitamin A and vitamin B3 (niacinamide) for overnight regeneration, and remember you should not mix niacinamide with products that are acidic and have a pH below 4. Products with high levels of acid such as L-ascorbic acid, AHAs (alpha hydroxy acids such as lactic or glycolic acid) or BHAs (beta hydroxy acids such as salicylic acid) may be too acidic and react with retinol (a common form of vitamin A) and niacinamide.

When the acidity of a product is too high, niacinamide and retinol undergo a chemical reaction and they no longer work effectively, so you really need to think about how you combine your ingredients.

*   *   *

So there you have it: the 'ABC team' of essential cosmeceuticals. These little gems literally feed our skin from the outside! We all need a skin regulator (A), a multitasker (B) and an antioxidant fortifier (C) every day to achieve true skin vitality.

chapter 4

A spotlight on sunlight

Sunlight plays a significant part in accelerating the skin's ageing process, and when sunlight combines with environmental pollution you have an ageing cocktail. (I'll go into detail about the effects of the environment on our skin in chapter 14.) Protection from sun damage is more complicated than simply applying sunscreen to your skin once a day. To understand just how harmful the sun's rays can be, let's begin by shedding light on (sorry, I do love a pun!) the different types of sunrays.

UVA rays

UVA rays are like 'solar ninjas' because the damage they cause can't be seen immediately. They penetrate deeply into our skin — to the dermis, where the cells that make our youthful collagen and elastin live — and directly damage these living cells. I remember UVA as 'A' for 'Ageing'. Worse still, UVA can cause nasty mutations in our cells that can lead to melanoma and other skin cancers.

UVA rays generally result in tanning rather than burning. It's UVA that's used for tanning in solariums, which thankfully have now been banned. I rue the day I visited these skin cancer incubators disguised as tanning salons in the '80s. Hindsight, hey?

How to protect yourself from UVA rays

When you buy sunscreen, always make sure it's 'broad spectrum': this means it protects against both UVA and UVB rays.

The 'PA' rating on sunscreens is a broad UVA protection rating. The higher the PA values, the better the UVA protection. The PA rating isn't accepted worldwide, but it's currently the best indicator in many global regions for UVA protection.

Table 4.1: PA rating and UVA protection

PA rating	UVA protection
PA+	Some UVA protection
PA++	Moderate UVA protection
PA+++	High UVA protection
PA++++	Extremely high UVA protection

Not-so-fun fact

UVA rays can get through your windows, so you're not protected in your car. That's why we're usually more aged on our driver's side than our passenger side.

UVB rays

UVB rays aren't insidious like UVA; they like to make their presence felt by turning you into a lobster!

Damage from UVB rays manifest as sunburn and unlike UVA, which penetrates deeply, these rays only reach the top layer of the skin (the epidermis). Nonetheless, UVB rays are bad: they can lead to skin cancers by causing mutations in living cells. Remember, UV 'B' is for 'Burning'.

How to protect yourself from UVB rays

For maximum protection against UVB rays, there are specific sunscreen ingredients designed to block these burning rays. But remember, this will only protect you from the damage on the surface of your skin that makes you burn and not the deeper damage from UVA rays. It's relatively easy to measure the effectiveness of the UVB protection we can achieve from sunscreen in a lab test because we can see it on the skin of our subjects — their skin turns red after a certain period of time when the UVB protection from the sunscreen has worn off. And this is the basis of that special UVB protection rating called SPF.

SPF explained

I'm constantly surprised at the emphasis people place on the SPF (sun protection factor) of sunscreens. It's only a measure of UVB protection and has nothing to do with UVA protection. You need protection for both.

Here's the lowdown on SPF.

The acronym 'SPF' is a measure of how long it takes you to get sunburned with sunscreen on, compared to how long it takes you to burn without sunscreen. If your skin would burn without sunscreen in 10 minutes, by wearing an SPF 15 sunscreen you'd be protected from burning for

150 minutes (15 × 10). This is a general rule only and not an exact measure because the time of day and amount applied are also important. Note that you only get 3 per cent more UVB protection from an SPF 30 than you do from an SPF 15.

Moreover … I'm getting on my soapbox again … I'm really concerned that smart consumers are led to believe that using a very high SPF sunscreen will protect them all day. SPF 50 only gives you 2 per cent more UVB protection than SPF 30, yet it lulls us into a false sense of security that we have a shield of armour against all UV damage. Wrong! Remember those sneaky UVA rays? Well, not even SPF 100 would protect from them so don't think for a second that you're good to go all day. While you're tanning on the beach, those UVA rays are infiltrating your cells, destroying your precious collagen and causing you long-term damage. Remember to look for UVB *and* UVA (broad spectrum) protection.

This chart shows how increasing the SPF only has a small effect on the number of UVB rays that reach the skin. Interesting, hey?

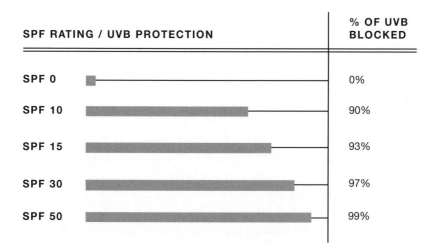

SPF RATING / UVB PROTECTION	% OF UVB BLOCKED
SPF 0	0%
SPF 10	90%
SPF 15	93%
SPF 30	97%
SPF 50	99%

UVC rays

UVC rays are toxic: they damage and mutate DNA. However, we don't need to worry about this scary wavelength of light because it's absorbed by our precious ozone layer and doesn't actually reach our skin. We just need to make sure we don't further destroy the ozone layer... but that's a whole other topic!

(A note about vitamin D)

We all know it's important to get enough vitamin D. Vitamin D is vital for our bone health, and the best source of this vitamin is sunlight. Short bursts of gentle sunlight became even more important during the COVID-19 pandemic as we were all spending so much time indoors! It's okay to get a few minutes of sunlight a day in summer as long as it's not between 11 am and 3 pm. Also, make sure you eat foods high in vitamin D such as eggs and fatty fish, or take quality vitamin D supplements.

Other types of damaging rays

Over the past few years scientists have been studying the negative impact of other, lesser known solar rays such as infrared radiation and high energy visible (blue) light.

Infrared radiation (IR)

Infrared radiation (IR) — aka infrared light — is a new enemy of the skin. IR comprises a whopping 54 per cent of all radiation from the sun. IR is also produced from laptops, electric ovens, hair dryers, microwaves and even certain lightbulbs. The heat generated from IR may be the cause of the condition known as 'laptop rash', where the skin presents with red or brown blotches in areas of heat contact with home computers. We now know that IR directly ages the skin and cosmetic chemists have coined the phrase Infra'aging (IR-induced skin ageing).

You know I can't help myself, so here's the cool science. ☺

Just as there are three categories of UV light—UVA, UVB and UVC—there are also three categories of infrared light: IRA, IRB and IRC. The different types of IR penetrate into the skin at different levels. Infrared A—aka 'near infrared'—penetrates into the dermis and is the most damaging category of IR.

IR and the heat created from this type of solar radiation have been shown to contribute to breaking down collagen and elastin in our dermis, and this loss of firmness and elasticity results in sagging skin and wrinkles. IR can also create cell-damaging free radicals, overheat the skin, and create inflammation and redness.

How to protect yourself from IR rays

We need to look beyond UVA/B protection when it comes to solar protection. We know that IR is blocked by zinc oxide and iron oxides (the natural pigment in mineral makeup). These are used in mineral makeup and physical sunscreens to guard against IR damage. There's also a great new botanical ingredient called *Polygonum aviculare* that's able to protect the skin by helping prevent the breakdown of collagen and elastin caused by IRA exposure. This ingredient can be considered a supplement to IR-filtering sunscreen ingredients.

More research is being conducted on the effects of IR and more is being discovered about the extent of damage it causes and the level of protection required to prevent it. I'm sure we'll be seeing more suncare products in the future that look beyond UV protection.

High energy visible (HEV) blue light

So, we now know that UVA, UVB and infrared radiation can be damaging to the skin. But wait... there's more! Scientists have also been alerted to the negative impact of blue (or HEV) light on the skin. Before you buy blue-light glasses or don a ski mask in front of your computer screen, let's dive into the facts about blue light.

What is blue light?

Blue light is also referred to as high energy visible (HEV) light. In terms of geek-speak, high energy visible light refers to the higher frequency, shorter wavelengths of light in the violet-blue band of the visible light spectrum (380–500 nm).

Most blue light comes from the sun (it constitutes between 20 and 25 per cent of the light the sun generates), although HEV is also emitted from televisions, laptops, desktops, smartphones and some types of lightbulb (particularly LEDs).

The science

Scientific evidence points to the conclusion that HEV light harms our skin cells by causing free radical damage, just like UVA and UVB. Furthermore, blue light has been linked to direct damage to the mitochondria, the 'mini organs' in our cells that provide all the energy we need to perform every function in our bodies.

HEV exposure can affect the genes in our skin, directly impact our natural response to inflammation, and reduce our ability to repair and heal the skin barrier. Blue light also alters normal melanin production, which may help explain why some individuals with melasma suffer from hyperpigmentation despite using high levels of sunscreen (which provides UVA and UVB protection, but no HEV protection).

Many people freak out over the dangers of being outdoors, but indoor light can also negatively impact our skin. There's a new buzz phrase called 'screen face syndrome', but is this really a thing and do we really need to worry about our televisions, tablets and smartphones? Current research shows that exposure of up to one hour on a device emitting blue light can cause free radical damage in skin cells; however, there are no studies (to date) reporting on the long-term effects of blue light from devices.

As a scientist, my recommendation is to minimise your total daily exposure to HEV, particularly the natural blue light from solar radiation.

The amount of HEV emitted by devices is only a fraction of the intensity of HEV light emitted from the sun: you'd need to be in front of your smartphone for 10 hours to equal 15 minutes of blue light exposure from the sun. If you're looking at screens every day, it can't hurt to add some blue light protection to your skincare routine, and if you spend time outdoors you definitely need to protect yourself from the four damaging wavelengths: UVA, UVB, infrared (IR) and HEV.

How to protect yourself from HEV light

So, what can we do to protect against HEV damage to our skin? Thankfully there are a couple of powerful ingredients that can be used in makeup and skincare to protect the skin from blue light:

- *Mineral makeup containing iron oxides.* A few years ago I spoke at the Australasian Academy of Cosmetic Dermatology on the benefits of mineral makeup. I referred to the protective benefits of iron oxides (at over 4 per cent dosage) to filter and prevent penetration of blue light. After my presentation I was inundated with questions from dermatologists wanting to recommend skincare and makeup for their patients with melasma and other forms of hyperpigmentation. I advised them to ensure mineral makeup has over 4 per cent of iron oxides.

- *Skincare with HEV protection.* Antioxidants neutralise free radical damage generated from blue light, so look for products containing green tea, vitamin C and lycopene. Lycopene from tomatoes is my number one blue light ninja because it filters the blue light wavelength and neutralises free radicals.

Sorry to sound like a mum, but it all comes down to moderation. In controlled doses, blue light can help with acne and other skin disorders. It also helps us be more alert and can elevate our mood. It's definitely worth minimising your daily exposure to blue light and protecting your skin and eyes if you're exposed to solar radiation.

Mythbust: skin types according to colour and ability to tan

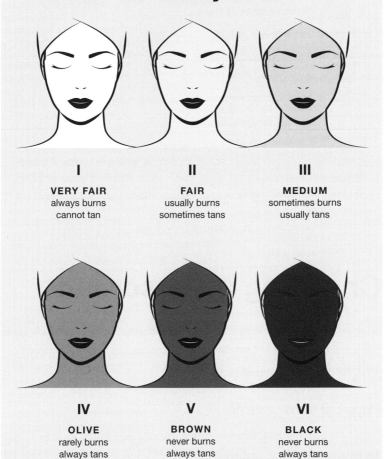

I	II	III
VERY FAIR always burns cannot tan	**FAIR** usually burns sometimes tans	**MEDIUM** sometimes burns usually tans

IV	V	VI
OLIVE rarely burns always tans	**BROWN** never burns always tans	**BLACK** never burns always tans

If you've ever had a skin consultation or laser hair removal, you've probably had your skin colour categorised according to what happens when you go out in the sun or tan.

(*continued*)

This categorisation is called 'Fitzpatrick skin typing' and it works like this:

- Type I: always burns/never tans
- Type II: always burns/rarely tans
- Type III: sometimes burns/tans moderately
- Type IV: rarely burns/tans easily
- Type V: never burns/brown skinned
- Type VI: never burns/very dark brown or black skinned.

So what does this mean for you? Anyone can get skin cancer, but if you're type I or II you're at the highest risk and you should avoid direct sun exposure unless you're protected with a hat, clothing and/or sunscreen. But don't be lulled into a false sense of security if you have naturally darker skin: melanoma can affect anyone, so always opt for protection.

Choosing a sunscreen

So now I've shed some light on sunscreens, it's time for you to make informed choices based on the facts. There are two broad categories of sunscreen: physical and chemical.

Physical sunscreens

Physical sunscreens are based on naturally occurring minerals from the earth and include zinc oxide and titanium dioxide. Zinc oxide is my absolute favourite because it's the only sunscreen ingredient that's able to protect effectively from both UVA and UVB rays. Most sunscreen ingredients are great at protecting against one and not the other, so you'll often find a cocktail of sunscreen ingredients in a chemical sunscreen product because they have to act together to be effective. Our hero zinc oxide does it all in one! And as a bonus, it also protects us from harmful infrared rays and calms down sensitive skin. As a formulator, I feel you need a minimum of 20 per cent zinc oxide in a moisturising base to provide good everyday protection.

Physical sunscreens sit on top of the skin and provide a physical barrier to harmful UV rays. The zinc oxide acts like tiny mirrors and reflects the light directly off the skin. It also absorbs some of the light on the surface, but doesn't let it penetrate the skin.

You need to remember the physical sunscreen rule: 'You move it, you lose it!' Technically, this barrier can remain on your skin for hours if you don't touch your face, but if you rub your skin or get it wet, the barrier will slide off. You *must* reapply to be protected.

I like to formulate with zinc oxide and titanium dioxide in sunscreens, and I also love using these ingredients in makeup foundations because they protect against UVA and UVB, reduce irritation and redness, and I can use them as a mineral-based white pigment.

Chemical sunscreens

I actually hate this term because it's very misleading. *Everything* in the world is in fact a 'chemical': water, air, metals, synthetics, even completely natural ingredients. They loosely call these sunscreens 'chemical' because they're not 'natural' like the mineral/physical category. Chemical sunscreens are also sometimes referred to as 'organic' sunscreens, but this is also misleading because they're not organic in the 'grown without pesticides', and so on, sense that most of us are familiar with.

Fun fact

The term 'organic' is a scientific term referring to chemicals that contain the element carbon. Since all 'chemical' sunscreens contain carbon (physical sunscreens don't) they're also called organic sunscreens.

The main feature of 'chemical' sunscreens is that they absorb into the skin — they don't sit on top like their physical counterparts. They absorb UV light and via a chemical reaction convert it to heat, which is released from the body. Chemical sunscreens can be found in the bloodstream and breastmilk hours after application and have been linked to allergic reactions, sensitivity and even hormonal disruption. Furthermore, many chemical sunscreens — such as the popular oxybenzone and avobenzone — have been banned by the FDA in many regions, including Hawaii, due to their damage to marine life and coral colonies. I choose to only formulate with mineral/physical sunscreens.

Sunscreen for kids and babies

When I became a mum in the early '90s my life was suddenly flipped on its head. All of a sudden everything was about my kids — especially what they put on their bodies and in their mouths — and I became hyper aware of all ingredients. What baby shampoo should I use? How can I find a baby wash without sodium lauryl sulphate (SLS)? What sunscreen is best? Back then the choices were more limited, but thankfully today there are some great options for 'safe' baby products and sunscreens.

The sunscreen choice for your baby is important because there are many sun-protective products marketed for babies and children that may not, in fact, be ideal for fresh new skin. The rule of thumb with babies and children is to limit exposure to potentially irritating chemicals in all body products, and keep it simple. Most companies focus on fragrance-free and the addition of anti-irritant ingredients like aloe vera and chamomile, but they fail to consider the potential irritancy of the sunscreen ingredient itself. Many chemical sunscreens, including oxybenzone, 4-isopropyl-dibenzoylmethane, PABA (para-aminobenzoic acid), avobenzone and cinnamates, have been linked to skin rashes and allergies. The skin of babies and children is more absorbent and more sensitive than the skin of adults, so you really need to understand your ingredients and read your labels to avoid those 'nasties'.

Mineral (physical) sunscreens such as zinc oxide and titanium dioxide are safer options for babies and children because they don't absorb into the skin. In fact, zinc oxide's use as an anti-inflammatory ointment dates back to 500 CE, and oldies like me remember using zinc oxide ointment on our babies' bottoms to help relieve nappy rash, and calamine lotion (which is a zinc oxide lotion) to help with the itch of mozzie bites. Because of its great anti-inflammatory properties, I consider zinc oxide as the best sunscreen option. It's such a clever mineral: it protects from both UVA and UVB rays and soothes fragile, young skin at the same time. Double yay for kids!

I generally don't recommend using any sunscreen on a baby under six months, but if there isn't an option *please* use a mineral/physical sunscreen over a chemical sunscreen, and absolutely avoid those sunscreen sprays: babies and children can inhale the fumes into their delicate new lungs! The best sunscreen for babies and children is shelter and sun-protective clothing, but if your child is exposed to damaging UV rays, the mineral sunscreen option is the ideal choice.

Mythbust: nanoparticles — what's with the hype?

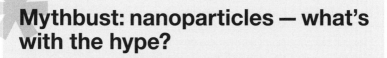

NANOPARTICLES SURE ARE TINY!

The size of a typical nanoparticle is...

...to a soccer ball as a soccer ball is...

...to the Earth.

I'm so over the media fear mongering around the use of nanoparticles in sunscreens and other skincare products. Consumers are terrified of nanoparticles and relate them to unsafe personal care products. You've been totally misled into believing that nanoparticles, as a general term, are ingredients that are dangerous and toxic if applied to the skin — it's simply not the case.

Here's why: a nanoparticle is defined as a particle smaller in diameter than 100 nanometres. One nanometre represents one billionth of a metre and is too small to be seen with the naked eye. To give you a better idea of how teeny weeny this is, 10 nanometres is 1000 times smaller than the width of an eyelash. Nanotechnology doesn't tell you anything about the safety or toxicity of the chemical characteristics of the particle; it merely defines its size.

It's the *type* of nanoparticle that may be dangerous, *not* the fact that it's a nanoparticle. There are thousands of types of nanoparticles that can be used in the beauty and drug industry, and some of them are undesirable, but others can be beneficial — even life-saving. Nanoparticles of lead in lipstick or makeup would be toxic to the skin, and nanoparticles of a toxic chemical such as arsenic would be fatal if inhaled or applied topically in a large enough dose. However, if you're having an asthma attack and need Ventolin, those nanoparticles of medication delivered to your lung tissue from your puffer may save your life. Both are nanoparticles. It's not the nanoparticle you need to worry about, but what the nanoparticle is made of.

There's been media hype over the past few years about the potentially harmful effects of the nanoparticles of zinc oxide in sunscreen. Studies have now concluded that zinc oxide nanoparticles don't penetrate healthy viable skin, and therefore don't present a risk to consumers. In 2019, the *Journal of Investigative Dermatology* concluded that repeated application of zinc oxide nanoparticles to the skin showed no evidence of penetration or toxicity to living skin cells of the epidermis. Furthermore, the tiny nanoparticles of zinc oxide tend to clump together in the sunscreen product and are therefore much bigger by the time they're applied to the skin.

As a scientist, I believe there's no problem in applying nanoparticles of zinc oxide to sunblock. The health and environmental benefits of zinc oxide in sunscreens far outweigh most of their chemical sunscreen counterparts.

It's essential to question the agenda of those who instil fear into consumers regarding nanotechnology. So, nanos are not necessarily no-no's!

It's ironic that humanity wouldn't exist without the sun yet it can also be one of the deadliest elements of our environment. There really is a lot more to protecting yourself from the sun than slapping on white goop and heading out the door. I hope I've given you the lowdown on choosing the best ingredients to protect your precious skin from all types of damaging rays and busted a few myths at the same time. Sun and dusted!

chapter 5

Dishing the dirt on good cleansing

The market has been flooded recently with different types of facial cleansers: foams, gels, oils, scrubs, micellar waters and balms. So which cleanser is ideal for your skin and what exactly should you look for?

Water-based cleansers

Water-based cleansers that contain surfactants attract oil and impurities to the skin surface so they can be easily removed. A surfactant is a scientific term for 'surface active agent'. It reduces the surface tension between the two 'phases' of the formula (such as the oil and water phases) so they mix better. There's an oil-loving part that traps the oil and gunk, and a water-loving part that easily rinses away with the water. Surfactants in facial cleansers basically degrease the skin's surface; they emulsify skin oils, makeup and impurities so they can be easily removed from the face. This type of cleanser includes foaming gels and non-foaming lotions.

HOW DO CLEANSERS WORK?

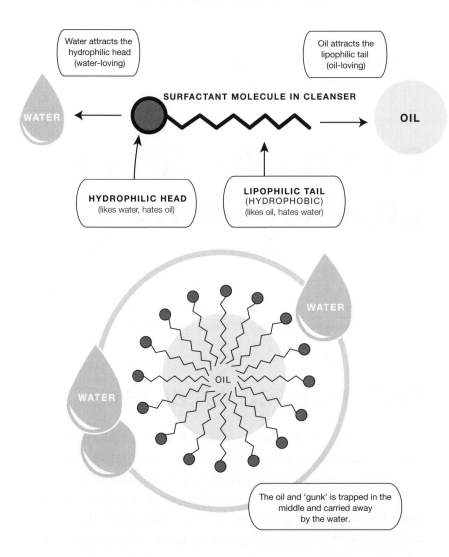

Water attracts the hydrophilic head (water-loving)

Oil attracts the lipophilic tail (oil-loving)

WATER

SURFACTANT MOLECULE IN CLEANSER

OIL

HYDROPHILIC HEAD (likes water, hates oil)

LIPOPHILIC TAIL (HYDROPHOBIC) (likes oil, hates water)

WATER

OIL

WATER

The oil and 'gunk' is trapped in the middle and carried away by the water.

Foaming cleansers are ideal for virtually every skin type, including normal, combination and acne-prone skin. Just ensure they're pH balanced and free of SLS and other potentially irritating surfactants.

Non-foaming lotion (or milk) cleansers are technically oil-in-water emulsions. These usually contain a lower level of surfactant with added emollient oils and are recommended for dry or mature skin. They're formulated in a mild, low-foaming milk formula that's gentle on fragile and dry skin.

The optimal pH for any water-based cleanser is around 5.6 (slightly acidic). This is the natural pH of skin, so irritation is minimised and our normal acid mantle is maintained. A good facial cleanser must be mild and not disrupt the natural barrier function of the skin, but at the same time be effective enough to remove excess oil, makeup and surface impurities.

Micellar waters

Micellar waters are creating a real buzz, but what exactly are these elusive 'micelles'? Micelles are ball-shaped clusters of surfactant molecules with the water-loving heads all sitting around the outside (where the water is), and oil-loving tails pointing inwards in the middle of the ball. These micelles break up when in contact with skin and act like magnets to attract and lift dirt, oil and makeup from the skin.

Micellar cleansing waters effectively remove traces of makeup, oil build-up and impurities without stripping the skin, and there's no need to rinse, making them the perfect on-the-go cleanser. My daughter loves a good micellar water when she's had a late night out and can't be bothered using a water-based rinse-off cleanser. Sorry to dob you in Georgie :) I personally prefer using a cleanser that requires rinsing because I don't like cleanser and makeup residue on my face, but micellar waters are a great alternative if you're too tired to do your usual bathroom routine.

Powder cleansers

Powder cleansers are an emerging trend that originated from Japan. They're simply a powder concentrate that requires the addition of water to create a cleansing foam. Powder cleansers have the benefit of a longer shelf life and are very convenient when travelling because there are no leakage risks. Look for powders that have been formulated without artificial fragrance or added colours, making them ideal for sensitive skin.

Exfoliating cleansers

Exfoliation is a necessary element of all skincare routines. There are two ways to exfoliate skin: chemical and physical exfoliation.

Chemical exfoliating cleansers

I don't believe adding a chemical exfoliating agent such as lactic or salicylic acid to a cleanser is effective. Acid exfoliants require a period of time to remove dead skin cells, which is why these ingredients should only be in products that remain on the skin surface for a longer period, allowing the exfoliation process to occur.

Physical exfoliating cleansers

Physical exfoliants are a better choice for rinse-off cleansing products, provided the particles are non-irritating and are suited to your skin type. Using rice powder or jojoba beads for exfoliation is a great choice for those with more sensitive skin. Be careful not to overuse physical exfoliants as they can be a little aggressive and can disrupt our delicate skin barrier if used too often. Many particles — such as some types of nut husks and coarse coffee grounds — are rough on skin. I personally use fine aluminium oxide crystals (the same ones used in microdermabrasion treatments) as a physical exfoliant once a week.

What to avoid in cleansers

There are some excellent cleansers on the market that really do deliver in effective cleansing without compromising our all-important skin barrier. As with any product, there are always certain ingredients and products that should be avoided.

The microbead controversy

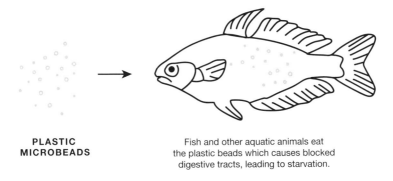

PLASTIC MICROBEADS

Fish and other aquatic animals eat the plastic beads which causes blocked digestive tracts, leading to starvation.

Microbeads may be microscopic, but they're creating serious problems for our aquatic environment. Commonly added to facial cleansers, these tiny plastic beads serve no benefit to the skin and are used as cheap alternatives to effective mineral- and plant-based exfoliants. And then they end up in our waterways and cause havoc with aquatic life. Avoid them at all costs.

Bar soaps

You know those annoying people who say 'I only use soap as my skincare routine?' I say *bah* to bar soaps! Bar soaps have a pH of around 9, which is way too harsh to be used on the face every day. Soaps are effective at stripping oil, dirt and impurities, and they are excellent hand sanitisers, but often destroy the natural acid mantle and can result in skin irritation.

Oil cleansers

Oil cleansing is a fad in the cosmetic industry based on the premise that 'oil dissolves oil'. Oil cleansing definitely removes and attracts the excess oil and makeup on the skin's surface, but you then have to remove this remaining oil from your skin. A layer of oil on the surface of the skin will prevent penetration of your important water-based serums, which is why facial oils and moisturisers containing oil should be the *final* step in your skincare routine, *not* the initial step. I don't subscribe to oil cleansing unless you're really good at removing the oil before adding the other elements of your skincare routine.

Active ingredients in cleansers

This is a pet peeve of mine. Cleansers are only in contact with the face for an average of 20 seconds before being washed down the drain. Adding active ingredients such as AHA and BHA exfoliants, vitamins or peptides to cleansers is a waste of money because there's very little time for these active ingredients to work on the deeper layers of your skin! If actives are added to a cleanser formula they must be rapidly penetrating. Leave your actives in your serums and moisturisers!

(My advice on cleansers)

- Choose the cleanser that's best suited to your skin type and lifestyle.
- Don't waste your money on cleansers with unnecessary active ingredients.
- Don't get caught up on 'fad cleansing rituals'.
- Avoid soaps and cleansers with harsh ingredients such as artificial fragrances and sulphates.
- Avoid cleansers and exfoliants with synthetic microbead technology.

Serum or moisturiser?

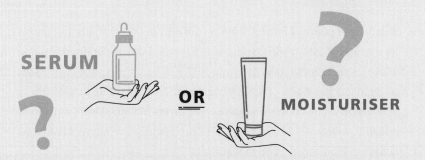

SERUM OR MOISTURISER

The three-step cleanse/tone/moisturise routine is truly a thing of the past, but as serums and elixirs evolve in the skincare market it's becoming more challenging to navigate the minefield of skincare steps. So, do you need a serum, a moisturiser or both? Let's break this down so you can spot the differences and figure out what will be best for your skin.

Serums

We've entered the era of the serum. Over the past few years serums have soared into the market to become the new essential in your twice-daily skincare routine, but with such a wide range of serums, all varying in quality and targeted skin concerns, which one should you choose and exactly what are they designed to achieve?

Serums are very specific in what they do: compared to a moisturiser they're lighter and much more readily absorbed into the skin. They're lighter in texture too, and almost always formulated in a water (or aqueous) base.

Serums are a method of achieving the concentrated delivery of cosmeceutical ingredients that target specific skin conditions such as dehydration, lines and wrinkles, redness, irritation, pigmentation, congestion and blemishes. Many of the active ingredients — such as L-ascorbic acid, niacinamide and many peptide ingredients — are water soluble and are very small molecules, so they're easier to deliver in a water-based serum formulation than a moisturiser would be.

For a list of the most popular ingredients found in serums, see appendix A.

Moisturisers

I like to think of serums as the power boost for the skin, and moisturisers as the thing that locks the serum in while providing skin moisture and adding a few more necessary goodies. Moisturisers can range in consistency and are usually milk, lotion or cream based. They're designed to lock in moisture, lubricate the surface cells and protect from surface damage, and in the case of physical sunscreen moisturisers, protect from UV ray penetration.

In general, a moisturiser is a creamy emulsion. A skincare emulsion is a mixture of water-based ingredients and oil-based ingredients that are mixed together to make a creamy product that's prevented from separating by an emulsifier.

Golden rules for using serums and moisturisers

1 Thinnest to thickest

After cleansing, always start with your lightest, thinnest product before moving onto your heaviest, which means your serums should always be applied *before* you moisturise! Some serums are made in a lightweight but thicker gel formulation, but this should still be considered as the lighter product and applied before a moisturiser.

2 Serums should not be used to replace moisturisers

Quality serums are all about the delivery of specific active ingredients such as vitamin C (L-ascorbic acid), vitamin B3 (niacinamide) and peptide solutions in doses designed to make a difference to the appearance and health of the skin. But you'll still need a moisturiser to lock in these wonderful cosmeceuticals, increase skin hydration and protect from environmental damage. Serums and moisturisers are both necessary.

3 Serums = value for money

Serums may initially seem expensive for such a small quantity of product, but a little goes a long way. You should always apply serums sparingly (but don't forget your neck) and they should be totally absorbed after two minutes.

High-quality options in particular should represent a high value per millilitre as they're often formulated with expensive active ingredients.

4 Not all serums are created equal

Department store and pharmacy brands often don't incorporate sufficiently high levels of active ingredients in their serums to create any visible change in your skin. It really is a matter of trust in a brand and doing your homework to ensure the ingredients are added for true skin benefits and not just a marketing claim — you really do get what you pay for.

5 Look for the science to support the claims

Ask your qualified dermal therapist or dermatologist for guidance and education on clinical data to support ingredient claims. Department store retailers aren't medically trained in educating their clients on addressing specific skin concerns, so seek the advice of specialists to help you choose the right serums and devise a skincare regimen that suits your skin and its requirements.

Remember, cleansing is a vital step in your skincare routine. It's the preparation for your other products. You wouldn't paint a door before sanding it; a clean canvas is essential before adding the active ingredients that truly make a visible difference — but choose wisely!

chapter 6

Facial exfoliation: what, why and when?

Exfoliation is the removal of dead surface skin cells that cling to the skin's outermost surface and become trapped in the pores, and it is a vital process for good skin health. Our skin is designed to exfoliate naturally at regular intervals. In fact, in healthy young adults a whole new skin surface is created every 30 days. How cool! But as we age this natural exfoliation process becomes slow and we end up with a rough, uneven, dull skin surface. Younger acne sufferers have the opposite problem: they have an overproduction of new skin cells that get trapped inside the pores and give birth to zits if excess oil and bacteria are present.

This chapter gets beneath the surface of exfoliation (sorry again!), and while the whole body is designed to shed and renew, I'll be focusing on the face.

Why exfoliate?

If our natural processes of exfoliation are disrupted, becoming either too fast or too slow, we need to rely on additional external methods of exfoliation to improve the condition of our skin. It's particularly important to remove dead surface skin to encourage new cell production; when the new cells are removed from the top of the skin it sends a feedback message to the cells deeper down to reproduce fresh new cells.

Exfoliation also removes sun-damaged and hyperpigmented skin cells that sit on the top layer of the skin, and it helps unclog pores and clear up acne and blemished skin.

So which exfoliants should you use in your skincare regimen?

Chemical exfoliants

These are usually available as skin serums. Alpha hydroxy acids (AHAs, such as lactic acid) help remove dead surface cells and improve natural moisture levels, and beta hydroxy acids (BHAs, such as salicylic acid) help to unclog pores and reduce inflammation.

When using a chemical exfoliant it's best to avoid glycolic acid (which can be irritating) and opt for lactic acid in combination with salicylic acid for decongesting the pores. There are also very gentle non-acidic exfoliants available that are based on yeast and soy amino acids.

Physical exfoliants

These exfoliants are basically scrubbing agents which physically remove the surface dead cells. There are many materials used for physical exfoliation, such as rice bran, jojoba beads, walnut husks, coffee grounds, sugar and salt. One of the best physical scrub agents uses aluminium oxide crystals, the same material used in microdermabrasion machines, which are able to effectively remove surface roughness and dead skin build-up, particularly around the T-zone. When exfoliating, it's important not to scrub too vigorously because physical exfoliants can damage the delicate skin surface and may cause irritation or fine blood vessels to be visible.

(A note about mixing ingredients)

You should never mix acids such as lactic, L-ascorbic and salicylic acids with vitamin B serum (niacinamide) and retinol, as acids cause these ingredients to be less effective. The rule of thumb is to use retinol and B at one time of the day (usually in the evening) and exfoliating acids at another time of the day under your sun-protective moisturiser or makeup.

Chemical peels by professionals

Chemical peels are a popular and effective form of skin therapy and another method of higher-level exfoliation. They can be used to reduce congestion, address pigmentation and minimise fine lines.

Peels preformed in a clinic can be light and superficial, or deeper and therefore capable of causing dermal skin wounds that require monitored healing. Deeper peels must only be performed under expert medical supervision.

Light chemical peels should be performed by a qualified skin therapist and generally involve the use of alpha hydroxy acids (AHAs) such as lactic and glycolic acid, and beta hydroxy acids (BHAs) such as salicylic acid. Peels can vary in strength from 20 per cent AHA up to 60 per cent AHA for more tolerant skin types. Always be guided by your skin therapist for the best course of treatment for your skin type and concern.

Clinical peels are an important element of skincare; however, they're not a 'one size fits all' treatment. Peels come in many strengths and forms and you must always seek the advice of a qualified skin professional before embarking on a series of chemical peels with a trusted therapist.

My top FAQs on peels

What are the best ingredients for peels?

For AHAs I prefer to formulate with lactic acid over glycolic acid because lactic acid is a larger molecule and is less likely to penetrate the epidermis and cause skin irritation. Lactic acid is also a natural skin hydrator and is less likely to cause surface dryness.

Salicylic acid is a great peel agent due to its ability to penetrate the pore and reduce inflammation. Even clients with sensitive skin will benefit from low-level salicylic acid peels (5 per cent or less).

I also like mandelic and malic acids as these AHAs can offer additional skin benefits such as regulating oil, improving barrier function and reducing uneven skin tone.

Stronger peels such as Jessner and trichloroacetic acid (TCA) must be applied with caution, but the results can be very effective, particularly for acne, pigmentation and fine lines.

Who are the best candidates for peels?

Generally those who suffer from acne, congestion, blackheads, sun damage and fine lines will benefit from peels. For acne, the lactic acid removes the top layer and salicylic acid (BHA) penetrates the follicles to help unblock pores, reduce inflamed skin and remove trapped oil and dead cells. For those suffering from surface pigmentation and sunspots, AHAs help lift the surface cells which hold the uneven surface pigmentation. Clients with fine lines will find that a series of AHA peels will cause a reduction in the appearance of fine surface lines because exfoliation causes the skin to regenerate new cells more efficiently and remove rough surface cells.

Is one peel enough?

Unless one strong, deeper peel is performed under controlled medical supervision, no. Best results will be achieved through a series of six to eight fortnightly to monthly peels, rather than a one-off treatment. It's recommended to have lighter peels over three months than one aggressive peel that may cause damage to the skin. Many clients commence with low-level peels (lactic acid 20–30 per cent) and gradually increase the peel strength over the series, up to 60 per cent if tolerated. A qualified skin therapist will advise you on a suitable level for your skin type.

Can anyone have a peel?

Not everyone is suited to chemical peels. Peels should never be performed on those with darker skin tones, particularly those of darker Asian, Middle Eastern, African, African-American and southern European ethnicity because they're prone to skin pigmentation after the skin has been damaged, and a peel can set up a minor wound on the skin. This condition is called post-inflammatory hyperpigmentation (PIH) and is challenging to treat.

Can skin be over peeled?

Have you ever noticed older skin that has the appearance of candle wax? This may be the result of over peeling. Having too many peels of overly aggressive treatments can irreversibly thin the skin, and may even permanently remove your natural protective pigment. Always err on the side of caution and have peels performed by reputable therapists. Remember, peels are designed to address a skin concern; once the concern is controlled or the desired results are achieved, the treatment should cease. Maintenance treatment can be performed as needed.

Physical exfoliant scrubs should only be used twice weekly (unless otherwise recommended by a skin specialist).

When should I exfoliate?

The frequency with which you exfoliate using skincare products depends on your skin type.

Physical exfoliant scrubs should only be used a maximum of twice weekly because the particles can irritate the sensitive skin surface, and people with sensitive skin and skin redness shouldn't use a physical exfoliant.

Rules for exfoliating

In general, the rules for exfoliating according to skin type are:

- *Acne and congestion:* use a chemical exfoliant daily until the acne is controlled, then reduce usage to alternate days. Avoid the delicate eye area and don't use at the same time as vitamin B3 serum or retinol. You can add a physical exfoliant too, but no more than twice weekly, focusing on the T-zone and avoiding broken skin.

- *Dry skin:* exfoliate once or twice a week with a chemical exfoliant, and once a week maximum with a physical exfoliant. Don't use a physical exfoliant on the same day as a chemical one.

- *Normal skin:* weekly chemical exfoliation is sufficient to remove dead surface cells. You can add physical exfoliation fortnightly or as needed.

- *Sun-damaged/pigmented skin:* daily chemical exfoliation is recommended to remove the surface sun spots and continue until the skin appears more refined and brighter. Then do it twice a week for maintenance. Use a physical exfoliant weekly or fortnightly if you have congestion in the T-zone.

- *Ageing skin:* use chemical exfoliation once to twice a week. Add physical exfoliation fortnightly or as needed for minor congestion in the T-zone.

In my opinion, your daily home regimen has more impact than what can be achieved with occasional clinical treatments. While an experienced skin therapist can produce visible results with the correct treatments, it's possible to achieve excellent results, and improve skin tone and texture, with high-quality home exfoliation ingredients.

chapter 7

Intelligent makeup: minerals do more than rock!

When I was nine years old I spent my pocket money on supermarket cream, eyeshadows and lipstick, and I'd spend hours painstakingly applying it with a fine paintbrush to my walking doll Alice. Maybe that's where my passion began! Alice looked like a Goth in the beginning, but by the time I was 11 she didn't look too bad thanks to my paying close attention to magazine models.

Fast-forward a few decades and I'm still as passionate about makeup, but my knowledge has given me the privilege of helping real women and not walking dolls!

We women wear makeup for roughly 10 hours a day, and the chemicals in our makeup are in constant contact with our skin. So, it's my personal mission to help educate you to make informed and healthy choices when it comes to selecting your makeup.

In the early '70s mineral makeup was launched, and over the decades cosmetic scientists have revolutionised the cosmetics industry to create makeup that works in synergy with and offers real benefits to our skin. They took the lead from Cleopatra, who used natural earth pigments to highlight and enhance her features.

Mineral makeup must offer women active ingredients and protection from harsh solar rays without the addition of questionable ingredients. Makeup should work with, not against, our skin. It should be functional and offer more than just surface improvement; mineral makeup must be intelligent, and the positive 'side-effect' is it should make you look freaking awesome!

What should mineral makeup contain?

With so many brands out there it's no wonder women are confused about what minerals really are! Minerals are inorganic substances derived from the earth.

I recently saw a brand of mineral makeup call itself 'organic' — that's an oxymoron! Organic ingredients are plant-derived from living 'organic' matter, and minerals are broadly based on rocks (minerals) that have been in the earth for thousands of years and don't contain living matter. Sure, you can add a few 'organic' ingredients, but minerals are the exact opposite of organic.

Mineral makeup should contain naturally derived mineral (inorganic) ingredients that, when formulated correctly, are great for your skin.

High-quality minerals can offer the same visual results as non-mineral synthetic makeup, but with added skin benefits and safe ingredients.

Minerals adhere to the skin like a veil and act like tiny mirrors, reflecting and scattering light to protect the skin and give it a luminous appearance. They harness the natural properties of the earth to provide coverage, camouflage and protection. When it comes to formulating mineral makeup, ingredients should not block pores or cause irritation. The best mineral makeup combines with zinc oxide, titanium dioxide and iron oxide as natural pigments at the correct dosage to provide UV, blue-light and infrared solar protection if used as primary ingredients.

What are the main benefits of mineral makeup?

Pure mineral makeup allows the skin to function correctly: to excrete toxins and absorb moisture from the atmosphere. Mineral makeup should act like a second skin, as well as provide physical, broad spectrum protection for the skin.

The water-resistant properties of minerals allow women to sweat, exercise and even swim with their makeup staying on throughout the day, provided they don't rub it off. The minerals only come off when removed with a soft cloth and gentle cleanser.

To protect against UVA, UVB and infrared rays, use mineral sunscreen that has high levels of zinc oxide and titanium dioxide (I like using at least 18 per cent zinc oxide/titanium dioxide in liquid foundation, and 40 per cent zinc oxide/titanium dioxide combined in cream, pressed compact and loose mineral formulas).

Zinc oxide is also a natural anti-inflammatory, which makes it an ideal option for people with sensitive skin or who are prone to breakouts. I've often seen young girls with acne switch to a high-quality mineral makeup and their condition has significantly improved with no other change to their skincare routine.

It has recently been discovered that the natural iron oxide pigments used in quality mineral formulas are highly beneficial to the skin, whereas most traditional makeup brands use artificial food, drug and cosmetic (FD&C) dyes that offer no benefit to the skin. At levels of 4 per cent and higher in a formula, iron oxides act as effective filters against harmful blue light.

But beware … not all minerals are created equal. As the mineral trend has gained momentum, many companies have jumped on the bandwagon and created inferior quality makeup that has tarnished the reputation of true mineral makeup. Cheap fillers such as talc bulk up the product and give a cakey, dry finish, which has given many women the misconception that loose powder minerals are drying. Good quality loose minerals should actually make the skin appear hydrated and dewy.

Mineral makeup should *not* contain questionable ingredients such as:

- cheap fillers and bulking agents (like talc)
- dimethicone (which can cause skin breakouts)
- bismuth oxychloride (this is a potential irritant that is used as a shimmer agent)
- artificial colours (FD&C bases)
- artificial fragrance
- paraben preservatives.

Mineral makeup is continually evolving. Minerals are now being combined with active ingredients and antioxidants to formulate high-quality cream foundations and skin camouflage products. Advances in natural colour technology also mean minerals are now available in a greater variety of more natural tones, and are able to suit almost any skin type. New milling and production techniques now produce a finer grade product with superior coverage, texture and environmental protection. Yay!

I believe mineral makeup is a logical extension of a good skincare regimen. If you invest in good skincare, why would you negate all the benefits by plastering inferior makeup on your face for the next 10 hours?!

Applying mineral makeup

Loose or pressed mineral makeup should always be applied over a lightly moisturised face to ensure even adhesion of the mineral particles to the skin. I recommend applying minerals with a densely packed kabuki brush that doesn't shed! Load the kabuki with a small quantity of loose minerals, and apply with firm circular motions over the face and neck. Work rapidly over the face to ensure even coverage. For natural results, it's also best to apply minerals in light layers rather than one heavy layer. Minerals provide a natural base which can be built up to achieve an airbrushed finish.

The 7 deadly makeup sins

1

80s time warp with sparkly neon-coloured eyeshadow (Watch out for massive shoulder pads too!)

2

Jaw 'tidemarks' — using the wrong colour foundation

3

Applying concealer too heavily and not blending properly

4

Overdrawn lips and unblended lip liner

5

Harsh blush and bronzer lines — Blend! Blend! Blend!

6

Over-plucked 90s brows

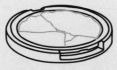

7

Using cheap makeup. See make up as an extension of your skincare routine.

Having been in this industry as a female cosmetic chemist for over 20 years I've seen some weird and wonderful beauty trends come and go. Makeup has undergone its own massive makeover over the years, particularly with the advent of minerals. Makeup is designed to enhance, not alter, your appearance. Too often I see young women with dark, over-bronzed faces or older ladies caking it on, making them look even older. As a makeup tragic, here are my top tips and tricks to avoid the most common makeup blunders.

1 Being caught in a time warp

Many of us in our forties and fifties have been caught out still using the same makeup techniques and colours we used in our twenties. Times, trends and techniques have certainly changed, and as we age my top tip is 'less is best'. As Coco Chanel said, 'Take it off, take it off, take it off!'

We can't expect that the makeup we used when we were in our twenties will still be appropriate as we get older. As we age, our skin will appear dryer and those dreaded fine lines begin to infiltrate, so subtle enhancement with a dewy complexion is key. Heavily applied foundation, shimmery eyeshadows and bright colours will instantly add years to your look! Opt for hydrating bases, soft natural eyeshadows on the lid and crease, and choose subtle brown eyeliner instead of harsh black tones.

2 Jaw 'tidemarks': using the wrong colour foundation

Choosing the correct shade for your skin tone creates the basis of your makeup. That's why it's called 'foundation'! Don't get stuck in the rut of using one shade of foundation all year round. Your skin will change with the seasons — even without lying in the sun — and your foundation should adapt. Choose a foundation in your lightest tone for winter and a darker tone for summer, and mix the two between seasons, or use a matte bronzer to deepen your winter foundation. If you're unsure, I'd suggest getting matched by a makeup professional.

It's fine to go a little darker in summer as long as it blends with your natural neck and jaw tones, but using a dark foundation will certainly not enhance your natural skin tone or make your skin look any healthier.

Don't match your foundation to the inside of your wrist — it's simply not the same tone as your face. For a perfect match, choose a shade that blends directly into your neck or jawline. Also, remember to use the correct brush: a kabuki brush to blend loose minerals and a foundation brush to blend creams and liquids.

My best advice is blend, blend, blend … then check and blend some more.

3 Getting carried away with concealer

Avoid overusing concealers: your foundation should be able to conceal 90 per cent of skin imperfections. Concealing is a necessary final step to creating a flawless base, but it should never be obvious. Always blend, blend, blend!

How to use concealer

- Colour correction should be applied first (before foundation) to even out skin tone. Apply sparingly with a small concealer brush and blend using dabbing movements with your ring finger. Next, apply skin tone concealers over the top of your base colour. To cover minor blemishes, use a concealer that's slightly lighter than your foundation.
- Apricot-toned concealers are perfect for concealing bluish, dark under-eye circles, and green-based concealers are ideal for camouflaging redness.
- Apply concealer sparingly to the base of your eyelid to brighten the area and make your eyes seem more awake.
- Don't use concealers that contain ingredients that may congest the skin:
  - avoid comedogenic oils, petroleum-based oils, and artificial colours
  - mineral concealers are ideal.

4 Overdrawn lips and visible lip liner

If you wish to create the illusion of fuller lips, applying lip liner and lipstick far over the lip line is not the way to go. Here are my tips for enhancing your natural shape and creating a perfectly defined pout:

- Preparation is key. Apply an overnight lip treatment and gently exfoliate lips with a toothbrush and mild physical exfoliant scrub.
- Apply loose minerals or setting powder sparingly to the lips as a primer to create a blank canvas.
- Choose a lighter lip colour or gloss to give the illusion of larger lips.

- Line lips with a liner slightly darker than your lipstick using small, feathery strokes. Avoid overdrawing more than 2 mm from your natural lip line and blend inwards to avoid a visible line.
- Apply a thin layer of lipstick with a brush and blot with a tissue.
- Follow with a light dusting of setting powder.
- Apply another thin layer of lipstick with a brush and blot again.
- Apply a dab of highlighter to the cupid bow of the lips and blend.
- Clean up the edge of the lip line with a light tone of concealer and blend with a small cotton tip or ring finger.

5 Harsh blush and bronzer lines

With blushers and bronzers a little goes a long way! Start by very lightly sculpting out the cheekbone with your bronzer, then go in and subtly build up the tone of your blush in light layers on the apples of your cheeks and temples. Harsh, unblended streaks are not a good look. Contouring takes practice and using the correct blending brush is vital. Soft 'bunny tail' brushes are excellent for applying blush, and a slightly denser brush is best for contouring. Don't forget to blend!

6 '90s brows

Thin, over-defined brows are out. Today's brows are natural and fuller. If you don't trust yourself to create the ideal shape, consult a trusted eyebrow therapist to give you the brow best suited to your face. I've been using the same 'brow queen' for years and I've never looked back. Thanks Katia. ☺

Once you have the brows in shape it's time to define them with makeup.

- Apply a matte brow powder or brow pomade to fill in and define:
    - blondes and light brunettes look best with a taupe tone
    - dark hair looks best with a deep, chocolate tone
    - avoid any browns with a reddish tone.
- Use a flat, slanted brush to define your brows.

- Apply using light sweeping strokes in the direction of the hair. Of course, I recommend mineral-based pigments. You can even use a taupe-coloured eyeshadow (no shimmer) for blonde eyebrows or chocolate for darker hair.
- Set with a small amount of hairspray on a dry mascara wand.

7 Using cheap makeup

When it comes to makeup, you really do get what you pay for. Quality mineral makeup is the makeup of choice today, but as we've seen, many companies have jumped on the mineral bandwagon and created inferior 'faux mineral products'. Quality mineral foundations should behave like a second skin and produce a dewy glow with natural coverage that can be gradually built up in layers. To get the best results, it's wise to choose makeup that does more than just enhance: it should actually benefit the skin.

The key to having a radiant glow is using products that enhance and benefit your skin and applying them using the correct techniques. Makeup can be a huge confidence booster, so find a range that suits your skin type and tone, and most importantly, have fun with it. At the end of the day, it's about making you feel truly great in your skin!

I consider mineral makeup as an unsung hero of skincare. If formulated properly, it's really the final step of a great skincare routine. And snap … it can also make you look totally awesome!

chapter 8

Nerd-out time

This chapter contains some very important ingredients that are a great addition to most daily routines but not part of the essentials 'A Team' (Vitamins A, B and C). Let's call these ingredients part of the 'reserve team'.

The information in this chapter is pretty 'sciency' but bear with me cos everyone needs a good nerd-out sometimes.

Peptides

These clever little chemicals can be made into fabulous cosmeceutical ingredients, but the term 'peptides' is grossly misunderstood and overused. I'm often asked if a certain serum or moisturiser contains 'peptides' without the person understanding what they are or how many millions of peptides we formulators can choose from to make a skincare product. It's a buzzword that most women believe needs to be in products, but they're mind boggled when they learn how peptides actually work on the skin.

An amino acid = one single pearl

A peptide = a few amino acids or pearls

A protein = lots and lots of amino acids strung together like a pearl necklace

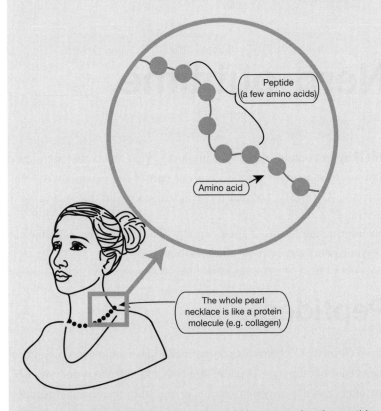

Peptide (a few amino acids)

Amino acid

The whole pearl necklace is like a protein molecule (e.g. collagen)

If a protein is a pearl necklace, an amino acid is one pearl and a peptide is a few pearls. 'Peptide' is simply a group (2+) of amino acids. The amino acid is the basic building block of a protein. There are 20 different amino acids that make up proteins in humans, and they can be assembled in hundreds of millions of different combinations. A protein is a large and complex molecule of over 50 amino acids, and is able to either perform a function in our body (e.g. a hormone or an enzyme) or be part of the structure of the body (e.g. collagen and elastin).

In science, we term peptides as comprising between 2 and 50 amino acids: these are called 'oligopeptides'. Fortunately, the human skin is a great barrier to the penetration of bacteria, pollution and other nasties, but what happens when we want molecules in our skincare, such as a cosmeceutical peptide, to penetrate and make our skin healthier? It needs to be small enough to get in.

Soapbox time … companies boasting the presence of the protein collagen in their products to boost collagen production in the skin drive me to distraction. This is *so wrong*! Collagen has over 1000 amino acids, so good luck getting that in! Apart from being far too big, collagen won't stimulate more collagen. What you need is a teeny weeny peptide to signal the skin's fibroblast cells to *make* collagen.

There are dozens of different peptides used in cosmeceutical products. I use peptides with fewer than 10 amino acids because anything over this size has a huge problem with penetration, and because peptides don't like high temperatures I add them at the end of my formulation. Cosmeceutical peptides often have additional stabilising pieces added to the peptide to keep it from being broken down by our body's defences — it's all very sciency and wonderful!

New technology enables scientists to create tens of millions of different peptides in the lab, some of which will end up in your serums and moisturisers if they pass all the lab tests and the data stacks up. There are some innovative labs currently creating peptides that are able to perform many beneficial skin functions, such as stimulating collagen, reducing the appearance of uneven pigmentation, reducing redness, reducing inflammation and reducing lines of movement such as crow's feet and frowns.

There are three types of peptide used in formulas:

1. *Signal peptides* tell a cell to do something like make more collagen, elastin or hyaluronic acid.

2. *Carrier peptides* help to transport an important mineral like copper or magnesium to a cell so that it can function more effectively.

3. *Neuropeptides* such as the cosmeceutical peptide acetyl heptapeptide-1 — a seven amino acid peptide that helps to stop the nerve telling the muscle to move — have a direct effect on a muscle to inhibit its movement. This is really helpful for those pesky crow's feet as it helps to soften the appearance of wrinkles.

There's no doubt that peptides have a huge place in skincare, but it's important that we understand how diverse they are and how crucial it is that they actually get to the target site of the skin to create beneficial change.

Hyaluronic acid

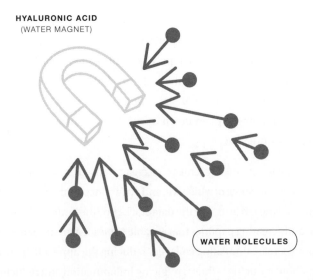

HYALURONIC ACID
(WATER MAGNET)

WATER MOLECULES

Hyaluronic acid (HA) is another must-have ingredient that keeps popping up in skincare products and the media. Despite its name, HA is not acidic: it's actually a type of sugar in a thick gel-like consistency that fills up the spaces between the collagen and elastin fibres in the dermis. HA acts like a hungry water magnet, soaking up 1000 times its weight in water! Cool, huh? HA is a lubricant and hydrator of the skin that's produced naturally by our bodies, and with nearly half of the HA in our bodies being in our skin it's worth a nerd-out.

HA: Q&A

Let's get started.

What does HA do?

Hyaluronic acid is crucial for keeping skin hydrated and youthful from the inside. As well as binding with water molecules, HA aids ingredient absorption, reduces inflammation, increases healing and aids in the communication between the living cells in the skin.

Is there a difference between hyaluronic acid and sodium hyaluronate?

You'll often see 'hyaluronic acid' or 'sodium hyaluronate' on your skincare labels because they're essentially interchangeable: sodium hyaluronate is the salt of hyaluronic acid, which is what's created as soon as you add water.

Does size matter?

Yes it does! There are many different sizes of HA available from suppliers and it's important for cosmetic chemists to understand the differences so they use the right ones in their formulations.

Large particle HA (aka high molecular weight (HMW)) doesn't penetrate the skin. It would be like trying to post a basketball in a letter box! These molecules sit on top of the skin and hydrate the dead surface layer by taking water from the atmosphere.

Tiny particle HA (aka sodium hyaluronate), which has a low molecular weight (LMW) works quite differently. These guys are small enough to reach a bit deeper to plump up the skin with water, which increases the suppleness and firmness, and they also trigger a healing response and fight free radicals. However, despite all the marketing claims, even the low molecular weight HA is too big to reach the living dermis so it's still just a great hydrator.

I prefer to use a mixture of small and large particle HA in my formulas so I can cover the skin surface and go a little deeper for added hydration.

How to use HA

Using a serum with HA without putting a moisturiser on top can make my skin feel dry, particularly if I'm in a dry climate, so as a general rule I always apply a moisturiser over the top of an HA serum to lock it in. If the outside air is very dry and the humidity level is low, the water from your skin can actually be attracted to the HA, not the water in the air, which will dry your skin out. Using a moisturiser to lock in the HA will stop this occurring.

With HA, more is not better. The recommended dosage in a serum is 0.5–2 per cent, and the only time you'd find more in a formula is if you were injecting it directly into the skin or using it with clinical skin needling treatments.

Fun fact

Most dermal filler injections are actually hyaluronic acid because they plump the skin from the inside using their special water magnet powers!

I do love this ingredient, but don't get caught up in the myth about the smaller particles working miracles in the dermis. HA is simply a great hydrator of the epidermis.

The good oil on facial oils

Facial oils are an important component of many skincare formulations. Although the majority of facial oils are nurturing and emollient, they're not technically considered 'active cosmeceuticals' because their effect is on the surface of the skin, where they hold in water and keep the skin feeling supple.

For formulators, oils must be selected for their individual characteristics and suitability for the end user, but not all oils are created equal, which is why it's important to understand the differences in their chemical structure, function in the formula, overall effect on the skin and comedogenicity. Unless you're armed with the correct information, you can easily make incorrect choices that may actually aggravate a problem you're seeking to treat. Worse still, the wrong oil may be unknowingly creating new skin issues and those dreaded breakouts!

There are numerous myths that oils are generally too 'thick' and 'heavy' for the skin and will inevitably lead to pore congestion and breakouts, but current skincare technology has evolved to the point where there are oils suitable for virtually every skin type and condition. The natural hydration levels of the skin can be increased with oil because it creates a physical barrier, preventing water loss from beneath.

For optimal skincare benefits, oils and moisturisers containing oils should be applied following a water-based serum because oil can impede the penetration of a serum's active ingredients by creating an impenetrable film on the skin's surface.

Completely oil-based products are often incompatible with moisturisers (which are made of water and oil emulsions) so a pure, lightweight facial oil should be massaged into the skin thoroughly either as a standalone moisturiser, or allowed to fully absorb before applying an additional moisturiser.

Oils must be used with caution and applied according to your skin type, and they should only be purchased in a properly formulated skincare product — not in their 'raw' state from the oil section of a grocery store. Food grade oils have a different purity level from cosmetic grade oils; you really do get what you pay for.

Oils used in skincare generally fall into one of the following six key categories:

1. *Comedogenic vs non-comedogenic:* The 'comedogenicity' of an oil is its pore-blocking potential, which is especially important when treating congested, acneic or inflamed skin. See the comedogenic table on page 233.

2. *Dry vs wet feel:* 'Dry' oils absorb within a few seconds with little trace of the oil and are usually more penetrating. They have a lighter consistency and give a silky feel to the skin rather than a slick shine. They're not heavy and greasy. Dimethicone is a common example of a 'dry oil'. One of the best lightweight 'active' oils in my ingredient library is olive-derived squalene because it's almost identical to human squalene and delivers high levels of antioxidants, as well as calming and skin-healing properties.
   Wet oils are heavier and more emollient and the oily feel lasts longer, but heavier oils are not necessarily bad guys for skin. Castor oil is one of my faves and is great for calming the skin. The active ingredient in castor bean oil is ricinoleic acid, which is antimicrobial, anti-inflammatory, a penetration enhancer and is excellent as a post-treatment oil. Although heavier in texture, it's not comedogenic so it can be used on acneic skin.

3. *Low molecular weight vs high molecular weight:* Low weight oils are usually liquid at room temperature and high weight oils are generally solid at room temperature.

4. *Occlusive vs emollient:* Occlusives form a protective barrier on the skin to prevent water loss, and emollients are oils which lubricate and soften the skin surface.

5. *Petroleum-derived or synthetic vs natural oils:* Petroleum oils are derived from crude oil and petroleum refining, whereas natural oils are derived from either plants or animals.

6. *Carrier oils vs essential oils:* Carrier oils are bulking oils and are usually vegetable based (e.g. almond oil, sunflower oil). Essential oils are concentrated and highly volatile (hence the aroma). They're plant based and are usually used in perfumes, aromatherapy and flavouring. I love to incorporate carefully chosen essential oils into my formulas because they have great benefits, but it needs to be the right type and amount of essential oil because some can cause irritation to sensitive skin.

Omega oils

The primary beneficial ingredients in most oils are the fatty acids, which are critical for skin function. Our bodies produce many fatty acids, but unfortunately not the essential fatty acids (EFAs).

The EFAs are:

- omega-3 alpha-linolenic
- omega-6 linoleic acid
- omega-9 oleic acid.

Applying these oils topically produces a number of benefits.

Omega-3 alpha-linolenic

These are the golden oils of skincare. They're essential for healthy skin and are often referred to as the 'good fats'. As well as helping skin appear youthful and healthy, they're responsible for the integrity of the cell membrane, which acts as a barrier to the entry of toxins, pollutants and microbes. Our vital cell membrane also provides a pathway for nutrients and active ingredients to enter cells and waste products to exit them, plus the cell membrane enables the cell to hold water. Foods rich in omega-3 fatty acids (salmon, tuna, walnuts, flaxseeds and chia seeds) also help to reduce production of our natural inflammatory factors, which contribute to disease and ageing.

Omega-6 linoleic acid

This fatty acid is critical in maintaining a healthy skin barrier to lock moisture and nutrients in and keep toxins and harmful microbes out. It promotes wound healing and reduces inflammation, but if it's deficient in the skin it has the opposite effect. Omega-6s can be found in meadowfoam oil, safflower oil, grapeseed oil, evening primrose oil, sunflower oil, pumpkin seed oil and soybean oils. Topical application of oils high in omega-6 can help reduce inflammation associated with eczema and dermatitis.

Omega-9 oleic acid

Omega-9, which can be found in squalene, meadowfoam oil, grapeseed oil and sea buckthorn oil, is highly effective in increasing hydration and reducing inflammation. Omega-9s can also act as penetration enhancers of other ingredients.

Can oil actually clean the skin?

Although it sounds like a contradiction, oils can make great cleansers because they dissolve the oil on the skin. The best cleansing oils are lightweight and economical varieties such as grapeseed and safflower oil, although I only recommend using these if you have dry skin, and you must follow them with a water-based surfactant cleanser to remove any oil film left on the surface. If oil is left sitting on the skin surface it will prevent the penetration of water-soluble active ingredients. Many people find this oil cleanse too time consuming, and I believe using a good gel-based cleanser is the fastest and easiest way to cleanse and remove makeup.

When oils go 'off'

We all know how horrible rancid olive oil smells. Well, facial oils also oxidise and have different stabilities and shelf lives. A rancid oil is packed with free radicals and will smell 'off' so it has no benefit to the skin. I always try and formulate with oils that have a longer shelf life, such as squalene and castor, macadamia, meadowfoam and jojoba oils. I also avoid oils that tend to turn rancid quickly, such as evening primrose, borage and rosehip oils.

(A note about oils)

When choosing to add oils to a skincare regimen they should be seen as a supplement, not the foundation. Cosmeceuticals in the form of vitamins A, B and C, peptides and other active ingredients are key when it comes to improving skin health. My advice is to choose oils for specific skin conditions. Check the shelf life and stability of oils in your products and think of the oils as the moisturising and emollient components of your daily regimen.

Antioxidants

Antioxidants are important for protecting our skin from cell damage and ageing. Although I consider vitamin C to be the essential antioxidant fortifier in all skincare regimens, numerous other antioxidants are part of our skincare 'reserve team' as they can help make the formula more stable and provide supplementary protection and other great benefits.

'Antioxidant': buzzword or reality?

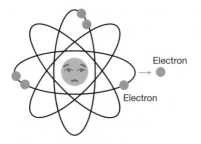

Electron

Electron

Lonely, unpaired electron

This is a free radical atom — it's really tiny and pesky! It's missing an electron and these guys like to be in pairs. So he wants to steal electrons from the other parts of the body and skin to make him stable and happy.

So, this guy is going to steal an electron from healthy skin cells, causing skin inflammation and the ageing of an innocent molecule.

But ... our antioxidant superhero comes to the rescue and donates its electron to the free radical. So, now the free radical is stable and no longer picking on our innocent healthy skin cells.

ALL IS GOOD IN THE SKIN AGAIN!

You can't read a skincare label or a healthy cookbook without coming across the concept of antioxidants. We all know that having antioxidants in our diet and adding them to our skincare is mega important, but do you know exactly what antioxidants are and why the heck they're so important?

Antioxidants are substances that neutralise or prevent oxidation, which is a chemical reaction that produces particles called 'free radicals'. Free radicals create an unfortunate series of events that can damage and even destroy cells.

Free radicals are tiny particles that can be atoms or molecules. Stable atoms and molecules have tiny, negatively charged electrons happily existing in pairs on their outside. These pairs of electrons are like happy satellites orbiting the core of the atom or molecule. Some particles exist without electrons in pairs, and these are unstable. When there's a particle with a 'lone electron' (without its buddy), it starts looking for an electron soul mate elsewhere to pair up with.

One of the best places to find an electron is the delicate membrane of the cells. This membrane is the first line of defence, and once the nasty free radical infiltrates the cell membrane it can launch a full-on attack on the nucleus of the cell, which is the home of the DNA and the blueprint of the cell. This is not good. The free radicals can also damage a clever little part of the cell called the mitochondria, which is responsible for making all the energy the cell needs to function and stay alive. Thus, the unstable atom or molecule picks on the poor innocent cell membrane of the skin, gets inside the cell and does all sorts of damage, like interfering with healthy skin processes and causing accelerated ageing. It can also kill a cell if the damage is too much for natural repair processes to kick in. This attack on the cells by free radicals is known as oxidation.

Enter the antioxidant! As the name implies, it works to counteract oxidation. An antioxidant is a molecule that has spare electrons that it donates to unstable free radicals — it's a generous and selfless entity. By giving up its electron to the rogue free radical, the cells are saved from attack and damage. That's why antioxidants are so important in protecting cells from solar damage, pollution and ageing.

There are numerous antioxidants available to formulators, but some are more potent than others. Here are the top five antioxidants I have in my laboratory:

1. *Vitamin C (L-ascorbic acid and ethyl ascorbic acid).* I recommend using this essential antioxidant in the morning to protect the cells from solar damage. Vitamin C is not technically a solar protector like sunscreen, but it is a perfect partner to your sunscreen as it protects the cells from free radicals created by solar radiation.

2. *Green tea extract.* I love this ingredient! It has multiple benefits for the skin, including neutralising free radical damage, reducing collagen breakdown and reducing pigmentation concerns.

3. *Lycopene.* This is a very powerful antioxidant that's derived from the skin of tomatoes. It's one of my top antioxidants because it protects the skin from blue light damage. Amazing, huh?

4. *Coenzyme Q10.* This antioxidant is an excellent choice because it helps to make other antioxidants, like vitamin C and vitamin E, work longer and more effectively. CoQ10 also protects from free radicals created by UV, IR and pollution.

5. *Vitamin E (aka D-alpha tocopherol).* Don't be fooled! This ingredient won't necessarily improve your skin, but it's great for stopping other ingredients in the product from oxidising. I often use it to stop the other oils in my moisturisers from going rancid. Beware of false claims on products that 'added vitamin E will be great for the skin', especially if it's at the lower end of the ingredient list.

6. *Caffeine.* The is a multifunctional ingredient but is also considered an antioxidant for the skin.

Mythbust: the benefits of a daily 'caffeine fix' for your skin

Caffeine has a positive effect on the skin when applied topically. It's an anti-inflammatory, it constricts enlarged blood vessels and it's used in skincare products to minimise the appearance of facial redness, which can help those who suffer from rosacea (a chronic facial redness in the skin caused by dilated blood vessels — more on rosacea in chapter 23). Caffeine also helps to reduce the appearance of cellulite when applied to the skin because it can reduce the fat content within human fat cells. Caffeine interferes with the activity of a specific chemical messenger within the cells known as phosphodiesterase (you'll probably never need to say this tongue twister). The human body uses this clever enzyme to prevent the breakdown of body fat, and caffeine inhibits phosphodiesterase and therefore helps the body to burn off the deposits of fatty tissue that may contribute to cellulite. The challenge is to get it to reach the deeper fat layers of the body, but certain treatments like skin needling can achieve this.

In addition to its anti-inflammatory and fat-fighting benefits, caffeine is also touted for its powerful antioxidant properties when used both topically and orally. Research suggests that both oral and topical caffeine may assist in repairing UV damage, and studies have found that caffeinated green tea and caffeinated black tea prevent sun damage, and even repair UV damage. Decaffeinated teas, however, do not have this effect.

Adding caffeine as an active ingredient to skincare products may help with cellulite, skin redness and solar skin damage. So...that morning coffee fix may not be a vice after all!

This selection of 'reserve team' ingredients really shouldn't sit on the bench for too long. They're great ingredients to add to your daily regimen and encompass literally thousands of different peptides, antioxidants, oils and other ingredients that will benefit so many specific skin concerns. The active ingredients discussed are only a small sample of all the options available and there are new ones created and discovered by cosmetic chemists every day. I truly love how dynamic this field of science is!

For those of you who made it to the end of this chapter: welcome officially to the SkinGeek Club!

chapter 9

What's really in your bathroom cabinet?

You're shopping for a new moisturiser and you care about the substances you put on your body, but when you turn the product over you're faced with a list of over 50 chemicals. Why so many? And why is the main one water?

There are over 10 000 ingredients approved for use in personal care products, and most products contain anywhere from 20 to 60 ingredients, so an average woman who uses 12 products a day (including dental, hair, body and face products) will apply over 500 different chemicals to her body every day. That's why it's important to know if these ingredients are actually good for you!

Deciphering an ingredient list is challenging. You're juggling claims, ingredients, symbols, buzzwords... how are you meant to analyse it all?

It's a minefield! I recently reverse-engineered a popular department store moisturiser (it shall remain nameless) that sold for over $400 a jar, and was gobsmacked by the inferior ingredients in the product — and the technology used to create it had remained virtually unchanged for decades. Grrrr ...

My advice is to put the made-up marketing buzzwords, promises and the whole gamut of persuasive language aside and check out exactly what's in the product through the ingredients list. Don't be seduced by misleading statements about the product containing a certain active ingredient that will create a visible change in the skin — an active ingredient needs to be at an effective dosage according to scientific data and testing to work. Many companies put a whiff of an ingredient in so they can use it in their marketing, when it needs to be at a much higher dosage to be effective.

Then there's the terms 'natural' and 'organic' with claims of purity — when only a few ingredients are actually organic! And while I'm on my soapbox, what's 'natural' anyway? This is the most overused term in skincare. Almost every cosmetic ingredient needs to be purified or slightly modified to be fit for adding to a skincare product, so it's hardly ever exactly the same as the ingredient that was originally picked from a tree. So is it still really 'natural'?

I know I sound like a cynic. I'm actually a glass-half-full kinda gal, but I'm so over all the hype and misinformation ... hence this book!

What will you find on a label?

Labels are jam-packed with information. Most of it is extremely useful and must be included by labelling law, but there's some 'white noise' too. Hopefully this section will help you decode your labels more effectively.

A product label must include:

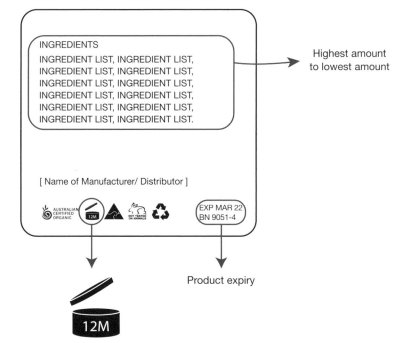

COMPANY LOGO

Product name

product tagline/ description

℮ size ml / size fl oz.

INGREDIENTS
INGREDIENT LIST, INGREDIENT LIST,
INGREDIENT LIST, INGREDIENT LIST,
INGREDIENT LIST, INGREDIENT LIST,
INGREDIENT LIST, INGREDIENT LIST,
INGREDIENT LIST, INGREDIENT LIST,
INGREDIENT LIST, INGREDIENT LIST,
INGREDIENT LIST, INGREDIENT LIST.

Highest amount to lowest amount

[Name of Manufacturer/ Distributor]

AUSTRALIAN CERTIFIED ORGANIC   12M   NOT TESTED ON ANIMALS   EXP MAR 22 BN 9051-4

Product expiry

12M

(Period after opening symbol)

- the company logo

- the product name

- a tagline (usually a concise description)

- a full ingredient list with INCI (International Nomenclature of Cosmetic Ingredients) names in descending order

- the size/net contents

- the name of the manufacturer and/or distributor

- the expiry date or time to use from when you open the product:

  - If you see a symbol with a lid above a jar with a number followed by an 'M', it tells you how long in months the product is okay to use after opening.

  - The expiry date is the date when the product is no longer fit for use. This is particularly relevant to eye products as you can get a nasty infection by using an expired mascara, for example!

Some labels also include:

- *product claims: 'free of'.* What companies leave out of their products is often as important to the consumer as what they include. Because clean science is so important to me as a scientist and a woman who's committed to health, there are numerous ingredients I classify as 'nasties', but the decision to purchase products that are 'free of' certain ingredients is ultimately a personal one, and yours alone.
I have my opinion on certain ingredients and their safety profile, and while many other companies sometimes promote selling by fear, I prefer to simply choose the safest options that have minimal negative impact on human health.

Typical 'free of' claims include:

- SLS/sodium laureth sulphate (SLES)
- sulphates
- parabens
- silicones

- FD&C dyes
- phthalates
- formaldehyde
- PEGs
- oxybenzone sunscreen.

I choose not to formulate with the above ingredients.

SKINCARE SYMBOLS DECIPHERED

RECYCLABLE

AUSTRALIAN MADE

CRUELTY FREE

ORGANIC

PERIOD AFTER OPENING

- *various symbols*, including 'Recyclable', 'Cruelty free', 'Organic' and 'Australian made'.

- *hypoallergenic or dermatologist tested*. Any good formulator will always create products with the lowest irritancy profile, but we can never guarantee that nobody will react to a product or ingredient. There will always be individuals who will react negatively to a certain ingredient when 99.9 per cent of the population won't. So when a product is touted as hypoallergenic or dermatologically tested, don't be fooled... it doesn't give a guarantee — nor does it imply it's endorsed by dermatologists!

Decoding the ingredients

If you're not up for a serious dose of nerdiness, please go and make a cuppa and skip to the next chapter... no, please *come back*! This is really important information.

All skincare products should have a full ingredient list either on the product itself or inside the packaging. Now to decode it. There's an urban myth that if it can't easily be pronounced, chances are it's harmful. This is rubbish! D-alpha tocopherol, for example, sounds very complicated but it's really just good-old vitamin E! When you read any accurate ingredient list it will state all ingredients in INCI. This is what's legally required to be stated on labels. Many products have trademarked or buzzword ingredient names created by a marketing department, but they should not be found on your product's labels without being accompanied by the official INCI name. The INCI name ingredient list can seem very sciency and overwhelming at first, but bear with me — it'll all become clear soon. For example, a common variety of lavender essential oil should be listed as 'Lavandula Angustifolia Oil', but some companies also add the word 'lavender' in brackets to help the consumer recognise the ingredient more readily.

The order of ingredients

All ingredients on your label must be listed in order of highest to lowest dosage. Water will usually be the first ingredient, as serums and emulsions nearly always need water as the main ingredient, so don't think you're being duped by the cosmetic company.

As you progress down the ingredient list, the dosage of ingredients becomes lower and lower, which is important to note.

Let's consider the addition of acids and alcohols. Some acids — such as lactic, malic and mandelic acid — are added in significant doses (sometimes at 10 per cent or more) to act as active exfoliants on the skin. But acids such as citric acid may also be needed in very small amounts to adjust the pH of the formula to make it more skin friendly. Alcohol is another good example. I often use a small amount of alcohol (under 3 per cent, which is not drying to the skin) to dissolve another ingredient in the formula. So if you have sensitive skin and you're worried about acids or alcohol, check where they are on the list. If they're low down, chances are they're a very low dose.

When you get down to the ingredients that are included in the product at 1 per cent or lower, they can be listed in any order — and this is where it can get misleading. For example, an active ingredient to reduce the appearance of wrinkles may be needed in a formula, according to the clinical data, at a dosage of 3 per cent to create the desired result. Some companies may just add it in at a 0.5 per cent dosage to say it's in there for marketing, and position it at the top of the 1 per cent or less group of ingredients so it appears to have a higher dosage. Sneaky!

Whether the dosage of an ingredient to make the desired change in the skin is 5 per cent or even as low as 0.2 per cent (and this is sometimes the case), I believe it's the ethical responsibility of cosmetic companies to always use the correct recommended dosage of active ingredients so they create the desired results.

The best way to decode your ingredients list is to use the website www.ewg.org. It gives a safety profile rating of any ingredient you put in the search engine, so you can be empowered to make your own decisions on which products you buy. It's a good general reference to help you keep your bathroom cabinet as free of nasties as possible. A lot of skincare companies don't like this website because it highlights the toxicity of their products, but I think it's a fantastic resource for the general public to learn about the ingredients in their skincare products. Search for an ingredient, then click on the image of its chemical makeup to read all about it. Also, remember that you need to look at percentages on labels. Bear in mind that some ingredients, while harmful in high doses, are harmless when used in tiny doses. Sodium hydroxide, alcohol and lactic acid are good examples of this. As mentioned previously, sometimes they're needed in minute quantities (less than 0.5 per cent) to adjust pH or make another ingredient dissolve. And please, don't let this website make you fearful. It's about being aware of repeated long-term exposure and not allowing many of the undesirable ingredients to build up in your system over time. If there are safer alternatives, then I choose clean!

What ingredients are in moisturisers?

As well as product ingredients needed for skin health, there are other ingredients (called excipient ingredients) which make the product elegant, function properly, and not break down or become contaminated. These ingredients include:

- *solubilisers* — used to make some ingredients dissolve in others, usually oils in water. They're usually found at the lower end of the ingredient list. For example, polysorbate can be used to solubilise essential oils.

- *thickeners* — used to give elegance to a product and improve its consistency. They're usually found in the middle to upper third section of the ingredient list.

I like to use naturally derived thickeners such as xanthan gum, hydroxyethyl cellulose and guar gum. Synthetic thickeners are very popular and carbomer is a clean, safe synthetic alternative. Mineral thickeners aren't as common, but can also be used to absorb water and oil in the formula. Examples include silica and bentonite, which are often found in clay masks and makeup.

- *emulsifiers* — fundamental in making a product containing oil and water stable so you don't get a layer of oil sitting on top of your product. If I add oil to water in my products, no matter how much I mix and shake, they'll keep separating unless I use an emulsifier to reduce the surface tension between the oil and water molecules. Science is so cool!

  Emulsifiers are generally found in the middle of the ingredient list, and two or three emulsifiers are usually needed in combination to make a lotion stable.

  There are literally thousands of emulsifiers, with new ones presented to me by ingredient companies every month. I personally avoid emulsifier or solubiliser ingredients with polyethylene glycol (PEG) as there are cleaner alternatives I prefer to use. Some of my faves include cetyl alcohol, cetearyl alcohol, stearic acid, cetearyl olivate and sorbitan olivate.

- *preservatives* — essential in all products because they prevent the product from being contaminated by bacteria, mould, yeast and fungi, thus contributing to the shelf life and safety of a product.

  If you see the claim 'preservative free', or if the preservative is being 'hidden' under another category or name in the list, you should question the quality of the product. Don't be fooled, grapefruit seed extract and essential oils may be okay at boosting the preservative activity of a product, but they're not strong enough to be used as a standalone preservative.

  Preservatives are generally used at a dosage of 1 per cent or less so they'll appear at the lower end of the ingredient list, but some need to be as high as 5 per cent.

  Preservatives have come under scrutiny recently and there are numerous preservatives I choose not to formulate with. Selecting a preservative can be challenging because many are very sensitive to the pH of the formula and can also be reactive with other ingredients. A combination of preservatives is often needed to provide the best level of protection of the product. My favourite preservatives with a good safety profile include:

  - benzoic acid and its salts (for example, sodium benzoate)

  - benzyl alcohol

  - dehydroacetic acid and its salts

- sorbic acid/potassium sorbate

- caprylyl glycol

- ethylpropanediol

- phenylpropanol.

Here is a list of preservatives that I don't use in my lab due to their less than favourable wrap in our industry:

- parabens: propylparaben, methylparaben, butylparaben, ethylparaben, isobutylparaben and isopropylparaben

- DMDM hydantoin

- BHA (butylated hydroxyanisole)

- triclosan

- methylisothiazolinone (MIT)

- bronopol (2-Bromo-2-Nitropropane-1,3-diol)

- urea-based preservatives: imidazolidinyl urea & diazolidinyl urea.

- *fragrance* — can include thousands of chemicals, most of them unpronounceable! And when I say chemicals, I mean that even natural essential oils contain 'chemicals'. Remember, everything is technically a chemical, even all the natural stuff.

   I prefer to avoid synthetic fragrances not derived from plants in my formulas because many contain allergens and phthalates to make the fragrance last longer. Phthalates (or diethyl phthalate) have been linked to hormonal disruption and are banned in some regions. They're on my 'no-no' list. Artificial fragrance (not botanically based essential oils) is generally a concentrated ingredient or group of ingredients, and will usually be found low down on the ingredient list. Often the word 'parfum' or 'fragrance' will indicate that the fragrance is artificial and not naturally derived. Fragrance in skincare is considered the number one potential irritant or allergen, so 'fragrance free' is the best option if you're highly sensitive or allergy prone.

   Essential oils are naturally derived from plants and don't have added phthalates. But beware… essential oils can be irritating unless the formulator really understands how to use them. The dosage is critical, and using over 4 per cent in a skincare product can be risky. There are also some essential oils, like bergamot, that can react with sunlight and cause skin reactions (bergamot needs to be free of the chemical bergaptene to avoid this reaction). Some essential oils also need to be avoided if you have highly sensitive skin or are pregnant.

Other essential oils, like lavender, are anti-inflammatory and help reduce irritation if used at the correct dosage, and rosemary essential oil is a great natural fragrance which also acts as an antioxidant to stop the oils in the product going off. Essential oils will usually appear in the lower third of an ingredient list as they should generally be added at less than 5 per cent.

- *antioxidants* — prevent free radical damage. I use antioxidants for two functions in my formulas:
  - as active ingredients to fight free radicals in the skin. Vitamin C, green tea, lycopene, CoQ10 and alpha lipoic acid are the top five skin antioxidants that I formulate with for great skin benefits (when added at the correct dosages). Dosages of different antioxidants vary so they can appear anywhere on the list, but generally should not be within the bottom 10 per cent of the ingredient list.
  - to help keep my formula stable, because added antioxidants stop the oils, butters and waxes from going rancid (and I try to use stable oils with a longer shelf life as well). One of the best examples of a common antioxidant used to stop oils going off is vitamin E (aka D-alpha tocopherol, tocopherol or tocopherol acetate). This will usually appear in the lower third of the ingredient list. Many companies tout vitamin E as being an active antioxidant ingredient for the skin in their formula, when it's only present at around 1 per cent to stabilise the oils. It's all marketing spin!

- *humectants* — a fancy word for hydrating agents. Humectants are water-loving ingredients that attract moisture into the skin like a magnet. They can either draw water from the lower layers of the skin (the dermis) to the upper layers (the epidermis) or draw water from the skincare product or the atmosphere into the skin to improve hydration. When the top of the skin is more hydrated, there's less flaking and cracking and the skin looks more luminous. Hydration also helps to keep the barrier nice and strong so it's better protected from harsh environmental extremes.

  Most humectants, with the exception of hyaluronic acid, which is usually needed in smaller doses, will usually be found in the top third of the ingredient list.

  My favourite humectants are glycerin, betaine, sodium PCA, sodium lactate, sorbitol, hyaluronic acid, aloe vera and lactic acid.

  I don't formulate with propylene glycol (because it has been linked to skin sensitivity, and it also increases the ability of the skin to absorb other ingredients, which may be undesirable) or PEG (polyethylene glycol).

PEG is also a penetration enhancer, and there have been reports of PEG containing potentially harmful impurities. Again, don't freak out — the problem isn't single exposure to these questionable ingredients, it's repeated long-term exposure.

If there's a risk associated with an ingredient, as a scientist who is committed to skin health, I'll always try to source a safer alternative.

- *emollients* — all the yummy oils and butters that I love to add to my lotions, moisturisers and balms because they help moisturise, smooth and lubricate the skin. Unlike humectants, which attract water, emollients moisturise by filling in the gaps between dead skin cells that are missing their own oils. This softens the skin and helps prevent the loss of water from the skin surface. Occlusives (discussed earlier) are a type of emollient that helps form a protective barrier on the skin surface to prevent water escaping.

  Depending on the type of emulsion, oils and waxes can appear high on the list or in the lower third. Thick balms and body butters have oils and waxes in the top third of the list, and some balms may be 100 per cent oil based. Lighter lotions and milks have more water and a lot less oil so the emollients will appear lower down.

  The list of oils and butters to choose from is almost endless! Examples of emollients include:

  - plant oils and waxes (fun fact: jojoba oil is really a liquid wax!)
  - animal oils (vegans and cruelty-free advocates must look out for these on the labels)
  - shea butter.

  Don't be scared off by long chemical names like triglyceride, myristate, palmitate or stearate — many of these emollients are great for the skin and provide great moisturisation.

  Here are some examples of thicker occlusive emollients mainly used for barrier healing and dry skin because they create a layer on the skin surface to prevent moisture loss and the entry of many nasties like pollution, grime and some microbes:

  - *petroleum jelly/petrolatum/mineral oil* (I prefer not to use petroleum-based ingredients. Petroleum products offer no cosmeceutical benefit to the skin and they may contain traces of undesirable contaminants if the ingredient has not been refined properly)
  - *beeswax*
  - *lanolin* (this ingredient is both an occlusive emollient and a humectant)

- *vegetable waxes* (candelilla, carnauba)
- *castor oil* (I love this one! Castor oil contains ricinoleic acid, which is great for reducing inflammation).

- *colour pigment* — a very popular additive to many skincare products, though usually not needed for performance. In makeup, however, this is a totally different story. For simplicity's sake, let's cover the three broad categories of colour:
  - *artificial FD&C or D&C colours (also referred to as 'lake' pigments).* These pigments are derived from coal tar, which is a by-product of petroleum refining. The FDA has passed FD&C dyes as safe to use in cosmetics, but I prefer the overall safety profile of mineral pigments. There's evidence linking some FD&C dyes to cancer, and there are tight regulations as to the amount of toxic lead or arsenic they contain.
  - *naturally derived mineral pigments.* These form the foundation of mineral makeup (pun intended). Mineral pigments include:
    - *iron oxides (e.g. yellow, red, brown and black iron oxide):* I love using these as they also protect the skin from UV and blue light damage (at the right dosage)
    - *zinc oxide and titanium dioxide:* they offer both UVA and UVB protection while producing a natural white pigment for makeup
    - *mica:* these come in a huge variety of grades and colours, and I love this natural mineral pigment because of its ability to reflect light, camouflage flaws and provide pigment without artificial dyes
    - *manganese* (purple)
    - *chromium oxide* (green)
    - *ultramarine* (blue).

  Mineral pigments may not have the huge colour palette of the artificial FD&C colours, but they have more staying power and are more resistant to heat and light.

- *natural colours* — these are usually plant based and include beet (red/purple), sweet potato extract (red), chlorophyll (green) and turmeric (yellow).

  FD&C colours are highly concentrated and will usually appear on the bottom of the ingredient list. Minerals like zinc oxide and mica are usually needed in higher quantities, so they will appear in the top half of the ingredient list. For example, zinc oxide may appear at the top of the ingredient list in mineral foundation and sunscreen (it's the white base).

Iron oxides (e.g. red iron oxide, yellow iron oxide, brown iron oxide) are used to create the deeper colours and skin tones and will usually appear in the bottom third of the list.

Natural pigments can appear anywhere on the list, but are usually in the lower 20 per cent.

- *pH adjusters* — ingredients used to make the product pH friendly for the skin. Our skin naturally adjusts to a pH level of around 5.6, which is slightly acidic, to ensure our outer barrier is functioning properly and working in synergy with those vital bacteria.

  When I'm making a serum or moisturiser, the product often doesn't end up with the ideal skin-friendly pH in my beaker. If it's too acidic I add something alkaline, and if it's too alkaline I add an acidic ingredient to adjust it.

  These pH adjusters are only used in tiny quantities, usually less than 0.5 per cent, so they're nothing to worry about in terms of irritation to the skin. They're usually found in the lower part of the ingredient list.

  pH adjusters are commonly used. If it's too alkaline, citric acid and lactic acid are added. If it's too acidic, triethanolamine and sodium hydroxide (I prefer to use this ingredient due to the higher safety profile at the very low doses needed to adjust pH) are used.

- *active ingredients* — tricky to categorise because actives can be present anywhere on the ingredient list. These are the ingredients that really make a difference to the skin: the vitamins, peptides, marine actives, botanical actives…the list goes on.

  The crucial thing here is whether the formulator is using the correct dosage of the active to make the desired change in the skin according to the clinical tests and data provided by the ingredient supplier. Again, just adding a whiff for marketing claims is not what we scientists are about. We aim to make a difference, and use the dosage to do just that!

If you'd like to read a moisturiser ingredient list comparison of a moisturiser I'd happily formulate in my lab versus one I deem as questionable, see my 'Moisturiser-off' in appendix B.

Mythbust: a word about toners

Toner

Toners are so '80s! The old cleanse/tone/moisturise routine should be archived as one of the great beauty routine myths. Apart from the fact that the majority of toners contain high doses of alcohol, which can disrupt our surface acid mantle, toners provide *zero* skin benefit.

I'm guilty of using a toner when I was in my early twenties because I mistakenly thought it would close my pores, and it was great at removing those last traces of pesky makeup. *Wrong!* Pores will look smaller if there's less oil in them and if the skin around the pore is young and full of collagen and elastin to make it tight and spring back. There are some great new cosmeceuticals in serums that will do an excellent job at reducing the size of large pores. And as far as removing the last traces of makeup goes…I think I should have either done a better job of cleansing in the first place or chosen a better quality cleanser that actually worked. It's not rocket science!

If you want a true skin 'balancer' to use before your serums, I suggest a prebiotic/probiotic pre-serum, which will do a great job of balancing the skin before adding your serums and moisturisers.

My advice? Ditch the toner and focus on a serum with active ingredients that are suited to your specific skin concerns.

I soooooo enjoyed writing this chapter. I gave it to one of my girlfriends for her feedback while I was writing this book. She found it so useful that she printed it out and kept it in her handbag as a reference for future skincare purchases. Knowledge gives you the power to make choices without all that marketing hype.

chapter 10

Lifestyle tips of a clean science nerd/ beauty tragic

I start my day with a non-startling alarm jingle of 'Over the rainbow' on my Samsung. I'd love to say I'm one of those people who springs out of bed at the crack of dawn every morning, but I'm a snuggly bed lover who loves a weekend sleep-in! Those weekday morning workouts are a killer, but the feeling I have walking home from a power walk or the gym is so worth it!

I can't function without my first morning cuppa, and it has to be a strong one. I try to exercise every day, alternating between pump classes at my local gym, a brisk morning walk around my local park or a zingly 15-minute routine on my vibration trainer! Yes … I love this machine. It keeps by muscles firm and stops me losing bone density as I age. The technology was originally developed for NASA astronauts to maintain muscle mass in zero gravity. As I always say, 'if it's good enough for NASA, it's good enough for me.'

Breakfast is my favourite meal of the day and I'm a creature of habit. I love my egg white omelette with mushrooms, spinach and avocado, but if I'm in a rush I'll go for Greek yoghurt and berries.

I start every day with a handful of supplements. As I'm getting older (and I see that as a privilege) I really focus on my inner health and look for supplements that I don't believe I have enough of in my normal dietary intake. I consulted a naturopath at Gwinganna Wellness Retreat last year and he was really happy with my choices, so here's my list:

- green tea antioxidants

- sea buckthorn oil fatty acids (unfortunately I can't have fish and fish oil)

- zinc

- magnesium

- chlorophyll

- esterified vitamin C

- vitamin D

- ubiquinol

- probiotics.

Every other day I spend 15 minutes under my home LED machine, which really wakes up my skin cells and helps to repair and regenerate my skin at a cellular level. I do 5 minutes on yellow light as a preparation, then 10 minutes on red light for rejuvenation. While I'm under the light I try to meditate using one of the meditation apps on my phone (I use Insight Timer and Smiling Mind). Let me be open here: I'm probably one of the worst meditators *ever*! I feel like Dory from *Finding Nemo* with my thoughts darting here and there every minute. But I'm putting in the effort, even though it's really not my strength, because I know how great it is for my mind.

I usually work from home for a couple of hours each morning before heading into my lab and head office. I find I can focus on my writing, formulating and articles without distraction. In fact, that's what I'm doing right now.

When I'm not travelling for work I love spending time with my work team — they're family to me. We all have huge mutual respect for one another and we truly work collaboratively. We also know how to laugh and … sidenote … our Christmas parties are legendary!

My office time is spent working with my team or at my desk doing research, and I always try to make time for a healthy lunch. My team are often shocked by the amount of chicken salad I can consume in one sitting. And I can't get through the day without at least two almond milk chai lattes (Prana Chai is amazing, people). It feels like such a treat!

I spend my evenings with my wonderful partner, my kids or my friends. I'm very social, but I also recognise the need to have quiet nights at home. I also have at least five alcohol-free days a week.

My favourite night in is homemade pumpkin and ginger soup and a good Netflix doco. I'm obsessed with nature docos — isn't David Attenborough's voice the best? I also love historical dramas and have become invested in the *Outlander* series (and not only because Jamie is easy on the eye).

You snooze … you don't lose!

I've recently made a big shift in my habits and I go to bed before 10 pm! Last year I thought I was sleeping my life away if I went to bed before midnight, but the research I've been doing on sleep has reframed my thinking. I've discovered the importance of deep sleep for body and brain restoration and the thought of losing brain function terrifies me. I even monitor my sleep with a Fitbit now and use downloaded white noise to help increase deep sleep. Melatonin is my other secret weapon if I'm jetlagged. This natural hormone is highly recommended as a regular supplement for the over forties for metabolism and general health.

The secret's out: my skincare routine

Now for my 'secret' skincare routine. Being a cosmetic chemist, I have a plethora of products to choose from. I could make my regimen super complicated but I really only focus on the anti-ageing essentials and a few added extras weekly or fortnightly. Because my book is not brand focused, I'm going to keep it general. I'd like to empower you to make your own informed product choices.

TERRI'S ANTI-AGEING FACIAL SKINCARE ROUTINE

Morning

1. Cleanse in the shower with my ultrasonic silicone cleansing brush. I always use an SLS-free pH-balanced cleansing gel.

2. Five minutes of rolling over my face with my home needling device. This roller has 0.5 mm fine plastic needles, which create channels so my serums can get into my skin more effectively and I get more bang for my buck!

3. Apply a prebiotic balancer tonic then anti-ageing serum containing anti-ageing peptides, new cell stimulants, collagen and hyaluronic acid stimulators.

4. Apply vitamin C serum to protect against all those free radicals that attack during the day.

5. Apply eye serum.

6. Apply anti-ageing moisturiser.

7. Apply mineral makeup sunscreen (at least SPF 30 and PA +++).

Evening

1. Use SLS-free cleansing gel with a muslin cloth to remove my makeup really well. The muslin gives me a gentle exfoliation.

2. Five minutes of rolling with my home needling device. I hate standing in one place for too long so while I do this I walk around the house doing my one-handed chores: loading the washing machine, stacking the dishwasher …

3. Apply vitamin A serum.

4. Apply vitamin B serum.

5. Apply eye moisturiser.

6. Apply anti-ageing moisturiser.

Weekly or fortnightly

1. *Gentle scrub:* to polish my skin and fight those blackheads.

2. *Anti-ageing mask:* I love my pamper nights when I can veg out, binge on Netflix and be kind to myself. I leave the mask on while I sleep and wake up with baby skin.

3. *Mini peel:* I do this every fortnight. I mix 20 per cent L-ascorbic acid crystals with 80 per cent exfoliating AHA/BHA serum and leave it to do its magic overnight. I don't use my other serums and moisturisers on that night, except for my eye cream.

(Don't do this mini peel if you have sensitive skin, and don't put it too close to the eyes.)

I like to think of my morning and evening skin routine as taking the time to love myself. I've really worked on my self-esteem over the years and I take the time to devote to self-care and nurturing. It feeds my mind and my soul, and makes me my best self inside and out!

Travel tips for holiday-ready skin

This isn't related to the skin, but please indulge me. I travel so much and I'd love to share a few travel tips in addition to the ones that follow.

Sidenote travel hacks

Here are some hacks that you might find useful if you're a traveller like me.

1 *Shower cap shoe protectors*

I always travel with hotel shower caps on my shoes. If you think about where the bottom of your shoes have been you'd *never* leave them to touch other things in your suitcase. I collect shower caps in every hotel so I always have a *big* supply!

2 *Multi-outlet power board for your hotel room*

All you need is one universal adaptor plugged into the multiple outlet power board you brought from home and bingo! You're all set.

3 *Luggage cover*

If you want to keep your suitcase looking like new, invest in a lycra luggage cover that you can easily recognise on the carousel. Those baggage handlers can be pretty rough and my Samsonite needs to go the distance...literally!

4 *Packing cubes*

These are an absolute *must*. I have different-sized zip-up cubes for daily clothes, workout wear, undies and accessories. Most of them go straight into the drawers without unpacking. It makes travelling so much more organised!

5 *Order more hangers when you check into the hotel*

One of my pet peeves is that there are never enough coat hangers in hotels, so I always ask for an extra dozen to be sent to my room when I check in. Please don't judge, but I nearly always need them all.

6 *Remove those pesky luggage stickers with eucalyptus oil*

Who wants to look at luggage stickers? Eucalyptus oil is great for easily removing them. I also use eucalyptus oil to clean the wheels of my luggage after a trip...If you really stop to ponder where those wheels have been you would *never* put your suitcase on your bed. Am I weird?

Long-haul travel skin tips of a beauty tragic

INTERNAL HYDRATION

... I'd recommend consuming about 250ml of water every hour, which also helps to combat skin puffiness and bloating.

250ML

LIPS

...A hydrating barrier style lip treatment will ensure you arrive with plump luscious lips.

EYES

... Use hydrating eye drops (I like Systane drops).

FACIAL HYDRATION

...Apply moisturiser every 2–3 hours on long flights WITHOUT FAIL, and remember to rub any leftover moisturiser into your hands.

CLEANSING

... Thoroughly cleanse your face with an SLS-free cleanser and a cloth in the aeroplane bathroom, or micellar cleansing water and cotton pads is the perfect way to cleanse from your seat.

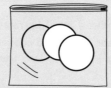

NOSE

... I apply an occlusive balm with a cotton bud inside my nose every couple of hours ...

KEEP MOVING

... Stand up to stretch your legs every hour, and wear compression socks if necessary.

FOOD

... I like to take my own unprocessed snacks such as nuts, seeds, fresh fruit, veggie sticks and yoghurt.

HYGIENE

... I suggest carrying a sanitising gel and wiping the surfaces around your seat area and the bathroom.

SLEEP

... Wear a comfortable eye mask that's not too tight ... Use earplugs or noise-cancelling headphones ... If you shape the seat headrest firmly to the side of your head you will minimise side movement and won't wake up with a sore neck ... Wear really comfy, warm clothes ... If you have problems getting to sleep try herbal or natural remedies such as valerian or melatonin.

SIDENOTE TRAVEL HACKS

1. Shower cap shoe protectors

2. Multi-outlet power board for your hotel room

3. Luggage cover

4. Packing cubes

5. Order more hangers when you check in ...

6. Remove those pesky luggage stickers with eucalyptus oil

AFTER THE FLIGHT

Try to adjust to the new time zone if you are staying for more than a few days.

Facial hydration boost ... I always apply an overnight hydrating mask when I first hit the hotel room.

I do a lot of travelling, mainly for business and a bit for pleasure. Long aeroplane trips can really take a toll on my skin. I remember arriving in Heathrow one morning and my skin felt like a cornflake! We really need to give our skin extra attention when we're in the air, so here are my top tips for long-haul skincare.

The air inside the cabin of a plane usually has a humidity level of under 20 per cent, which is significantly lower than humidity on the ground (between 30 and 65 per cent), so it's very important to maintain natural hydration levels. The first place to show signs of dehydration is the skin, so you need to apply skincare products which both add and hold moisture within the skin.

Internal hydration

Always ensure you're hydrated on the plane and *never* refuse water. Avoid alcohol, cola, carbonated drinks and coffee as these are natural diuretics which will lead to further dehydration. If there's less water in your blood when you're dehydrated, the concentration of alcohol will be slightly higher. This causes quicker intoxication and increased potential for a hangover. I'd recommend consuming about 250 mL of water every hour, which also helps to combat skin puffiness and bloating.

On-board

Travel light and don't forget to take no bigger than 100 mL containers for liquids for international flights. Here's my in-flight hydration kit:

- *Lips:* a hydrating barrier style lip treatment will ensure you arrive with plump, luscious lips. Your lips are the first thing to dry out in low humidity.
- *Eyes:* use hydrating eye drops. Contact lens wearers should switch to glasses during air travel.

  A cosmeceutical eye serum will add hydration, and some contain ingredients that will reduce puffy eyes.

  Hint: for an in-the-air eye treatment, soak thin cotton pads in a lightweight eye serum, add a little water to the pads, pop them on your eyelids and place your eye mask over the top while you sleep.
- *Facial hydration:* apply moisturiser every 2–3 hours on long flights *without fail*, and remember to rub any leftover moisturiser into your hands. You might need to use a slightly richer moisturiser to lock in the water in the dry cabin air.

- *Cleansing:* I can't think of anything worse than travelling for hours with a face full of makeup! I always cleanse as soon as I board. If you can be bothered, it's best for your skin if you thoroughly cleanse your face with an SLS-free cleanser and a cloth in the aeroplane bathroom, or micellar cleansing water and cotton pads is the perfect way to cleanse in your seat. If you don't want to carry a 100 mL travel bottle of micellar water, pre-moisten four cotton pads and pop them in a snap-lock bag. Wipes are another great option, but make sure they aren't packed with nasties and artificial fragrance.

- *Nose:* I know this sounds weird, but I hate that dry-nose feeling when I travel! Keeping the nasal lining moist will reduce the chance of nosebleeds and prevent nasty bugs penetrating your nasal cavity. I apply an occlusive balm with a cotton bud inside my nose every couple of hours, but I do try to do it when no-one's looking. ☺

- *Keep moving:* deep vein thrombosis (DVT) is a serious and dangerous concern during long-haul flights. People most at risk include those with circulation problems, diabetes, the aged and those with clotting disorders. Stand up to stretch your legs every hour, and wear compression socks if necessary.

- *Food:* due to the higher pressure in the cabin you're more likely to experience bloating and digestive problems. Avoid carbonated drinks, rich foods or foods that contribute to bloating such as cauliflower, onions and legumes. Plane food is pretty average so I like to take my own unprocessed snacks such as nuts, seeds, fresh fruit, veggie sticks and yoghurt.

- *Hygiene:* interestingly, it's not only the dry air in the cabin that can make you ill, it's the surfaces around your seat and the bathroom. Aeroplanes are considered one of the most unhygienic places, with aeroplane toilets having exceptionally high levels of E. coli bacteria. Tray tables are also a major source of microbial contamination, and can even be contaminated with cold, Coronaviruses and influenza virus. I suggest carrying a sanitising spray and wiping the surfaces around your seat area and the bathroom. It may seem a bit OTT, but the last thing you want to do is ruin a good holiday or work trip by getting sick.

  Also, baby wipes are very handy for travelling. A few wipes will freshen you up when you don't have access to a shower. Try to buy ones without chemical nasties, artificial fragrance or parabens.

- *Sleep:* this is my biggest challenge on long-haul flights. Here are my top travel tips for getting the best sleep:
  - Wear a comfortable eye mask that's not too tight (you can get really good contoured ones online).
  - Use earplugs or noise-cancelling headphones (check for comfort before buying!). Even without music the earphones mute external noise,

and you'll sleep so much better if you can drown out the background noise. Find some comfy noise-cancelling ear buds and download some soothing ambient sounds to cut out background noise.

- I personally find the U-shaped neck pillows uncomfortable! If you shape the seat headrest firmly to the side of your head you'll minimise side movement and won't wake up with a sore neck. There are some great travel pillows you can try as well.
- Wear really comfy, warm clothes. Girls, no tight jeans, high shoes or uncomfortable underwear. It's not the time to be a style icon.
- If you have problems getting to sleep, try herbal or natural remedies such as valerian or melatonin.

After the flight

To reduce the severity of jetlag, try to spend roughly 15 minutes in direct sunlight without sunglasses on soon after landing.

If you're staying for more than a few days, try to adjust to the new time zone. I take low dose (5 gm or less) melatonin before bed to help reset my natural sleep rhythm.

Facial hydration boost

As a final tip, I always apply an overnight hydrating mask when I first hit the hotel room. This mask is perfect for rebalancing hydration levels and plumping up dry skin.

It's totally okay to have a vice (or three) but I really do try to be the best version of myself by focusing on a daily routine geared towards optimal health. This, of course, means adopting a skincare routine that I liken to brushing my teeth every day: I *never ever* miss it! But it also means looking after sleep habits and not allowing long-haul travel to get in the way of feeling and looking my best.

chapter 11

The eyes have it!

The eyes are a major part of your skin routine. This is one of the first areas of the face to show ageing or even illness, yet we often ignore our little peepers.

Common eye area skin concerns

The eyes truly are the focal point of the face but the ravages of time, environment and lifestyle directly impact the appearance of this delicate area. The skin around the eyes is markedly different from the rest of the face, which is why we need to treat the eyes differently when choosing skincare and treatments. The skin around the eyes is 10 times thinner than other areas of the face, and is further thinned as we age due to loss of collagen, elastin and hyaluronic acid. And just to add another challenge, there are fewer oil glands under the eyes and on the eyelids so moisturisation and adequate hydration is essential as we age. The eyes are one of the first areas to age with the appearance of crow's feet, crepiness and sagging eyelids.

There are some common eye conditions that are worth understanding further.

Milia

Milia appear as tiny, hard, white raised lumps that are often confused with hard whiteheads. These bothersome bumps are created because of our skin barrier protein, keratin, becoming trapped under the skin. Comedogenic oils and waxes can cause blockages under the skin and lead to milia, and it can also develop when our skin's natural exfoliation process is disrupted. If you're prone to milia you should avoid heavy eye creams and opt for lightweight eye serums. Applying vitamin A will help improve cell turnover to prevent congestion, and gentle non-abrasive exfoliants will also help to slough away the surface skin and address milia effectively.

Milia are very stubborn, and it's really important to *never* squeeze or pick the delicate skin around the eyes. Using the right skincare ingredients may resolve the problem, but deep milia need to be removed with needle excision by a qualified skin therapist.

Dark circles and puffiness

Dark circles under your eyes can be a genetic condition that's difficult to treat. However, it can also develop from illness, ageing, a big night out or lack of sleep. Dark circles are caused by blood pooling around the eyes—it's more obvious as we age because the skin around the eyes becomes thinner and more delicate.

Effective skincare needs to target the walls of the tiny blood vessels, called capillaries, because if they're stronger the blood will not appear to 'pool' around the eyes and the dark circles are less obvious. One of the best ingredients for addressing dark circles is vitamin A and a peptide ingredient called acetyl tetrapeptide-1, which both help with dark circles and puffiness.

Puffiness is caused by poor blood and lymphatic circulation around the eyes. If you wake up puffy you can give yourself a one-minute lymphatic eye massage to direct the excess fluid away from your eyes.

A one-minute eye massage for puffy eyes

1

Use light tapping motions in a circle around your eyes with your middle and index finger. Be careful not to pull or drag the skin as this may cause more swelling.

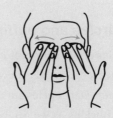

2

Start at the inner corner of your upper eyelid and progress outwards along the browbone towards the temple.

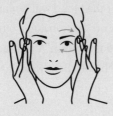

3

Move inwards now, just above your cheek bones and towards the corner of your lower lid and bridge of your nose.

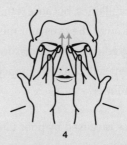

4

With your middle fingers, press upwards firmly just on the inner edges of your eyebrows near the bridge of your nose.

5

Finish with light pressure, using middle fingers just above the inner corners of your eyes.

This massage drains away the excess fluid that makes your eyes look tired and puffy.

1. Use light tapping motions in a circle around your eyes with your middle and index fingers. Be careful not to pull or drag the skin as this may cause more swelling.

2. Start at the inner corner of your upper eyelid and progress outwards along the browbone towards the temple.

3. Move inwards now, just above your cheekbones and towards the corner of your lower lid and bridge of your nose.

4. With your middle fingers, press upwards firmly on the inner edges of your eyebrows near the bridge of your nose.

5. Finish with light pressure, using the middle fingers just above the inner corners of your eyes.

Another old, tried and tested treatment that I love is applying cold tea bags to your eyelids, eye bags and any puffy skin around the eyes. The caffeine helps to constrict the vessels around the eyes and reduce puffiness.

One of the causes of more obvious bags under the eyes is ageing, thanks to the rubberband-like ligaments under the eyes becoming stretched and loose and no longer supporting the fat pads under the eyes. Treatments for this include injectable fillers and lower eyelid surgery.

Fine lines and wrinkles

Avoiding sun damage is one of the best ways to slow down fine lines and wrinkles around the eyes, but there are a number of ingredients and treatments to address them as well. Vitamins A, B3 (niacinamide) and C (L-ascorbic acid and ethyl ascorbic acid) are the all-stars of collagen stimulation and increasing natural hydration levels, and acetyl octapeptide-3 is a great peptide ingredient that relaxes facial muscles to reduce the appearance of crow's feet.

Anti-wrinkle injections are very popular too. Medically trained professionals can successfully reduce the appearance of crow's feet and lift the brow area for a subtle eye lift, but unfortunately this is only a temporary solution and treatments need to be repeated every few months.

Eye care

My top tip for eye care is to use a home needling roller device.

Roller devices help penetrate your active ingredients into the skin around your eyes, and home roller devices are gaining popularity. The daily use of a home skin roller with shallow needles (no more than 0.5 mm long) will dramatically improve the penetration of your products, particularly active serums. At-home rollers with needles made of fine plastic polymers are an ideal choice because they're very comfortable and sturdy, and can be used close to the lash line. Simply cleanse, roll the device over your skin in an even pattern and apply your active serums and moisturiser. The order is simple:

1. cleanse

2. roll

3. serums

4. moisturiser.

Don't forget to do this morning and night. You can even switch off your laptop, load the dishwasher or pull back the bedsheets while you roll. Gotta love multitasking. ☺

Non-surgical eye treatments

The best non-surgical rejuvenation options to reduce lines and crepiness around the eyes are clinical skin needling (collagen induction therapy (CIT)), fractional laser, radiofrequency treatments, plasma, medium-depth peels (performed with extreme care around the eyes) and anti-wrinkle injections.

There's also a treatment which uses fine heated needles that's very similar to skin needling, except these needles are heated to 400 degrees Celsius. The treatment effectively stimulates new collagen production, and there's less risk to the eyes and less discomfort than from laser treatments.

My vote goes to conventional needling and heated skin needling as I've had both treatments. I had six conventional needling treatments several years ago with a needle-pen device, and the results appeared best after 9 to 12 months. More recently I had two heated needle treatments, which did leave me under cover for a few days, but I've definitely noticed an improvement to the skin on my eyelids and under my eyes since.

With conventional medical skin needling, a series of at least eight treatments, done fortnightly or monthly, will significantly improve the appearance of fine lines and skin texture around the eyes. Heated skin needling isn't as common, but four- to six-monthly treatments are recommended. I'll admit, it's a bit ouchy, but it's a great non-surgical way to rejuvenate skin tone and texture.

Lush lashes

Lush, long, fluttering lashes can do wonders to enhance our eyes. Lash extensions are very popular, but long-term application can severely damage your natural lashes for months. Some glues are highly allergenic and can cause long-term eye irritation. I personally experienced this. After my third session of extensions, I began to have shortness of breath, severe nasal congestion and eyes so swollen that I could barely see out of them. It took me and my lashes weeks to recover, and despite new, more gentle glues on the market, I've been traumatised for life! If you're fortunate not to experience sensitivity to glues, my advice is to use lash extensions for the short term only, and visit a lash extension specialist.

Eyelash growth promoters, both synthetic and botanical, are another option. Be guided by your skin therapist for the best lash promoter—the right product can improve the appearance of your natural lashes in just a few weeks! The trick is to be committed and apply the serum at least once daily.

The biggest minefield for short-term lash enhancement is mascara. There are hundreds of formulas and brushes promising volume, length, clump-free, waterproof… the choices are endless! But beware of artificial pigments—such as FD&C dyes—as they can have a negative impact on the health of the lash follicle with prolonged use. My advice is to lash out (lol) for special occasions with sexy artificial lashes or uber-volumising mascara, but for day to day wear, invest in products with a clean ingredient profile and to opt for mineral pigments rather than FD&C dyes.

Diet and lifestyle for youthful eyes

Your skin is a product of both external and internal influences and your eyes are no exception. Here are some simple tips to optimise the appearance of the skin around your eyes:

- Avoid squinting and solar damage (UV and IR) by wearing sunglasses.

- Reduce your salt intake as this contributes to excess fluid retention and puffiness.

- Take adequate vitamin C and oral iron supplements as this may help reduce the appearance of dark circles.

- Adopt a low sugar regimen to avoid glycation (collagen cross-linking creating crepey skin).

- Consume seeds, nuts and fish rich in essential fatty acids. The skin loves EFAs.

- Drink more water and include green tea as part of your liquid consumption.

- Get at least seven hours of sleep each night.

- Keep alcohol intake low as it leads to skin dehydration.

Skincare for great eyes

So, what's the best option for addressing the eyes? As always, use your trusty vitamins A, B3 and C, and add your anti-ageing peptides. I also recommend a home needling device (0.25 to 0.5 mm in length) for really helping those ingredients reach the target cells around the eyes. These rollers are generally thought of as devices for the face and neck but there are great benefits to using one around the eyes and even on the lids if you're very careful. And, of course, protect those delicate little peepers from sun damage every day with good-quality sunnies, a sun-protective moisturiser and a UV and IR blocking mineral makeup.

Ultimately, the aim is to be the very best version of you at any age. Remember that the skin around the eyes is highly sensitive and requires products specially designed for the eyes that avoid high levels of artificial fragrance, SLS and alcohol.

* * *

With the right products, treatments, lifestyle and advice, it's possible to have eyes that literally light up the room.

chapter 12

Nutrition for great skin

I wish the only answer to great skin was great products, but they're only part of the equation. Skin health is multilayered, involving quality skincare products, nutrition, exercise, sleep and a positive mental attitude. Your diet is extremely important in the fight against premature ageing, obesity and disease.

The sugar epidemic

Research has shown that consuming high levels of sugar contributes to a higher risk of dying of heart disease, and those who regularly eat foods high in sugar and refined carbs have a 10 per cent higher risk of dying from any cause compared to the average person.

Inflammation is directly linked to high glycaemic index (GI) diets, and excess sugar consumption can lead to visible 'broken' capillaries, loss of skin elasticity, dark circles and puffy eyes. High sugar diets will also increase the severity of inflammatory skin conditions such as rosacea, eczema and acne. Ever noticed how much 'puffier' your face looks at Christmas time, after a few days of pudding and mince pies?

Sugar puts excessive stress on your adrenal glands and the additional cortisol depletes the skin and body of vital nutrients, increasing testosterone, which stimulates excess oil production and lowers natural immunity. It also directly affects mood and can be linked to anxiety and depression.

Sugar and refined carbs can make your skin appear wrinkled due to a process called glycation. Glycation is a reaction that takes place when simple sugar molecules such as fructose or glucose become attached to skin proteins (collagen and elastin) deep in the dermis, which causes the skin protein fibres to become stiff and malformed. When those proteins hook up with renegade sugars, they become discoloured, weak and stiff, which manifests as wrinkles, sagginess and loss of elasticity. Signs of glycation include those fine criss-cross lines on the face, neck and under the eyes.

On a microscopic level, glycation produces toxic compounds called AGEs (advanced glycation end-products). These substances result in internal free radical damage to the supportive collagen and elastin, which are responsible for making your skin look firm, springy and supple.

Sugar also suppresses the production of human growth hormone (HGH). Humans have natural levels of HGH in the bloodstream, and while I don't recommend injecting or consuming HGH (and yes, this happens!!), it's a vital hormone. Natural levels of HGH keep our body in optimal condition and regulate muscle mass, bone density, metabolism and heart function.

So which types of sugar should we steer clear of? Corn syrup is the biggest culprit; it has extremely high fructose levels and is very addictive. Many qualified nutritionists believe corn syrup is to blame for the obesity epidemic, particularly in the USA.

To keep your refined sugar levels down, avoid the following in your daily diet:

- corn syrup (especially high fructose corn syrup)
- agave nectar
- barley malt
- white sugar
- brown sugar
- fructose (1–2 pieces of fruit per day is okay)
- caster sugar
- raw sugar
- demerara sugar
- dextrose
- dextran
- fruit juice
- honey
- lactose
- maple syrup
- molasses
- rice syrup
- sorbitol
- treacle
- golden syrup.

As a general rule, read the label to ensure it contains less than 5 per cent sugar/refined carbohydrate (which is less than 5 grams per 100 grams).

And the less processing of any food the better. Although fruit contains fructose, the nutrients and fibre in raw fruit far outweighs the negative effects of fruit sugar—a piece of fruit and a cup of berries a day is ideal.

What's the best sugar alternative?

Stevia is my choice. Stevia is a herb that's 200 times sweeter than sugar and is the ideal choice for 'clean food' sweetening. Recent studies have shown stevia to benefit patients with high blood pressure and diabetes, and it has no negative impact on blood sugar levels. Stevia reduces dental plaque and has also been associated with increasing collagen production when applied to the skin and lips.

I find the most palatable type of stevia comes from the purest tips of the herb (Reb A). The 'Natvia' brand is, in my opinion, the most pleasant low-calorie natural sweetener currently available in Australia. (I have no commercial affiliation to Natvia by the way.) The secret is the natural sugar alcohol (erythritol) combined with the high quality stevia, which enables Natvia to be used by the spoonful without the aftertaste that's often experienced with stevia alone.

Overall, the best advice for a healthy diet is to keep it simple and fresh—your carbohydrate intake should come from whole grains and raw fruits.

Eat well for great skin

My advice as a cosmetic chemist is to consume a balanced diet with minimal processed food, quality supplements as required, and a quality cosmeceutical skincare regimen to specifically target your skin concerns. I'd love to say topical skincare is the only solution, but you must also address your skin from the inside out.

When it comes to living and looking my best, I try to practise what I preach. I take several supplements daily for my general wellbeing (these include green tea, resveratrol, curcumin, chlorophyll, sea buckthorn oil, esterified vitamin C and vitamin D). I also try to eat a healthy diet of fresh fruit and veggies, seeds, yoghurt, 'good' fats and protein. Coffee is my biggest dietary vice and I do drink alcohol socially. I avoid processed carbs, sugar and trans fats but still allow myself a 'blowout' junk day occasionally! I also try to exercise daily for at least 30 minutes because I spend a large chunk of my day sitting in my lab or office. I use a standing desk to help correct my posture and boost my energy levels throughout the day. There's recent evidence that intermittent fasting can increase your lifespan and slow down the ageing process, but more studies need to be performed.

Today's Western diet is very high in processed foods and our soil has become depleted of many essential minerals and nutrients from over-farming the land, which is why most adults will benefit from supplements. However, it is advisable to consult a reputable nutritionist or qualified naturopath for the best advice. I also advise against taking cheap vitamins when choosing supplements. This is often a case of 'you get what you pay for'.

There are critical dietary factors that are scientifically proven to affect the way we age. Genetics, sun damage, pollution and smoking all accelerate ageing, and research has proven that the glucose and fructose present in common foods we consume daily directly affects the collagen and elastin proteins in our skin. Glycation and glycotoxins can actually produce and accelerate the formation of wrinkles.

The science

Glycation (or glycosylation) is the result of the chemical bonding of a protein or lipid (fat) molecule with a sugar molecule to form what's known as AGEs (advanced glycation end-products). This results in collagen and elastin proteins in the skin becoming stiff and rigid, like a tiny cornflake, inside the skin. The resulting sugar-protein complex is discoloured, malformed and brittle and manifests as wrinkles and loss of radiance.

Lucky youngsters are constantly able to produce healthy new collagen and get away with a higher sugar diet. However, as we age we're less equipped to produce our own collagen and elastin and a poor diet high in sugar will directly influence the appearance of wrinkles.

The solution

Reduce or totally remove the following foods from your diet:

- sugar (sweets, dried fruit (these are really high in sugar!), fruit juice)

- alcohol

- refined carbs (pasta, pastry, white rice, bread, processed flour)

- processed carbs (chips, pizza, etc.)

- fresh fruit in excessive quantities.

Fructose is fruit sugar that creates AGEs, so limit your fruit to two pieces a day. Fresh berries are the lowest in sugar and are a great source of antioxidants so you can have more of these.

There are many 'hidden sugars' in packaged food. The general rule of thumb is the less processing the better, but if you're eating processed food try to analyse the back of your product labels and choose foods that are low in sugar (less than 5 per cent is my golden rule).

Dietary recommendations for great skin

So, avoiding sugar and processed food will certainly reduce the formation of AGEs. But what foods are truly beneficial for improving skin tone and texture at any age?

Skin superfoods

In my scientific opinion, the greatest skin superfoods are fresh vegetables, at least 8 to 10 cups a day of a variety of colours—and minimise cooking time or eat them raw. In particular, romaine lettuce, kale (which must be a super-food cos it tastes so hideous), broccoli, spinach, watercress, endive, tomatoes (rich in the antioxidant lycopene, which is great for blue light and UVB repair), red cabbage and asparagus.

Fun fact

Tomato paste or sugar-free tomato sauce is a fantastic source of lycopene because it's concentrated tomatoes.

Omega fats

Omega-3, 6 and 9 fats (in the correct proportion) are great skin oils. Omega-9 fatty acids are not considered essential fatty acids because our bodies make them. Omega-9s are great for regulating our metabolism. Our bodies can't make omega-3 and 6 fatty acids so they need to be eaten, which is why they're called 'essential'. We naturally consume extremely high amounts of omega-6 in our Western diet—for example, sunflower and soybean oil, which are cheap and plentiful—which throws out the ideal ratio (4:1) of omega-6 to omega-3 fatty acids. We currently consume a ratio of around 16:1, and because we're not genetically adapted to cope with this ratio this leads to excess inflammation in the body.

So we really need to eat more omega-3s for optimal health to get the ratio back to the 4:1 range. Omega-3s are essential for our heart, brain, metabolism and our largest organ—our skin! Here's a list of foods high in the omega-3s:

- salmon
- sardines
- oysters
- walnuts
- flaxseeds
- flaxseed oil
- chia seeds
- krill oil
- almonds
- sea buckthorn oil.

Other great foods to eat

Pulses (lentils and beans) are a great way to get healthy plant protein in your diet to help build collagen and elastin. Also great are split peas, chickpeas and lima/pinto/black/broad beans.

Whole unprocessed grains, teas high in flavonoids, oatmeal, oat bran, brown rice and wholegrain pasta are excellent sources of B vitamins and anti-inflammatory nutrients.

Herbs and spices are healthy and delicious. Ensure they're fresh if possible (not dried) and grown in a pesticide-free environment. Here are my faves:

- *ginger:* great for immunity and gut health

- *turmeric:* use this superspice in as many hot dishes as possible. The research has shown that turmeric switches on cancer fighting genes! But you need to heat the turmeric to activate it. I've stopped taking turmeric supplements and started cooking with it every day.

- *garlic:* a natural superfood!

Green tea is also a potent antioxidant and great for boosting metabolism.

Follow these simple guidelines and you'll have great skin at any age!

See appendix C for a selection of 'great skin' recipes.

Mythbust: collagen supplements and collagen in skincare

Collagen is the scaffolding of our skin. It helps the skin maintain a firm and youthful appearance. It's continually produced by skin cells, but this slows as we age and other factors, such as UV and IR light, pollutants, cigarette smoke and dietary deficiency can destroy, damage and retard collagen production. So, we're all on the hunt for anything that will increase the collagen in our skin.

As a scientist, I seriously question the growing market for collagen-based skincare and collagen nutritional supplements and powders. This is marketing myths at its best! There's no medical evidence to suggest that adding collagen to skincare or taking collagen supplements will improve your skin quality or reduce the appearance of wrinkles deep within the skin.

Collagen in skincare

It's biology 101: collagen molecules are large, complex proteins—far too big to penetrate the skin. One of the most important elements of effective skincare is the ability of the ingredients to penetrate the skin barrier to create a physiological change in the skin, and collagen is a massive protein molecule that's far too large for this. It's the tiny amino acids in skincare products (aka peptides) that can penetrate and make a difference, not massive protein molecules. Collagen in skincare products is a total waste of money!

Collagen supplements

There's a rising market, particularly in Europe and Asia, for collagen supplements and drinks. Please give me a break! Oral collagen supplements can't journey from your mouth, through your digestive tract, to your skin cells. Collagen is simply a protein source. Have a piece of steak or a bowl of lentils instead … they have more flavour too!

Here's why collagen supplements don't work. Firstly, collagen is taken in through your mouth, from where it makes a pretty rapid journey into your stomach. Here the big collagen protein is broken down by stomach acid into the protein's tiny building blocks, the amino acids. At this point the molecule has been digested in the stomach and it's no longer collagen. If, by some miracle of biology, the collagen protein remained intact, by the time it reached your small intestine (where all the nutrients are absorbed and carried into the bloodstream) it would be too large to be absorbed through the gut lining anyway and would be passed out through the body as undigested waste.

In short, collagen supplements will always end up like any other protein source: as the basic amino acid components. Collagen doesn't break down into amino acids and get reassembled into collagen again in the blood vessels on the other side of the small intestine. All amino acids end up in the blood where they will later be assembled into one of the many thousands of different proteins that our body needs to function effectively.

My advice? Increase your protein with high-quality sources of meat, fish, eggs or legumes. All types of protein end up as those simple building blocks anyway, so don't waste your money on expensive collagen supplements. Neither collagen supplements nor topical collagen skincare will make any difference to your skin.

Supplements vs serums: should vitamins be taken orally or applied to the skin?

I'm often asked about the difference between applying cosmeceutical vitamins directly to skin or taking them as oral supplements to benefit the skin, so here's the scientific lowdown on some commonly used vitamins that can be applied topically and consumed orally.

Vitamin A

Topical

Vitamin A (aka retinoids) is considered the gold standard in terms of skincare. Topical vitamin A is used to treat many common skin disorders including acne, sun damage, hyperpigmentation and even psoriasis. Prescription forms of retinoids (e.g. Stieva-A, Retin-A and Differin) are highly effective but can cause negative side-effects such as skin dryness and irritation, and many patients stop using these prescription forms due to the side-effects.

Non-prescription retinol as a stabilised molecule, and hydroxypinacolone retinoate (HPR) are considered the ideal forms for delivering topical vitamin A with maximum stability and effectiveness and minimal irritation.

Oral

Vitamin A is a fat-soluble vitamin so it can accumulate in your tissues if taken orally in high doses. Standard low dose vitamin A supplements have been clinically evaluated in terms of treating skin conditions such as acne, and results suggest that low dose oral supplementation may be ineffective at raising whole-body vitamin A levels.

High oral doses of over 1000 IU (international units) of vitamin A can lead to severe side-effects such as headaches, blurred vision, skin dryness and even reduced muscle function. If you're recommended to take oral vitamin A therapy in high doses it must be closely monitored by your physician. High dose oral vitamin A is recommended if a patient is suffering from severe cystic acne and risks permanent scarring, but if you're pregnant you must not use it as it poses a risk to your developing baby.

So which is better?

Topical daily application of vitamin A can achieve levels up to four times higher than standard oral vitamin A supplementation, so for general skin improvement I believe that topical vitamin A, primarily in serum form, is the winner over oral vitamin A supplements.

Vitamin B3 (niacinamide)

Topical

Topical vitamin B3 is truly the multitasking skin vitamin. It's used to treat acne, inflammation, fine lines, dehydration and flaking skin, pigmentation and even to improve skin immunity. Niacinamide is able to work on so many levels when used topically, so everyone can benefit from it, and used in serum form it's my absolute fave!

Oral

B3 is found in a variety of foods including green vegetables, eggs, dairy products, meat, fish, milk and grains. This makes it very difficult to have a B3 deficiency in modern society with the diverse food choices available to us, so taking it orally is hardly ever necessary.

So which is better?

Studies from The National Institutes of Health suggest that B3 works more effectively on skin when used topically rather than orally, particularly for treating acne, redness and dehydration. Furthermore, because B3 is a water-soluble vitamin it's not stored in the body, so what's not used by the body is rapidly excreted. Topical B3 wins over oral for visible results with the skin.

Vitamin C

Topical

Vitamin C in the form of L-ascorbic acid is an essential component of skin health. It's the most abundant antioxidant found in the skin. It's critical for collagen synthesis, wound healing and protecting cells against solar damage, and it's a great skin brightener.

Topical application of vitamin C is an effective way to deliver L-ascorbic acid to the skin, as L-ascorbic acid crystals are readily taken up by skin cells at an acidic pH below 3.5. Because of the instability of L-ascorbic acid in water, it's best to purchase it as a dry, refined powder that can be mixed directly with a serum at the time of application.

New ethyl ascorbic acid is a great alternative to pure L-ascorbic acid crystals because most of this ingredient gets converted into L-ascorbic acid once it penetrates the skin, and you don't need a highly acidic pH like with the pure vitamin C crystals to make it work. New ethyl ascorbic acid is a better alternative for those who prefer the convenience of a serum or if you have skin sensitive to acidity.

Oral

There's a variety of vitamin C supplements on the market. In my opinion one of the best supplements for fighting internal free radical damage is the esterified form of vitamin C (C-Ester), because it's more readily available to the cells compared to traditional L-ascorbic acid supplements. Data suggests that oral vitamin C in sufficiently high doses is effective in protecting against UV free radical damage, and can aid in skin healing. When taking a vitamin C supplement it's important to ensure you couple it with other micronutrients such as vitamin E, iron and zinc.

So which is better?

Overall, the most conclusive clinically proven results for visible skin improvement are seen in topical L-ascorbic skincare rather than oral supplements. However, I still think taking oral vitamin C is a worthwhile additional supplement for skin health. My advice is to ensure you have a diet rich in natural sources of vitamin C (fruits and veggies) and ensure adequate levels of iron and vitamin E are consumed. So, if your diet is low in vitamin C, esterified vitamin C is an excellent supplement for general health.

* * *

Healthy skin is all about the balance of lifestyle and skincare. When it comes to my skin, I know that the best results will be achieved by applying my ingredients directly to the areas of the face, neck and body that I wish to treat. I also love my 0.5 mm home roller to really drive the skin vitamins in for maximum delivery.

As far as directly treating ageing and specific skin conditions, I believe that topical vitamins win the battle over supplements, but a healthy lifestyle is critical to skin health.

Great skin really needs to be approached from both the outside with topical skincare and environmental protection and from the inside with great nutrition. The two work in perfect synergy to help our largest organ work at optimal levels.

chapter 13

The healthy skin lifestyle

As we've seen, having great skin is a result of adopting a multilayered approach. Great skin depends on good lifestyle choices, including optimal nutrition, exercise and the correct skincare regimen.

Skin and exercise

As much as exercise is recommended for a healthy mind and body, some forms can contribute to skin damage and inflammation, working against that sought-after healthy glow. So, what's the best way to care for your skin if you enjoy a regular workout?

Are you over-exercising?

Dermatologists have speculated that excessive exercise can be damaging to the skin due to the free radicals created by cells placed under extreme physical stress. Ever wondered why some marathon runners look prematurely aged? Interestingly, it's not all about the sun. High-intensity exercise (close to maximum heart rate) for extended periods may have a negative impact on the skin. Just like everything, moderation is key, and it's important to mix up our exercise with cardio and weights, particularly as we age. Accelerated ageing from excessive and prolonged exercise results from the combined effects of internal free radical damage generated by exercise, stress, and solar and environmental pollution assaults.

The ideal cosmeceutical ingredients to combat this environmental and internal damage are antioxidants such as vitamin C (L-ascorbic acid or ethyl ascorbic acid) and vitamin B3 (niacinamide), to increase the internal immunity of the skin and strengthen the skin barrier from environmental damage.

The impact of exercise on your skin

In addition to free radical damage from excessive exercise, there's a lesser known side-effect of high-impact exercise. Any high-impact exercise, like running or regular tennis, causes a jolt to the joints and skin. Just as breast tissue is unsupported during high-intensity workouts, pounding the pavement can stress facial ligaments and damage the collagen and elastin in the skin, which leads to laxity and sagging. It doesn't happen overnight, but it's one of the downsides of regular running sessions. I used to be a 10-kilometre-per-day runner but I now prefer long walks, vibrational training, cross training and pump classes. I did think of creating a face sling to support my face while jogging, but it would look totally ridiculous! I'll stick to formulating. ☺

Is your skin overheating?

For most of us, exercise enhances the blood flow through our body, which provides positive nutrients for our skin while also removing cell waste products and toxins more efficiently. However, for those with skin pigmentation concerns such as melasma, you must be careful not to over-exercise. Overheating the body can excite those rogue melanocytes (the cells that produce pigment). Those suffering from rosacea also need to keep the temperature down because the blood vessels dilate to lose heat and this may contribute to increased facial redness. Low-impact exercise and swimming are the best choices for those with melasma and rosacea.

Is exercise making your breakouts worse?

This is a question I get asked so many times from people worried about their sweat creating more zits. Fun fact: sweat is sterile!

It's not your sweat that's causing breakouts, it's the moist environment and surface impurities on your skin that create an environment for bacteria to thrive in. Another common breakout associated with exercise is the blemishes on your chest and back, called 'acne mechanica' (yes, it's a thing!). It's caused by the friction between your wet workout gear and your skin, resulting in inflammation and clogged pores.

During your workout it's important not to touch your face—gyms are a source of bacteria and other microbes that lurk on the machine handles, weights and locker doors. Also be sure to tie up your hair so it's off your face because many hair products contain comedogenic (pore clogging) oils and waxes, which contribute to breakouts.

The ideal face products for your workout

For those who prefer outdoor workouts, your number one skincare product is sunscreen. Try to exercise before 10 am and after 4 pm to avoid the damaging solar radiation. The best ingredients to adequately protect you from both UVA, UVB, HEV (blue light) and IR radiation are zinc oxide, titanium dioxide and iron oxide pigments. Mineral sun protection with over 20 per cent zinc oxide is a must during outdoor exercise and high-quality, non-clogging mineral makeup with zinc oxide, titanium dioxide and iron oxide pigment is a great way of protecting while also getting your glam on while you work out! Plus… it's water resistant and sweat proof so your friends will envy your glow! After my workouts I always use a quality cleanser to wash away the makeup, sweat and impurities that build up.

Overall, the benefits of exercise for optimal skin health far outweigh the negatives. Just as our skin requires the right products, your entire body needs the right exercise and nutrition, so to achieve the best skin results ensure you're tailoring your exercise routine to your age and skin type. Regular low to medium intensity exercise, coupled with whole nutrients and antioxidant rich skincare, is the ideal way to maintain your healthy glow.

Alcohol, your skin and the rest!

There's always an excuse: It's Friday! It's Christmas! We're in 'iso'!… The list goes on, and I'm just as guilty of finding any excuse for a glass of bubbles or a voddie, lime and soda. I don't want to be a party pooper and there's no judgement, but here's the lowdown on how alcohol affects your skin.

Glycation

Sugars mixed with alcohol (tonic water, colas, juices and other sugar mixers) and high sugar wines are what cause glycation. The high levels of sugar in these drinks attach themselves to the collagen and elastin in the skin, causing stiffening and deformity. This leads to accelerated ageing and those fine criss-cross wrinkles around the cheeks and eyes.

Dehydration

Alcohol is a diuretic, making you lose precious water from your cells, which is why a night on the espresso martinis will lead to that parched, crepey look the next day. It can take a couple of days to restore your pre-binge luminosity.

Puffiness and bloating

Because alcohol is a diuretic, your body responds to the water loss by acting like a giant sponge and trying to hold onto it. That's why the next day you have eye bags, bloating and a puffy face. At this point we usually vow *never* to drink again!

Inflammation to the body cells

Alcohol produces skin-damaging molecules called aldehydes which can be super destructive to the skin and body because they attack the delicate cell membranes and the interior of our cells where all the vital processes occur. They cause an inflammation of the cells, making them vulnerable to disease, which is why people who consume large amounts of alcohol can regularly contract chronic organ damage and have trouble healing from skin damage. There's also a risk of permanent brain damage from excessive, long-term alcohol consumption because of chronic inflammation of the brain tissue and the blood vessels that supply the brain.

Dilation of blood vessels and facial redness

You'll often notice you look a little more flushed when you're drinking, and this is because alcohol causes your tiny blood vessels to dilate. Unfortunately, rosacea sufferers are more severely affected by alcohol because the blood vessels are less able to recover, causing more prolonged facial redness.

Lack of sleep

I recently went through a period of not sleeping well and I became focused (borderline obsessed) with my sleep patterns. My Fitbit monitors the stages of sleep and how long I'm in each state, and I noticed that when I'd had a few drinks my dream sleep (REM) and deep sleep phases were well below normal. Both of these phases of sleep are vital, particularly deep sleep, which is responsible for restoring the mind and body. Alcohol totally messes with sleep quality. Even a couple of drinks will have a significant impact on how your body and brain rejuvenate. This has given me even more incentive to have at least five alcohol free days per week.

Weight gain and the sugar myth

It's a myth that alcohol forms sugar in the blood. Vodka, gin and rum contain zero sugar!

Alcohol is actually converted to a chemical called acetate by the liver. The liver sees this as a toxin and tries to break down the calories from acetate before breaking down 'good' energy from the fat or sugar in food. Alcohol provides no nutritional value at all, which is why it's often called 'empty calories', and it slows down the burning of fat, which is why alcohol contributes to weight gain. It also interferes with blood glucose levels and affects sugar breakdown.

Cancer connection

Alcohol, even one to two glasses per day, has a direct link with cancer, especially of the mouth and throat. Alcohol suppresses the immune system, thus reducing the body's natural defences. As alcohol is broken down in our body one of the main by-products is a chemical called acetaldehyde, a cancer-causing chemical which produces reactive free radicals and damages the DNA in our cells. The by-products of alcohol can also cause our skin to have a reduced defence against solar radiation damage, which may increase our likelihood of contracting skin cancers.

Okay, reality check... Most of us like a couple of drinks on the weekend, and a Thursday night out with the girls is just that little bit more fun with a couple of chardis. I'm talking about moderation and smart choices. The resveratrol in red wine is actually seen as a benefit due to its antioxidant ability, but drinking three or more glasses of cab sav a night will quickly negate those benefits.

The effects of alcohol on the skin and your overall luminosity are clearly visible the morning after, but it's the long-term impact that we need to be mindful of. Like most things that tempt us but can be harmful, the key is moderation and knowing your personal limits.

Holy smoke! How smoking really affects your skin

Every day we're constantly assaulted by thousands of noxious chemicals from pollution and the atmosphere, and chemicals from cigarette smoke are some of the most harmful forms of skin pollution out there. Apart from known links to cancer and heart and lung damage, smoking really targets the health of the skin. The skin of a smoker is more prone to skin disorders such as acne, rosacea and psoriasis because smoking weakens the body's natural defences and immunity to infection and environmental challenges.

And there's more… the damage in the skin from puffing away builds up over time and can result in genetic mutations and even cancers in the skin.

If a smoker starts in her twenties, chances are she'll look 60 by the time she's 40. Believe me, I've seen it! When I had my Melbourne skin clinic I'd always be honest with smokers and let them know that any product or treatment results would probably not be significant if they smoked.

If you don't smoke, please read this section anyway because if you have a friend or family member who smokes I implore you to pass this information on. And if you're a smoker, please take the time to read this.

What does tobacco do to the skin?

As George Bernard Shaw so cleverly said, 'A cigarette is a pinch of tobacco rolled in paper with a fire at one end and a fool at the other!'. Here's a list of exactly how tobacco affects your skin and why you should tell your bestie, mum, sister or self to *stop now*!

- *Free radical damage:* cigarette tobacco causes massive free radical damage and oxidation to the skin tissues and blood vessels, and impacts blood flow to the skin so fewer nutrients are carried there and the process of removing toxins is less efficient.

- *Microbiome imbalance:* the presence of toxins in smoke also affects the natural bacterial balance in your body so the good bacteria suffer and your vital skin barrier won't work efficiently.

- *Reduced collagen production and increased collagen breakdown:* tobacco smoke has a direct impact on skin ageing, sagging and wrinkles because it stimulates the skin enzyme matrix metallo-proteinase (MMP-1), which destroys our precious collagen. It also slows down the ability of our clever fibroblast cells to make collagen.

- *Elastin breakdown and malformation:* elastin breakdown is also called 'elastosis' and is where the elastin in the dermis is destroyed or mutates, and it looks like yellow, leathery skin with deep wrinkles when the face is at rest. Elastosis can also be caused by the sun, but if you smoke it's greatly exacerbated and the visual results are obvious.

- *Dehydration:* cigarette smoke directly interacts with the surface skin cells and sucks out the water, so your weakened skin barrier will appear dry, flaky and often inflamed.

- *Appearance of 'smoker's face':* I can recognise the skin of a smoker almost instantly. The carbon monoxide in cigarette smoke competes with vital oxygen in our bloodstream. Carbon monoxide latches onto our red blood cells and pushes the oxygen out of the way, effectively suffocating our body from the inside. Smoke also depletes our vitamin C levels and the chemical toxins interfere with the skin's normal cell functions. All of this results in wrinkles, gauntness and a dull grey appearance.

- *Reduced ability to repair:* smoking totally exhausts the natural ability of our skin to regenerate and heal because the skin is already too busy fighting the free radical damage smoking has created. Tobacco also slows down the ability of the body to repair a wound because the blood flow is reduced, so all those healing nutrients and oxygen aren't getting to the damaged cells that need them. This is why smokers' scars are usually larger and more discoloured than those of non-smokers.

- *Increased risk of dermatitis:* there's an increased risk of dermatitis because the allergens in tobacco, and filters such as menthol and formaldehyde, can lead to allergies and severe skin irritations.

- *Increased risk of psoriasis:* there's a direct link between psoriasis and smoking.

I know smoking is one of the most addictive habits in our society. Still, after reading what it does to your skin, and knowing what it does to your health, please, please, please … if you smoke … I *beg* you, do all you can to kick the habit. I know it'll be hard, but your family, friends, body and skin will all be forever grateful.

*   *   *

There's no single magic bullet for great skin. It really is about making good choices and moderation. Look at your day-to-day lifestyle, try to adopt good habits and avoid overloading your body with toxins from cigarettes and excess alcohol.

chapter 14

The environment

'EnviroAgeing' is a new buzzword which describes the process of skin ageing that is influenced by outside factors such as solar radiation (UV, infrared, blue light) and pollution.

Defending your skin against urban aggression

My first encounter with serious air pollution was when I visited Shanghai, China. I was there for over a week and never actually saw the sky, let alone sunlight! The industrial smog was so thick that the locals permanently wore a face mask. My first thought was to get indoors and protect my lungs, but my lungs were only one organ exposed to this pollution pea soup. My skin, the largest organ of my body, was drinking in the air pollution every second I was outside.

I arrived home relieved to breathe in the clean Australian air, and over the years have learned more about environmental pollution and the dangerous cocktail that can form when sunlight is combined with even low levels of air pollution.

Sad fact

Over half the humans on earth live on just 3 per cent of the total land mass of our globe! The concentration of pollution in our cities is massive, and we need to take this problem seriously. As a scientist, I can say categorically that in addition to the normal climatic cycles that have occurred over millions of years without human intervention, global warming and climate change are happening and accelerating every month. This is a whole other category worth major consideration, but not my area of expertise. I do urge you to find all the information you can about the human impact on climate change and see if you can play your part in this big issue.

What is pollution?

Pollution is substances present outside the human body that are considered harmful or toxic. In terms of air pollution, a number of factors contribute, including those shown in this illustration.

POLLUTION SOURCES

Industrial and factory waste   Vehicles   Heating and cooling systems

Agriculture   Fuel burning   Cigarette smoke

Fuel burning

The main damaging type of airborne pollution is known as 'smog'. This term was coined in the early 1900s from 'smoky fog'. Today, smog is more scientifically defined as a type of pollution containing tiny particles that are less than 2.5 microns in diameter. One micron is one-millionth of a metre and 40 times thinner than a strand of hair. Tiny.

These tiny smog particles float about and make contact with the skin surface, creating free radical damage. This damage can cascade into a series of events resulting in disruption of the delicate skin barrier, inflammation, dryness, dullness and sensitivity.

There are also tiny airborne particles of toxic heavy metals such as arsenic, lead, mercury, cadmium and nickel. Heavy metals, like smog particles, attack the skin barrier and wreak havoc with the balance and health of our skin.

Can we protect against urban pollution?

As with solar damage, the aim of the game with urban pollution is protection. Thankfully we don't need to mask up! There's a marine exopolysaccharide, which is a sugar molecule made by a special bacteria living in sea water, called alteromonas ferment extract (AFE) that can act like a shield against urban pollution. It stops the smog from sticking to the skin by creating an invisible mesh, so the pollution simply slides off the skin when you cleanse at the end of the day. AFE is also able to bind to toxic heavy metals, so if they land on the skin it neutralises the effect so that there are no toxic by-products to damage the skin. Cool, huh?

But there's more ... what happens when smog meets sunlight?

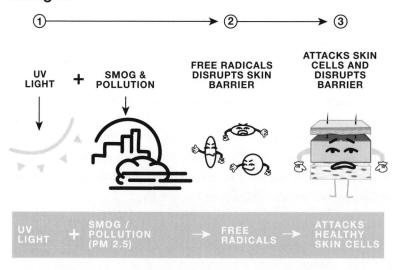

You may be lulled into a false sense of security when you live in an area of relatively low air pollution, but the truth is that any urban area is an issue: where there's urban pollution and solar radiation, it's a problem for your skin. Even in stunning Australia! When low concentrations of smog react with UV light, ground level ozone is created. This is a powerful free radical engine capable of causing DNA damage, barrier disruption, irritation and visible ageing. So beware ... even 'clean' cities like we have in Australia can be a problem if UV light is added to the mix.

Can supplements help?

Coupled with a good skincare routine, supplements can help reduce the negative impact of urban aggression. Opt for a diet high in antioxidants, or add oral supplements like lycopene, CoQ10, astaxanthin, resveratrol (which is found in red wine, yay!) and green tea extract. I'm not one for processed foods, but you can obtain high doses of lycopene from tomato paste or tomato sauce. I suggest looking for low-sugar or sugar-free sauce varieties to keep it as healthy as possible.

TERRI'S ANTI-POLLUTION SKINCARE ROUTINE

- Ensure you effectively and thoroughly cleanse morning and night with an SLS-free cleanser which is pH balanced. *Never* go to bed without cleansing!

- Apply daily sun protection to fight solar damage. Mineral makeup is ideal because high-quality minerals contain the following essential pollution fighters:

  - zinc oxide, which protects from UVA, UVB and infrared rays

  - titanium dioxide, which protects from UVA and some UVB rays

  - iron oxides (in mineral makeup at the correct dosage), which protect from UV, infrared and blue-light radiation.

- Look for alteromonas ferment extract (AFE) in skincare products. This will effectively combat the ageing effects of smog and heavy metals.

- Use topical antioxidants daily that will effectively neutralise the effects of free radical damage created by environmental pollutants. The most potent skin antioxidants include:

  - *vitamin C:* pure L-ascorbic acid crystals or stabilised serum. Protects the skin cells from free radical damage created by solar radiation.

  - *green tea concentrate:* this has been shown to reduce UVB skin damage.

  - *lycopene in the form of hydrolysed tomato skin extract:* this ingredient filters harmful HEV/blue light rays and reduces UVB redness.

Looking great in all climates

Our skin behaves differently when faced with different climates and environments, so when it comes to the seasons, we often need to reconsider our routine to suit the climate.

Winter skincare

When the climate is cooler, our blood vessels try to insulate us by becoming thinner and staying deeper in our skin to maintain our core blood temperature of around 37 degrees Celsius. This is why our skin looks paler in winter. We also need to be mindful of temperature fluctuations from our warm, and often very dry, cosy homes to braving the outside elements.

Stay UV protected

Don't let winter lull you into a false sense of security. Even though UVB (burning) rays aren't as intense in winter, ageing and deeply penetrating UVA rays are still as intense as during the summer—and UVA can even penetrate glass and clouds. UVA is also responsible for causing skin cancers, so it's important to use a broad spectrum sun protection moisturiser or mineral makeup. Preferably choose a product with a minimum of 20 per cent zinc oxide or a mineral makeup with high levels of zinc oxide and titanium dioxide to give you optimal UV protection during the day.

Hydrate inside and out

Central heating, temperature extremes and cold winds can wreak havoc on your skin and result in it drying and cracking. It's really important to use serums and moisturisers with high levels of hydrators such as hyaluronic acid, which binds 1000 times its weight in water, and high-quality, non-clogging oils such as olive squalene, shea butter, macadamia oil, marula oil and sea buckthorn oil to prevent moisture loss. My old favourite, vitamin B3 serum, increases the ceramide level in the skin, which makes it better at holding moisture and gives the skin a dewy glow during winter. B3 also strengthens the outer layer of the skin so the barrier is better able to cope with the environmental stress of winter.

Everyone needs a moisturiser in winter, but it's important to choose the right one for your skin type: oil-free or low-oil formulas for oily skin and enlarged pores; cosmeceutical-based products for ageing skin; low-irritant products for sensitive and irritated skin; and richer, emollient moisturisers for very dry skin.

Remember to stay hydrated in winter. If you can't handle glasses of cold water, opt for natural herbal teas or warm lemon and ginger infusions. Try a healthy hot chocolate with pure organic cacao (2 teaspoons), Natvia natural sweetener to taste (1–2 sachets) and skim milk.

Winter exfoliation

Gentle exfoliation is still necessary in winter, though not as frequently because your natural cell turnover can slow a little in the colder weather. Remember, don't excessively exfoliate or overuse harsh scrubs. A gentle abrasive scrub can be used weekly (especially in the T-zone) for normal, robust skin, but is not recommended for sensitive skin.

Chemical exfoliation with AHAs and BHAs is recommended once or twice a week, and if you suffer from sensitive skin try an acid free chemical exfoliant.

Body skin often becomes flaky and dry over winter, so remember to exfoliate your body twice a week. I use a loofah mitt in the shower followed by a non-greasy body lotion with niacinamide for added hydration.

Winter mineral makeup

Forget fake tans and embrace your natural skin tone in winter. Choose a shade of minerals that perfectly blend with the side of your neck to avoid the dreaded 'jawline tide mark', and take advantage of the natural UVA/B protection that good-quality mineral makeup offers during outdoor winter activities.

Remember the lips: they're very vulnerable to winter dehydration. Opt for a cosmeceutical lip treatment with ingredients that protect from wind damage and restore lost moisture from environmental damage.

Treat your dry hands and feet

Hands and feet really show the signs of winter dryness. Want to give your feet and hands an intense overnight mask? Exfoliate hands and feet with a gentle scrub and follow with the generous application of a thick occlusive moisturiser or overnight mask. Wear thin cotton socks and cotton gloves to bed and wake up with baby soft hands and feet. You can repeat this treatment for seven days for hands and feet rejuvenation. This treatment is not recommended if you have a new partner. ☺

Summer skincare

The harsh UV, infrared and blue-light rays, as well as the relentless heat of the summer sun, can leave your body dry, damaged and in need of replenishment. The skin is your body's first line of defence against the harsh external elements so it's important to keep it protected and hydrated. Here are my top tips for great summer skin.

Sun protection is key

This goes without saying! Even on a cloudy summer day when the UVB rays may not seem aggressive, your skin can be damaged by UVB, UVA, infrared and blue-light rays. Protect...protect...protect! Use your sunscreen and/or a high-grade mineral sunblock! This is uber important. Go back to chapter 4 for detailed information on sunscreen.

Drink up!

If you don't drink enough water in summer you'll suffer from dehydration, which is your body's way of telling you that it doesn't have enough water to support your vital functions—and remember, the skin is your largest organ! Our skin is 64 per cent water so keep your fluid intake up to keep that summer glow. Perspiring means you're losing water, so drink. Even mild dehydration affects brain function, mood and physical performance.

Did you know that drinking more water (roughly 2 litres per day) can increase your metabolism and burn an extra 100 (approx.) calories throughout the day? And that old myth that drinking caffeine in coffee and tea will dehydrate you is *absolute* rubbish — any liquids you consume (except alcohol) will add to the hydration levels of your body. The diuretic effect of tea and coffee is minimal compared to the benefits of drinking them. So have a cuppa and enjoy!

Moisturise your body daily

We often shower more in summer, which can strip the skin of its natural oils, so have an effective body moisturiser close at hand. Try to choose one with an added cosmeceutical benefit like vitamin B for hydration and barrier repair, or vitamin C for antioxidant protection.

Don't over-scrub your body

There are so many trendy scrubs on the market: be careful not to overuse them. Too much exfoliation removes the new skin cells and makes the skin more vulnerable to dryness and irritation. Weekly exfoliation is fine, and scrubbing mitts are great — especially for removing those last remnants of fake tan. Exfoliate in circular movements once a week using a loofah, mitt or gentle mineral scrub to help shed your dry, dead skin without removing your healthy skin.

Hot, steamy showers are a no-no

Steaming hot water can dry out the skin and temperature extremes can increase the appearance of fine blood vessels on the surface of the skin, so keep your showers short and not too hot. Also, avoid soap: it's very alkaline (pH of around 9) and can strip the natural pH of the skin. Most liquid cleansers and cleansing gels are around pH 5 to 6 so are a great substitute, but if you're sensitive, be careful that there are no other irritants in the ingredient list such as artificial fragrance, SLS or SLES.

Are you swimming in chemicals?

Chlorinated pools and spas contain chemicals that can strip the skin of good bacteria, moisture and natural oils, which can then cause irritation. After a dip, take a lukewarm shower to rinse off the chemicals — otherwise your skin may absorb them! The chemicals also ruin colour treated hair, so watch out.

Tanned skin isn't glamorous

Tanned skin is nature's warning that your skin is being damaged by UV rays. Sunbathing speeds the ageing process, causes wrinkles and sunspots, and most importantly, increases your risk of skin cancer! The best sunscreen is four walls and a roof!

Protecting our world

Unfortunately, the beauty industry is often guilty of ignoring the fragility of our planet, and many of the ingredients and the packaging used negatively impacts our planet. Thankfully, many companies are stepping up to do their part for the earth. Myself included! Let's put as much effort into making the best planet possible as we put into making ourselves the best possible.

Stats tell us that over 100 billion units of non-recyclable packaging are produced every year in the beauty industry. Eeek! This includes plastic containers, plastic coated card, foam, shipping packaging... and on it goes. I bet the guy who invented the first plastic polymer in 1907 didn't realise that his invention would still be lying in rubbish dumps 1000 years later... We're a lazy bunch and sadly over half of us simply can't be bothered using the recycling bin. And even if we're diligent, I've heard that the recycling industry is not what we think it is and so much of it ends up as landfill anyway. So, we clearly need to do our bit and take tremendous care with the packing and products we use.

Plastic microbeads

One of the big issues I'm passionate about is the use of plastic microbeads in so many face and body scrubs. I was introduced to this ingredient by a supplier several years ago and had a very bad feeling about it. With an intuitive concern about the effect these plastic beads may have on our environment, I chose to use biodegradable and mineral materials in my scrubs. As I predicted, years later these plastic microbeads are finding their way into our waterways, riverbeds and the bellies of our sea creatures! Thankfully these beads are now banned in most regions around the globe.

Synthetic glitter

All that glitters is not good! The other ingredient making news lately is plastic-based glitter in makeup and skincare. This ingredient is extremely common in commercial makeup and presents the same threat as plastic beads. The good news is the alternative mica-based mineral glitter is naturally derived and eco-friendly. Another great reason to choose high-quality mineral makeup. You can still sparkle with safety.

Ethical skincare

Palm oil has come under fire for a number of years because of the impact producing it has on our orangutan population, many other animal species and our forests, which supply the planet with life-giving oxygen.

Palm oil is the most widely used vegetable oil on earth and overproduction is wiping out our forests. Ethical skincare companies source palm oil from fair trade, sustainable sources.

Sustainable products and packaging

When I began packing my products to ship to my customers I wanted to find a way to reduce my carbon footprint. It's still a work in progress, but I've found a few ways to do my bit for the world. Here are some of the ways my packaging is sustainable:

- We use recyclable plastic and glass packaging for all our products.

- We provide refillable travel size packaging.

- We use 100 per cent recyclable paper and cardboard packaging and boxes for all of our products.

- We offer more sustainable 'semi naked' delivery packages.

- We use biodegradable outer packaging made of vegetable matter that's compostable in the garden. (This was a biggie for me.)

- All wrapping paper we use is recyclable.

- We use biodegradable cornstarch 'popcorn' style filling instead of plastic filling to fill the gaps in our boxed packages. You could probably eat this stuff!

- We provide calico washcloths and compostable konjac sponges rather than non-degradable, non-flushable facial wipes.

As an Australian business owner and a proud member of our planet, I'm committed to saving the environment for my tribe and future generations to have a greener and cleaner future.

What about our people?

Many industries exploit child labour to mine minerals and micas used in today's mineral makeup. I'm fiercely protective of children and will only source minerals from legal mines that use fair trade labour.

And our animal friends

Gaining the CCF (Choose Cruelty Free) accreditation was no mean feat. It means that not only must my products be free of animal testing, but every ingredient I formulate with (hundreds) must also be certified as cruelty free and not tested on animals.

I'm chuckling to myself now as I write this, because at my 50th birthday party my kids gave a wonderful speech and referred to my business as a side note: 'Mum doesn't test on animals, she tests on her kids!' Thanks James and Georgie for keeping it real!

Well, I vowed to be totally transparent in this book and I'll hold true to that. Back in the early days when I had products being tested in the lab I'd also hand out samples to all of my friends and family to trial them ... including my 'guineakids'! This gave me invaluable feedback on the elegance of the product before I took it to market. I really think people are so much better at honest feedback than rabbits.

Seriously though, I won't sell directly to regions that still perform animal testing on beauty products. There are now many alternatives, including creating artificial skin (which gives extremely accurate indicators of potential skin irritation).

Sustainable ingredients

As an Australian business owner and scientist, I owe it to my earth, and to you awesome people, to be mindful of every ingredient I formulate with. Ethics and safety are paramount.

Bioidentical ingredients

In the past decade scientists have come a long way in their creation of new bioidentical ingredients, and this is where I come back to my 'natural is not always best' mantra.

If we know that a specific ingredient sourced from nature is having a positive effect on the skin, and it's backed by data, then I believe it's more ethical to attempt to copy this active molecule in the lab than to pillage the land or sea for the natural ingredient. Creating these synthetic copies, which are identical to what nature created, doesn't put any stress on our environment and doesn't interfere with the delicate ecological chain. Synthetic is often more sustainable. Plus, creating synthetic bioidentical copies in labs also means that the ingredients will be 100 per cent pure, and won't contain any potentially undesirable contaminants. Win–win!

Protecting our oceans

The chemical sunscreen ingredient oxybenzone has been banned from use on the coasts of Hawaii and Palau due to its negative impact on coral reefs. This ingredient is one of the most common types of chemical absorbing sunscreen — chemical sunscreens that absorb into the surface of the skin. It is contributing to coral bleaching and DNA damage and is severely disrupting the entire marine ecosystem. The best alternative is zinc oxide and titanium dioxide in non-nanoparticle form. While zinc oxide and titanium dioxide nanoparticles are not considered dangerous in humans, there's concern that coral may be able to absorb these small particles, so it's better to opt for non-nano.

Plastic particles found in toothpaste, cheap makeup 'glitter' and as microbeads in exfoliating products also play havoc on our aquatic life and accumulate in their tissues. Plastic is certainly not fantastic!

Whoa! This was a meaty chapter (sorry vegans)! Our precious earth is all we have. We must respect it and be mindful of the impact of it on our skin. But we must also protect and preserve it for ourselves and our great-great grandchildren.

chapter 15

Skin under the microscope

When your skin looks great you can see the glow. While vibrant skin is visible to the naked eye, there's so much going on behind the scenes that we can't see. The surface of our skin and every living cell of our bodies resides in a microscopic universe that houses the blueprint of ourselves (our genes) — teeny tiny microbes that have a huge impact on the health of our skin and special cells that possess unlimited potential.

Epigenetics: our DNA is not our destiny

When I was a schoolgirl in Melbourne in the '70s I was passionate about biology and my biology teacher inspired me to pursue a future in science. My favourite subject? Genetics. The field of genetics has changed so much over the decades and what I studied has literally been turned on its head. We can now map the entire human genome, test for genetic defects that hadn't been discovered back then, and we now understand the role of a new area of biology called epigenetics.

Our genes are not our destiny and our DNA only plays a partial role in the way we look and feel. This is a huge relief to those of us who may have genes that dictate a predisposition to premature ageing — we can prevent this playing out through intervention with certain cosmeceutical ingredients and lifestyle modifications. We now know that many factors in our environment can 'tweak' the operating system of our genes, much like downloading an app on our phone can make our phone work more conveniently. These outside factors are known as epigenetic markers ('epi' and 'genetic' meaning 'above the genes') and these little guys can have a massive impact on our lives and our appearance.

So what is the epigenome?

Back to biology class. The epigenome is the information that lies above the genome or chromosomes. Our chromosomes are basically the strands of DNA in charge of holding our genetic information, which carries the blueprint for all the parts of us and our body processes.

A small piece of a chromosome is called a gene, and every gene in our body makes a protein that tells our body to make something or do something. We have genes for eye colour, hair colour, making collagen, making melanin ... and on and on it goes.

Our genes are shy little entities and can't do much without a gentle nudge from our epigenome. Think of our genes as the actors in a movie, and the epigenome as the director telling them what to do — whether to turn on, off, up or down. Any time a gene that creates collagen in our skin is turned on, that action is directed by epigenetics.

The impact of your genes

Here's something else we didn't know when I was in school and university: epigenetic signals from the environment (diet, surroundings and even behaviour) can be passed on to future generations without a single change to the genes in the cells. As bizarre as that may sound, what you put in your body today could have an impact on the wellbeing of your great-great grandchildren. Crazy, huh?

This fascinating field of epigenetics is now carrying over to cosmeceutical skincare and epigenetic skincare is booming. Cosmetic chemists can now harness ingredients that are epigenetically active, and with them reprogram skin cells on a genetic level for optimal health and a more youthful appearance. Amazing, right?

In terms of our skin, there are literally hundreds of genes responsible for its structure and function. For example, there are 40 genes responsible for collagen production, 200 genes related to antioxidants, 400 genes controlling inflammation and over 500 genes involved with skin hydration. By harnessing epigenetics in skincare we can be in control of how our skin genes are expressed and the destiny of our DNA.

Epigenetics in skincare

There are loads of incredible active ingredients that can direct our genes to improve our skin. Let's look at a few examples of ingredients that are epigenetically active.

Retinoic acid

This is a great example of an epigenetic cosmeceutical because it acts as a director of the genes of our skin cells.

(A note about retinoic acid) ───────────

Retinoic acid is the active form of vitamin A that works on our genes. Most non-prescription forms of vitamin A skincare products (e.g. retinol, retinyl palmitate and retinaldehyde) must be converted to retinoic acid in the skin before our skin cells can recognise and use it as a clever epigenetic molecule. Retinoic acid is the molecule that influences genetic processes in the very heart of our skin cells: the cell nucleus and the home of our genes.

So how does retinoic acid impact our DNA and genes? One main benefit is the effect it has on 'fixing' cells damaged by sunlight. UV light damages skin cells to the extent that mutations occur in the genes of skin cells, and retinoic acid can reverse this harmful mutation and direct the genes to repair the damage.

Retinoic acid also directs our genes to control the rate of epidermal cell production for the renewal of fresh, healthy skin, and is able to control oil production for acne sufferers and stimulate collagen production to make our skin look more youthful. This clever molecule is hands down my favourite ingredient because it acts as an epigenetic cosmeceutical in so many skin genes!

Hexapeptide-51

This cosmeceutical can reduce genetic damage from solar radiation, protect skin cells from ultraviolet damage and activate the genes for overall DNA repair. Clinical studies even show that this ingredient is able to epigenetically direct cells to behave as if they were 10 years younger!

Marjoram extract

Another exciting epigenetic discovery! Remember earlier in the book you learned that deep within your skin there's a vital cell called the fibroblast? This cell is responsible for making collagen and elastin, two proteins that give our skin firmness, density and elasticity. As we age, the fibroblast cells begin to age too, and they're less efficient at making the vital 'proteins of youth' so our skin loses its youthful tone. Cosmetic chemists have now harnessed the botanical 'marjoram extract' to epigenetically restore ageing fibroblasts! This is achieved through the purified active ingredient directing the gene responsible for collagen production to simply stay 'switched on'; it results in an 18 per cent improved density and a 15 per cent improved firmness in the skin.

Our skin genes are certainly not our destiny, and reprogramming can happen through our environment, nutrition, and ... yes ... even our skincare ingredients. The result is that we can direct the genes we're born with to make the best version of the skin we're in.

Our genes may be the doorway to the fountain of youth, but epigenetics provides the key to opening it.

Stem cells and growth factors in skincare: miracle or myth?

It sounds like sci-fi in a jar, but hundreds of skincare companies are espousing the virtues of stem cells and growth factors as the next wave in skincare and the key to the fountain of youth. So what exactly is all the buzz about? And do they truly deliver on their promises?

What are stem cells?

Stem cells are the basic building blocks of the body, kind of like the 'mother cell' from which all other cells are possible. A stem cell has the potential to become almost any type of cell in our body: blood cells, liver cells, bone marrow cells and collagen-producing cells, to name a few. As we age, the number of stem cells in our body reduces and we're less able to heal and regenerate new cells.

Stem cell therapy in skincare

Consumers expect stem cells to address visible signs of ageing. Stem cells in skincare products are expected to transform into cells which produce collagen and elastin (fibroblasts) to address wrinkles and rejuvenate the skin.

But can they go from jar to skin and perform such miracles? I think not.

Can stem cells survive outside the human body?

Stem cells can't survive outside the human body — for example, in a skin serum or cream — because the stem cells in skincare products are dead.

Keeping stem cells active isn't a simple procedure. Apart from sterile laboratory technology, stem cells need a perfectly balanced and specialised growth culture medium to remain active and alive, and these delicate cells can't survive in serums, creams or the air. Even if they could, they'd have to deal with the preservatives that are in all skincare products (or should be). The job of preservatives is to make sure living cells like bacteria, mould and fungi (that don't belong in the product) don't survive, so stem cells have little hope! If not stored properly, stem cells perish within minutes. And even if the cells could survive in a totally inhospitable skincare base, they can't be absorbed through the skin because of their large molecular size. Cells are massive compared to active ingredients. Again, it's like trying to post a basketball in a letter box!

Are plant stem cells valid?

There are numerous lotions and potions containing botanical (such as apple or pear) stem cells that tout their ability to reduce the appearance of wrinkles. But like human stem cells, plant stem cells are also vulnerable. They require the perfect growth medium to survive and are unable to penetrate human skin. And there's more... how can plant stem cells possibly be compatible with human cells? The species aren't even remotely related.

But... are stem-cell injections effective?

Some leading-edge clinics offer new treatments whereby the patient's stem cells are isolated and injected back into their face to stimulate the proliferation of new cells for rejuvenation or plumping. I believe this treatment can offer real benefits thanks to the stem cells and active cell components possibly still being viable (if the clinician is fully trained and knows what they're doing) and because they're using the patient's own stem cells (not something foreign). Some use a technique called 'deep freeze cryostore', in which a client's own stem cells are stored at very low temperatures so the cells are held in suspended animation and may be used in the future. When the face is pierced by the needle many times during stem cell injections, as with skin needling treatment, the skin has a minor injury and responds by going into self-repair mode, which stimulates the production of collagen.

Stem-cell treatment is an exciting new field of cosmetic medicine, but I must stress that it doesn't correlate with stem cells added to skincare products.

What about growth factors?

Growth factors are also creating a real buzz in the skincare industry. Stem cells actually produce small molecules called growth factors which may rejuvenate skin and address many signs of ageing. Growth factors are small protein segments and yes, these guys are often, but not always, small enough to penetrate the skin.

Growth factors act as chemical messengers and allow communication between cells in our skin and body. They can act as a control mechanism for wound healing and the regeneration of cells. They're fragile little entities. The method of preparing these growth factors from stem cells is highly specialised and must be performed in a laboratory; they can't be extracted by simply 'mashing' up the stem cells. Furthermore, these delicate growth factors need to be stabilised and protected by delivery systems such as liposomes, and they don't work effectively if applied directly to the skin.

Now here's where it gets a bit controversial. As a scientist dedicated to skin health, there are several things that concern me regarding the application of growth factors:

- *Growth factors aren't choosy:* if growth factors are applied to the skin, delivered correctly, and are small enough to penetrate and reach the target cells, they could stimulate many types of cells to regenerate, not just the target. My concern as a scientist is that growth factors may stimulate mutated and potentially malignant cells as well as the healthy cells — that is, they don't have the capacity to choose which cells they stimulate.

- *Growth factors can be too big to get in:* growth factors are essentially small pieces of protein making up an amino acid chain. The ideal number of amino acids that are able to penetrate the skin is around 10 or fewer. The most common growth factor applied to skin is epidermal growth factor (EGF), an ingredient that was released almost 20 years ago, and it's composed of 53 amino acids, making it very difficult to penetrate into the deeper dermis.

- *Plant growth factors aren't the same as human ones:* it's difficult to scientifically accept that a growth factor from an apple stem cell can be compatible with human cells. Growth factors which are chemically identical to human growth factors will be more effective, but may also stimulate malignant or premalignant cells. It's all about like-for-like compatibility, and being very selective with the target cell so they don't switch on rogue cells.

The future of stem cells and growth factors

Joint therapy and bone marrow transplants use stem-cell technology and this has proven successful and is now considered a viable treatment. However, overall stem-cell research is at an experimental stage and many therapies are considered controversial.

Stem cells used in clinical treatments will play a valid role in the future of skincare, but there are still many hurdles to overcome. In my scientific opinion, there's currently no effective method for delivering viable stem cells into human skin via a cream or serum.

Growth factors, on the other hand, can play a significant role in the future of skincare if more research is done to create safety, stability, delivery and effectiveness.

It's my belief as a formulator that the only truly safe and viable method for using growth-factor therapy is to stimulate the client's skin from within to produce their own growth factors in a controlled manner. There are currently some naturally occurring and laboratory produced peptides that can effectively stimulate the skin to produce its own internal growth factors that the body recognises as 'self', and these help rejuvenate the skin without turning on naughty rogue cells.

We're entering a 'brave new world' when it comes to harnessing stem cells and growth factors in cosmetic medicine, and we must tread carefully and be cynical about promises and claims. The future is exciting, but all clinical data and results must be fully validated for safety and efficacy before we invest in this technology.

Bacteria on our skin: the good, the bad and the facts

Did you know that there's an entire bacterial community residing on the surface of our skin that dictates the health of our skin?

A couple of years ago I was celebrating my son's birthday and chatting to his old school friend, who is now an entrepreneur. I love exchanging ideas with smart young people and Chris was excited about the prospect of using probiotics on the skin just like we use them for gut health. The conversation piqued my curiosity, so I set about learning more about this new frontier of skin therapy. Fast-forward to today and I'm even more passionate about using prebiotics and probiotics to improve the health and appearance of our skin. *Big* thank you to Chris H for your inspiration!

Happily living in our gut is a community of bacteria called the microbiome. We also have a microbiome on the surface of our skin, and this gang of bugs is vital for our skin health. Most people are aware of the importance of creating the ideal balance of bacteria in our gut, but we need to address the balance of good and bad bacteria on our skin too. Both impact the health of the entire body — even our brain function and mental health.

Fun facts

Here are some fun facts about the human microbiome:

- The human body houses trillions of teeny tiny microbes.
- These microorganisms make up to 3 per cent of the total weight of our body. Wow, that's a lot of little critters!
- The microbes in and on our body outnumber human cells by a whopping 10 to 1.

At a recent conference in New York on the skin microbiome, scientists suggested that it is so important it should be considered an organ. That begs the question: if the skin is considered the largest organ, then perhaps we should actually consider the skin microbiome as the largest organ of our body!

The skin microbiome is vital for nearly every skin function, including the strength of our barrier, and there are many factors that can severely disrupt the bacterial balance and skin barrier. These include:

- pollution
- climate extremes (heat, wind, cold, dryness, humidity)
- solar radiation (UVA, UVB, HEV and infrared)
- antibiotics (both oral and topical ointments and creams)
- personal care products:
  - strong acids found in glycolic or lactic acid cleansers or exfoliants
  - strong alkalis such as soaps
  - harsh surfactants with high levels of SLS and SLES
  - antibacterial washes that kill most bacteria on the skin surface, both the harmful and the beneficial species
  - excessive hygiene and sanitiser gels that are becoming the norm in most handbags
  - harsh preservatives in skincare products specifically designed to kill microbes.

All of these factors can cause bacterial imbalance, which causes barrier damage and results in redness, inflammation, poor skin immunity and sensitivity. Enter the new frontier of prebiotics and probiotics for the skin.

The benefits of prebiotics and probiotics for the skin

The huge benefits of taking oral probiotics are well studied, and the results can also be translated to topical application of probiotics in skincare, provided the formulations are stable. Like the gut, the health of the epidermis is largely dependent on the right balance and diversity of both beneficial and harmful bacterial flora. Clinical studies have shown that prebiotic and probiotic skincare can significantly reduce inflammation and redness, assist with balancing the pH of the skin and make the barrier more robust and able to cope with harsh environmental aggressors.

It's important to note that we still need 'bad' (pathogenic) bacteria, as well as good guys, to maintain a vigilant immune system.

Why are both prebiotics and probiotics important?

For the best results for your skin you need both. Prebiotics were first identified in 1995 as part of plant carbohydrates that couldn't be digested and act as a fibre source. Examples include certain parts of asparagus, leeks, broccoli, garlic, konjac root, dandelion root, apples, chicory root, Jerusalem artichoke and green, unripe bananas. My number one form of prebiotic in food is konjac root, which I buy as low carb noodles in the supermarket and serve with my homemade pesto or Napoli sauce. *Yum*!

If you're looking to up your daily intake of probiotics, then go for natural, unsweetened yoghurt, kefir (this is my fave because it's lactose free and mega-high in probiotics), miso, sauerkraut, kimchi, tempeh and kombucha. In terms of skincare, look for prebiotic ingredients on your label such as alpha-glucan oligosaccharide and purified inulin.

Both prebiotics and probiotics are great for your skin individually, but together they make magic! I like to use the garden analogy for prebiotics and probiotics. Prebiotics are the 'fertiliser' providing food to the skin surface. They enable the garden/skin to grow and flourish while inhibiting the weeds/bad bacteria. Probiotics are like the seeds that grow and flourish on the skin to make the whole garden healthy.

The benefits of prebiotics, for both topical skincare and gut health, increase the number and activity of good bacteria such as bifidobacteria and lactobacillus. The harmful bacteria can't use prebiotics as a nutrient source so the beneficial bacteria grow faster than the bad guys.

One of my favourite probiotics is the lysate of bifidobacterium. This active ingredient is great for improving the skin's ability to fight invaders. It improves the immune system of the skin, and it significantly reduces skin sensitivity, irritation, redness, dryness and fine lines. This probiotic ingredient is excellent at making the skin barrier stronger and more resilient, and addressing inflammation, which is the root cause of all negative skin conditions.

I believe that combining prebiotics and probiotics in a topical formulation can truly be a game changer in skin therapy for everyone.

Mythbust: living probiotic bacteria should be added to skincare formulations

Many new probiotic skincare products contain live bacteria which the companies claim have tremendous benefits for the skin. Scientifically speaking, the ideal formulation should not contain live microbes, but rather chopped-up pieces of the bacteria (technical term is 'lysates') containing the parts of the microbes that activate the positive changes in the skin.

You need the bits (lysate pieces) that make the change in the skin, not the whole bacteria, which will die in the jar! Whole, living bacteria won't survive the conditions of the product itself. Some ingredients, particularly the preservatives, are actually designed to kill microbes, so they're not going to decide to keep the good probiotic bacteria alive

(continued)

and kill the other potentially harmful bacteria in the bottle. The product packaging can also hinder keeping the bacteria alive — if oxygen comes into contact with a beneficial bifidobacterium, for example, it will die. So stick with products that don't have live probiotic bacteria.

So next time you look at yourself in the mirror and think, 'Yeah, looking on-point today girlfriend!' say a silent thank you to all those microscopic heroes that are working 24/7 to make you look and feel great!

chapter 16

Secret women's biz

Cosmetic injections are injectable substances designed to reduce lines and wrinkles on the face and neck. Thankfully this is 'not-so-secret women's business' and no longer a taboo subject. This chapter covers a brief overview so you can understand the difference between anti-wrinkle injections and filler injections and how they work.

Anti-wrinkle injections

When I started my career, having anti-wrinkle injections such as Botox® was a secretive business. Many women were having treatments, but were reluctant to admit it to their friends and partners. Today, it's considered a lunchtime procedure and many of us talk about it freely. Having Botox is a personal choice. I believe women should only consider Botox if it improves their self-confidence, not because of external pressures.

Many women turn to Botox when they begin to see those frown lines (aka number 11s between the eyes) and crow's feet. These are called dynamic lines: they're the lines that form when our face moves. Botox is recommended for these lines of movement, and not for lines and wrinkles that are always present. Anti-wrinkle injections can take up to a fortnight to show results, so be patient.

And there are medical uses for Botox too: helping with cerebral palsy, recovery after stroke, treating migraines and even excessive underarm sweating.

What is Botox?

Botox is a naturally derived substance from bacteria called *Clostridium botulinum*. In large doses this substance is toxic, but the doses used to treat humans has never caused toxic side-effects. In fact, Botox has been used to treat cerebral palsy in children for many years with no long-term side-effects, and the doses used on these children were much higher than the doses used for anti-wrinkle injections in adults.

Botox is actually a trade name of just one type of anti-wrinkle injection. There are other brand names, but Botox is the most popular type.

How does Botox work?

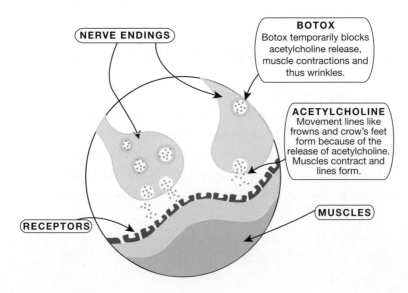

Botox works by preventing a substance in our bodies called acetylcholine from being released from the nerve cells that make certain muscles in our face and neck move and contract.

The injector must be very experienced and have a clear understanding of the anatomy of the face, otherwise things can end in tears with an uneven, droopy smile or eyebrows that looks like Doctor Spock from *Star Trek*!

How long does Botox last?

Botox can last up to six months, and repeated treatments can help the results last longer. Results do vary with different metabolisms.

What are the side-effects?

Serious complications with anti-wrinkle injections are rare, but bruising is common and resolves after 7 to 14 days.

Injectable fillers

Injectable fillers are a totally different type of treatment from Botox and other anti-wrinkle injections. Injecting filler is a cosmetic art form and injectors must have a thorough knowledge of facial anatomy and how the face naturally ages. I've seen women look 10 years younger with a good filler treatment! Injectors should treat each client as an individual and create a bespoke plan for them. The consultation process is paramount, and you should feel 100 per cent comfortable before proceeding.

What are fillers made of?

The most common type of filler uses hyaluronic acid, which binds 1000 times its weight in water. When the filler is injected into the deeper layers of the skin, it binds to water and adds volume to the face.

What are fillers commonly used for?

Filler is commonly used to enhance and increase the size and shape of the lips. I emphasise the word 'enhance' because I've seen many disasters where cosmetic injectors have overfilled the lips, creating the classic 'trout pout' where the lips are stretched so much that they look like they're about to explode!

Another area where the results can look artificial is with cheek fillers. When done poorly it can look like tennis balls have been implanted into the cheeks. Again, erring on the conservative side is always advisable, and cheek filler is only recommended when the mid face begins to sag and hollow. Filler can also be used on the temple areas and under the eyes to correct hollowing and the appearance of dark shadowing — I've even seen filler successfully used to perform an injectable nose job!

How long do fillers last?

Fillers can last from a few months to over a year, depending on the location of the filler and the individual metabolism of the client. Because hyaluronic acid loves water, you must stay well hydrated to get the best and most lasting results.

What are the risks?

The risks with fillers include over filling, asymmetrical results, irregular lumps and interfering with blood supply to the face. The risks are minimised with an experienced injector, but always discuss the possible risks with them before proceeding.

* * *

Cosmetic injectables are one of many medical treatments designed to restore a more youthful appearance to the face and neck. Although the risk is mitigated if you choose an experienced and qualified injector, it's important to have all the facts and realistic expectations about the results. My advice is to restore and not alter your features. Nobody wants to meet your lips five minutes before they meet the rest of your face!

chapter 17

What men want

I remember when I first started dating my partner. Granted he did have a skincare ritual of sorts, and he did use sunscreen (tick), but he really didn't pay much attention to what products he put on his face. He admitted that he used cheap supermarket body lotion as a facial moisturiser! Eeek!

Okay, just breathe Terri. He'll think you're a weirdo if you succumb to your nerdy urge to throw that cheap supermarket goop in the bin and start waxing lyrical about the benefits of vitamin B.

How to get your man onto skincare

So, when is the right time to have the 'skincare conversation' with your partner? It took me a few weeks before I picked my moment and broached the subject. I asked him if he used skincare (kinda already knew that), if he found it effective, and if he was interested in getting even better results. Hallelujah, he was receptive … and quite possibly a keeper. ☺

He knew I was 'in the biz' of skincare so he respectfully listened to my mini lecture on the benefits of cosmeceuticals and physical sun protection. To my delight he was open to using three products on his face every day!

I can happily report that my man is now a true skincare convert and his skin is glowing! He's even telling his guy friends about the benefits of good skincare. Beyond proud!

They say that when the student is ready, the teacher appears … and after reading this book, you'll make a great teacher! The thing with men is they want to know about good skincare, but they want to take on a minimalist approach. They're proud to finely tune their bodies at the gym so why wouldn't they take the next step and embark on a great skincare routine? This is where you come in, ladies. Take your man aside and gently introduce him to the possibility of skin fitness. Plus, if he has his own products he won't be stealing yours! It really brings a smile to my face when clients and friends lament over their partners sneakily using their precious serums and moisturisers. Cosmeceuticals are like personal trainers for the skin, and the right routine can be simple but very effective. Once men understand this, they can get hooked too.

Fun facts: male skin vs female skin

Here's how men's skin differs from women's:

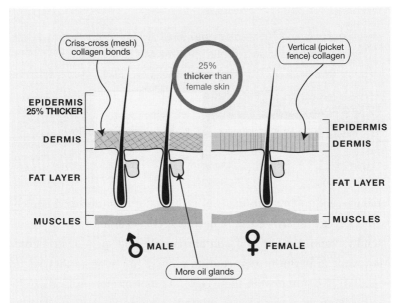

- Male skin is about 25 per cent thicker than ours and thins gradually with age, whereas the thickness of a woman's skin remains constant until about the age of 50, and after menopause female skin thins rapidly. The ageing process for men starts considerably later, but is also accelerated once it commences.

- The male dermis has a higher collagen density than the female dermis, making male skin appear firmer. The collagen fibres in men's skin form a tighter mesh; in women, they tend to run in a less dense, more parallel fashion. This may explain why some women appear to age faster than men of the same age under the same environmental conditions.

- A man's outer layer (stratum corneum) is 20 per cent thicker than a woman's. Thus, the male skin barrier function is slightly better at holding water and tends to be better hydrated than ours.

- Ageing men often exhibit less fine wrinkling but more deep facial folds than women. This is related to higher levels of fat loss with ageing men.

- Men have larger pores and produce 75 per cent more sebum. Since men don't enter menopause, their sebum production remains the same throughout their life, so again the skin is more protected from water loss. However, due to the higher sebum levels acne is more common in males.

- Males have more lactic acid in their sweat, which accounts for a slightly more acidic acid mantle — 0.05 lower pH than females.
- Men have more shaving-related skin issues, including ingrown hairs and razor burn. This is possibly due to their larger pore size.
- Men have naturally higher levels of testosterone, which results in increased collagen production, oil production and blood flow.

I believe embracing minimalism, style and straightforward choices is the key to satisfying the male market. Packaging must be user-friendly, sophisticated and contain simple and clear instructions. Men want to perform their routine quickly (on average they spend less than five minutes on their face). As men prefer products to be multitasking, it's important to minimise the number of steps in the male regimen and highlight the key ingredients and benefits to ensure product engagement.

A typical male skincare routine

A men's skincare routine primarily focuses on cleansing, exfoliating scrubs and multifunctional moisturisers with a recent growing interest in daily sun protective moisturisers, anti-ageing serums and eye products. With the increase of male personal grooming, the shaving cabinet will no longer consist of only deodorant and shaving cream as men place greater significance on their personal appearance. Yay to that!

TERRI'S STARTER ROUTINE FOR MEN

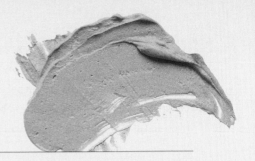

Cleanser

Make sure it's SLS 'nasties' free and foaming so it can also double as a shaving cream. They love two-in-one products.

Serum(s)

If I had to choose one for my guy, it would be vitamin B serum because of all the great benefits of niacinamide. If he's starting to become concerned about lines, get him onto an anti-ageing serum packed with peptides and other cosmeceuticals to boost collagen and hyaluronic acid.

Moisturiser

There are so many to choose from, but make sure there are active ingredients added because many moisturisers just sit on top of the skin and don't make a real difference. You might opt for a richer moisturiser if your guy works in an office environment because air conditioning and heating can really dry out the skin, or one for sensitive skin if he's prone to irritation or redness.

Sun protection

Need I go on about this? My preference is always for physical over chemical sunscreen, but whatever he chooses, don't let him go outside without protection.

Exfoliant

Men naturally exfoliate when they shave but many guys love the feel of a physical scrub. Even though their skin is thicker, a harsh scrub can still tear and damage the skin and cause visible redness with age, so choose a scrub with particles that are even in size and shape. Aluminium oxide crystals or dissolvable jojoba beads are great. I'd steer clear of large, rough seed and nut husks like walnut husks.

Whether male or female, looking your best at every age has a huge effect on self-esteem, and indirectly on personal success. That's the fundamental reason for using skincare. Ladies, help the special man in your life to invest in quality skincare and he won't look back!

part II

Skin conditions and concerns

'I have absolutely no issues with my skin' said no-one *ever*! Whether I'm out with friends or presenting at conferences I'm often asked about different skin concerns, and I know I love what I do because I never tire of answering questions. My team at work once laughed when I asked them to send products to the Uber driver I'd just met! So let's talk through the most common skin concerns and related skin conditions I've come across during my time in this industry. There's something in this section of the book for everyone, so dip into the parts that are most relevant for you.

chapter 18

Ageing

This topic is a book in itself... maybe my next one. It's also a personal concern of mine. Ageing technically begins around 25 (yikes!) and is well and truly underway by 40. Being a woman in her mid-fifties I believe that it's my right to be the best version of myself... for myself!

I'm constantly researching exactly what causes and quickens the ageing process, and what we can do about it. Alas, skincare isn't the magic bullet — it really is a balance of lifestyle, nutrition, genetics and skincare. You simply can't consider one without the other if you want to age with health and vitality. Exercise daily and have a diet of fresh fruit and veggies, good-quality protein, good fats and no added sugar. I'm no saint... I love a drink (or two) with my partner on a FriYay, and a daily coffee while people watching at my local café is a ritual. And I'm utterly *hopeless* at meditation but I do my best to be kind to myself and nurture my mind and body.

And, oh, hindsight. I wish I'd had the wisdom and knowledge I have now when I was young. In my final year of high school I would lie out on a reflective foil sunbaking mat, cover myself in SPF 0 oil and put lemon juice in my hair. I was basically a human salad dressing. When I was a uni student in the '80s I came home from a December trip to Europe and my then boyfriend picked me up from Melbourne airport and took me straight to South Melbourne beach. It was 35 degrees and I was armed with bathers, a towel and baby oil! I was alabaster white and I spent the day with my summer-bronzed boyfriend. I was so sunburned that I couldn't even open my swollen eyes the next day. Even my fingers were blistered!

In my late twenties I decided I would never sunbake again. I became vigilant about sun protection and the first product I formulated was a moisturising sunscreen. Unfortunately, it's the early incidents that have a profound effect on sun damage and our future skin health. Thankfully there are some ingredients that can actually reverse sun damage, but even these aren't miracle workers. Protection is the only insurance policy.

Genetics

Our genes are basically the blueprint of all the stuff that goes on in our bodies. Humans have 46 chromosomes packed with over 20 000 genes! They tell us to make blood, to make our eyes blue, to make collagen and every other function and component of the miracle that is within each of us.

Here's the good news: we're so much more than just our genes. Until recently, genetic testing was considered an accurate prediction of your future — thank goodness we have more control than that. Our environment has a significant bearing on how our genes are read and there are many factors that can turn our genes on or off, up or down. This is an exciting and relatively new field called epigenetics (you can read more about it on page 171 if you haven't already).

It's important to know about our genes and the areas of ageing or disease that we're predisposed to, but our genes are *not* our destiny and we're in more control of ageing than most of us realise. For example, we know that fair-skinned people, genetically, are more prone to skin cancer because of the type and distribution of melanin in their skin, but if fair-skinned people protect themselves from the skin cancer triggers (namely the sun) they'll significantly reduce their chance of getting skin cancer.

We can modify our behaviour, sun exposure, nutrition, stress levels and more, and these can all override our programmed genetics. Just because our genes say we're more likely to age faster doesn't mean we can't change the prophecy. Conversely, if we have genes that indicate we're unlikely to get skin cancer, that doesn't mean we're immune — if you push your luck and sunbake daily without protection you could get it.

External environment

A number of factors come into play when we consider how the environment influences visible ageing of our skin.

Sun

The sun is the number one enemy of human skin and will accelerate ageing more than almost any other environmental factor.

Not-so-fun fact

Roughly 90 per cent of environmental ageing is caused by solar radiation.

Pollution, smoking and nutrition

The sun's effect is followed closely by smog, cigarettes and highly processed foods. All these guys are free radical factories that instantly age and damage our fresh new cells. If you take identical twins with exactly the same genetic information and place them in different environments for 30 years, their visible ageing will be vastly different. If one twin smokes 20 cigarettes a day, eats junk food and is a diehard sun worshipper, she will look significantly older than her double who has opted for a healthy lifestyle. Go to chapters 12 and 13 for all my info on how to have a healthy diet and lifestyle.

Stress

I'm not going to bang on about stress and its obvious link to ageing because there are so many mindfulness books that help us lower our stress levels. Just look at how our politicians age 10 years in one term of office or during the COVID-19 pandemic for evidence! My one piece of advice is to not beat yourself up if you have trouble relaxing. Find that one activity that you lose hours in (mine is painting) and use it as your personal stress buster.

Skincare

Skincare counts as a major environmental factor to help wind back the years, but it only works if you choose the right ingredients. And remember, the most important skincare product for anti-ageing is... you guessed it, *sunscreen*!

Loneliness

This isn't an area of my expertise but it's *very* important and isn't discussed often enough. One of the biggest factors for ageing our cells is a lack of human connection. A Harvard study showed that one resoundingly common factor in people who live to become centenarians is human connection. Loneliness can be as damaging for your health as smoking. It doesn't necessarily mean having a romantic life partner, but rather having daily fulfilling human connection that gives you joy and purpose. So go out and make more real friends and watch that body clock reverse!

Internal environment

Our internal environment is all the processes that go on inside our bodies 24/7. Here are a few factors that are directly linked to ageing in our cells.

Disease and immunity

Let's break down the word 'disease': 'dis' + 'ease'. This is simply 'a lack of' ('dis') ease in the body. The best way of regaining the 'ease' or reversing disease is to strengthen our immune system. A stronger immune system means a longer cell lifespan and slower ageing. We can strengthen our immune system by lowering stress levels, eating foods that bolster our immunity and using skincare that increases our immunity to disease.

One of the best ingredients in skincare for increasing immunity is niacinamide (vitamin B3). Studies have shown that this ingredient has a direct effect on our skin's internal immune system to help us fight foreign invaders and make our skin stronger.

Glycation ageing

Glycation is considered as damaging and ageing to our cells as free radical attack. So what exactly is it? I briefly covered glycation in part I, but I want to dive into it in more detail here. Glycation is a very complex reaction in our cells involving a chemical reaction between sugar and protein. The result is damaging and accelerates our natural ageing process. Glycation ageing in the skin (forming AGEs or advanced glycation end-products) is the process of sugar circulating in our bodies and attaching itself to the fibrous collagen and elastin proteins. This forms abnormally brittle collagen and elastin fibres, and our structural collagen and springy elastin no longer work the way they should. Incidentally, this process of glycation not only attacks the proteins of the skin but has also been linked with other diseases like diabetes and Alzheimer's. We really need to prevent these renegade sugar molecules from hooking up with our youthful collagen and elastin to stop these AGEs being made.

The process is amplified when the chemicals in our bodies made from glycation react with UV light. This can cause a chain reaction of free radical attack on our skin, coupled with the collagen and elastin becoming stiff and brittle ... and all this shows up as sallow skin and wrinkles. Not pretty.

There are no natural body processes to rid the body of these glycation toxins, so they just build up in our skin and tissues over time and reduce that lovely springy support and elasticity. The visible result is that our skin looks crepey and crinkly ... sort of like a dried-up riverbed.

How can we fight glycation?

The bad news is that glycation is a natural result of the ageing process. But here's the good news ... We can slow it down and stop those badass AGEs in their tracks by cutting down on refined white sugar and fructose products like corn syrup. Read your labels! You'll be gobsmacked at the amount of sugar in your shopping trolley.

Since free radicals and glycation are a dynamic duo of ageing, antioxidants provide a great defence for fighting the ravages of glycation. I suggest high-quality antioxidant supplements. I take green tea, lycopene and astaxanthin daily, but your first port of call should always be a very colourful shopping basket with as much red, yellow and green as possible (and I don't mean cocktail sausages, Twisties and mint leaves!).

Collagen, elastin and hyaluronic acid loss

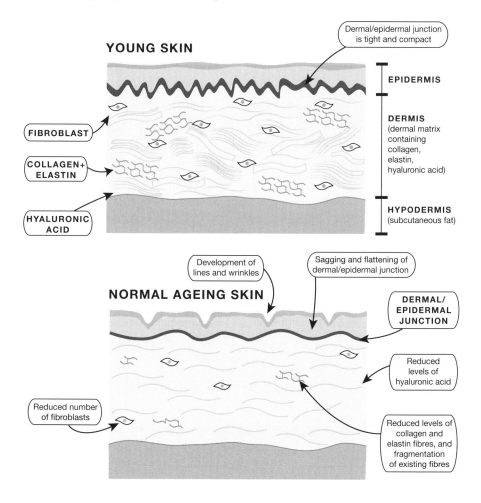

YOUNG SKIN

Dermal/epidermal junction is tight and compact

EPIDERMIS

DERMIS
(dermal matrix containing collagen, elastin, hyaluronic acid)

FIBROBLAST

COLLAGEN+ ELASTIN

HYALURONIC ACID

HYPODERMIS
(subcutaneous fat)

NORMAL AGEING SKIN

Development of lines and wrinkles

Sagging and flattening of dermal/epidermal junction

DERMAL/ EPIDERMAL JUNCTION

Reduced levels of hyaluronic acid

Reduced number of fibroblasts

Reduced levels of collagen and elastin fibres, and fragmentation of existing fibres

When we're young, our bodies make high-quality collagen and naturally break down the old collagen.

We look youthful because our collagen-making factory is working like a charm. If you're into accounting (not me) it's like a collagen ledger. Our overall collagen is 'in credit' when we're young (more collagen is made than destroyed) and 'in debit' as we age. A woman in her fifties actually produces 40 per cent less collagen than she did in her twenties. Other outside factors like the sun, pollution and smoking also cause loss and damage of collagen and elastin.

Elastin is a different story. This protein, which makes our skin bounce back, is really tough and hard to break down. We lose elastin more slowly than collagen, but unfortunately our skin isn't as good at making new elastin as it is at making collagen. We're better at keeping our elastin if we stay out of the sun because UV light speeds up its destruction. That's why sun worshippers tend to have skin that looks slack and has no 'spring back'.

As we age, the cells that make collagen and elastin (the fibroblasts) become lazy and sluggish, and our skin becomes thinner, saggy, less elastic and more dehydrated. The fibroblasts also produce naturally occurring hyaluronic acid, which moisturises our skin from the inside and makes it look plumper, and this slows down too. Just imagine a four-day-old balloon. You know how the surface looks when it starts to lose air? This is very similar to the volume loss from diminished collagen and hyaluronic acid in our skin as we get older. So let's get some air back in our balloons!

Boosting collagen

There are effectively two ways to fight the loss of collagen:

1. Increase the production of collagen by the fibroblasts through high-quality ingredients such as niacinamide, vitamin A, vitamin C, marjoram extract (which makes the fibroblasts more active and healthier) and peptides, which specifically target collagen production.

2. Reduce the destruction of your good-quality collagen. The best way to stop collagen destruction is to … sorry to sound like a broken record … *stay out of the sun* or *use sunscreen*!

Boosting elastin

It was a real challenge for me to find an ingredient that could actually boost elastin production because it's not as easy for our bodies to produce new elastin as it is to make new collagen. There's a new cosmeceutical peptide, acetyl tetrapeptide-2, that has been shown to increase elastin and collagen production, which is great news. There has also been evidence that the red light from LED machines helps stimulate elastin production (I'm personally a huge fan of LED treatments). Again, the best way to prevent the breakdown of elastin in our skin is by staying out of the sun.

Boosting hyaluronic acid

I recently found an active ingredient called saccharide isomerate that's able to boost the production of our own hyaluronic acid. This is great news because most products containing hyaluronic acid (and there are heaps on the market) can only hydrate the skin surface (the epidermis) — they can't penetrate deep enough into the dermis to signal the cells to make the skin's own hyaluronic acid. When the skin can make its own stuff you get a much better outcome.

Oxidation and inflammation of our cells

You know when you pick out one of those shiny, delicious apples from your fruit bowl and take a huge bite ... only to discover, to your disappointment, that you've chomped into a brown, mushy bruise! This is the oxidation of the apple, which happens when oxygen in the air penetrates the skin after it's been dropped. The oxygen molecules react with its cells and damage the tissue, creating darkened, oxidised flesh. The same can happen to our cells. The oxidation of our cells caused by free radical damage not only causes direct damage to the outer membrane of our cells, it also causes widespread inflammation, which directly impacts ageing! How ironic that free radicals can cause inflammation, and inflammation creates more free radicals, which can destroy our healthy cells. In fact, the effect of inflammation on the ageing of our cells is called 'inflammaging' — this is a known condition.

Inflammation wears two hats. On the one hand, it's important because it kickstarts our immune system when there are foreign invaders like bacteria, viruses and pollution. Our body organises its internal army to destroy or neutralise these invaders, and we often notice short-term redness, irritation or discomfort. However, sometimes our immune system goes into overdrive and constantly reacts to threats, leading to chronic inflammation from constantly putting our bodies under stress. When skin is constantly inflamed this stress eventually leads to disease, pigmentation, skin laxity and wrinkles.

Every skin disease has one thing in common: inflammation. Acne, rosacea, dermatitis and eczema are all underpinned by inflammation in our cells. So we really need to keep inflammation in check. There's a fine line between just enough inflammation to fight a bacterial disease in our body, and too much inflammation, which damages and ages our cells irreversibly.

The best way to tackle inflammation at the source is to make sure your skin and body are in the best shape possible to fight the good fight, which means having a good reserve of antioxidants in our bodies from food, and staying away from environmental situations that cause the vicious oxidation/inflammation cycle. Protect yourself from environmental toxins and chemicals that aren't safe for your skin, and avoid damaging sun exposure.

According to my research, some of the best anti-inflammatory cosmeceutical ingredients are aloe vera, allantoin, niacinamide (my old fave), Canadian willowherb, bisabolol (in chamomile), beta glucan, sea buckthorn oil, blackcurrant seed oil and peptides: acetyl hexapeptide-49 and acetyl tetrapeptide-40.

TERRI'S FAVE SKINCARE ANTIOXIDANTS

Green tea extract

Green tea contains a long-named chemical called epigallocatechin gallate or EGCG. It's actually a type of polyphenol, and scientific research confirms that EGCG can significantly reduce free radical damage and inflammation in skin cells. Drinking green tea is great, but it has also been found that black tea has a similar amount of polyphenol antioxidants. I love formulating with green tea — not only does it add an injection of antioxidants to the skin, it also helps to make the formulas more stable by preventing the oxidation of other ingredients. Win–win!

L-ascorbic acid

Totes love this ingredient! I won't go on any more about it — I discussed it on page 28.

Lycopene

Lycopene is a type of carotenoid and is another supercharged antioxidant. Studies have shown that tomato-derived lycopene significantly reduces the damaging effects of UVB radiation, and it's also able to defend that precious outer cell membrane from free radical attack in a similar way to L-ascorbic acid.

Telomere shortening and ageing

TELOMERES ARE JUST LIKE SHOELACES

PHASE 1 — Brand new cell

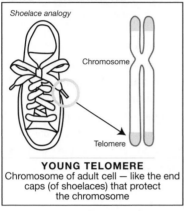

Shoelace analogy

Chromosome

Telomere

YOUNG TELOMERE
Chromosome of adult cell — like the end
caps (of shoelaces) that protect
the chromosome

**PHASE 2 — Cells divide and telomere
gets shorter**

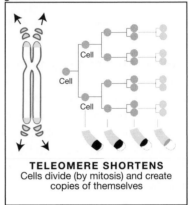

Cell

Cell

Cell

Cell

TELEOMERE SHORTENS
Cells divide (by mitosis) and create
copies of themselves

**PHASE 3 — Cells stop dividing and
eventually age or die**

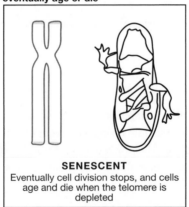

SENESCENT
Eventually cell division stops, and cells
age and die when the telomere is
depleted

The telomere is a little 'tag' that sits on the end of every chromosome in
every living cell of our bodies to protect our DNA. Think of a telomere
as the end of a shoelace that protects it from fraying. Every time the cell
divides and produces two new healthy cells in our bodies (this process
is called mitosis), the telomere gets a bit shorter, and when there's no
telomere left the cell stops dividing, ages and eventually dies. So the
shorter the telomere, the more aged our cells are. (This is not related to
our actual age in years, but rather our genetic age.)

How can we keep our telomeres long?

Though there are some new products on the market containing the ingredient telomerase, which is involved in keeping our telomeres from shortening, the jury is still out for me. As a scientist I know that telomerase is also crucial for maintaining cancer cells and I'm concerned that this ingredient may have an impact on skin cancer cells if applied directly to the skin. More research must be done.

In terms of having a telomere-preserving lifestyle, it's definitely not rocket science. Studies have shown that up to 45 minutes of moderate exercise three times a week, a diet high in the good omega-3 fats, reduced exposure to pollution, intermittent fasting and reduced stress levels can contribute to maintaining your telomere length and turning back that genetic clock.

Genetic repair and ageing

We know that our genes give our bodies all the messages they need to perform all functions and exhibit all of our characteristics, from how hairy our legs are to directing the complex process of digesting our breakfast.

But sometimes things go wrong. These messages (genes) can be messed up so the message is either interpreted incorrectly, or not interpreted at all. This is called a mutation. A mutation is a random event where the DNA of a cell changes abnormally, and when the cells divide this mutation is passed on unless the cell is repaired, destroyed or put to sleep.

There are special DNA repair enzymes in our bodies that are like our personal DNA handyman. Every minute there are genetic errors made in thousands of our cells, but before you freak out, our cells are so clever they can activate our own internal Airtasker. The repair enzymes are activated and they fix our DNA so it's business as usual. However, as we get older, so does our internal handyman. He (or she) limps around the body and becomes less efficient at fixing the damage. When this unrepaired DNA accumulates in our skin cells it looks like wrinkles, sagging, loss of elasticity, dryness, pigmentation and more.

How can we keep our 'DNA handyman' in check?

In order to keep those repair enzymes functioning we need to look after our internal health by doing all the stuff we know but often ignore, like eating well, exercising, sleeping well and nurturing our brain and mental health.

In terms of skincare, there's one cosmeceutical I discovered a few years ago that I believe has real merit in repairing damaged DNA. It's a peptide called acetyl hexapeptide-51 amide. Sorry for the big sciency words, but this is how ingredients appear on labels if you want to look out for them.

It's been discovered that people who live to be over 100 have higher levels of a substance in their cells called FOXO3A, which is able to repair damaged DNA before it has the chance to divide and make copies of faulty cells. This FOXO3A factor is like the guardian of the genes. It activates a genetic repair process, stimulates the production of internal antioxidants, and if the cell is beyond repair it kills it. It's very important that defective genes aren't replicated.

This peptide (acetyl hexapeptide-51 amide) actually mimics the way our own bodies protect and repair our damaged DNA by imitating FOXO3A (aka our DNA handyman). This little wonder protects the genes in our living skin cells (keratinocytes, fibroblasts and melanocytes). Tests also show that this ingredient, at the right dose, reduces the ageing process of human fibroblasts (the cells that make our collagen, elastin and hyaluronic acid). In fact, the cells treated with this cosmeceutical acted as if they were 10 years younger! In a clinical trial, scientists intentionally damaged the skin of volunteers with harmful UV rays. The skin treated with this cosmeceutical showed that there was a significant reduction in genetic damage of the skin cells. Pretty compelling stuff!

Is ageing a controllable state?

There are many theories of why we age, and none of them can be considered in isolation. I believe that all of the elements of ageing are intertwined and we need to address as many as we can to be the healthiest version of ourselves. A combination of lifestyle, nutrition and skincare gives us the best ammo to fight the ageing process from both inside and out.

TERRI'S TIPS FOR AN ANTI-AGEING SKINCARE ROUTINE

An anti-ageing skincare routine should focus on the major factors that need to be addressed, which I call 'the three Ts' of skin ageing. They are:

1. tone
2. texture
3. tightness.

If you study exactly how a face ages, there are gradual changes in all three factors. 'The three Ts' have crept up on me over the past 20 plus years. My eyesight started to deteriorate in my mid-forties (yes, another frustrating aspect of ageing), so I need my trusty 10x magnification illuminated makeup mirror to put a magnifying glass on my three Ts!

Let's look at the best skincare routine for each of the three Ts.

1 Uneven skin tone (brown and red)

This can look like hyperpigmentation in the form of dark patches or spots, as well as redness.

Brown

A woman who has significant sun damage, hyperpigmentation ('hyper' means excess) and varying skin tone over her face will be perceived as older than the same face with a more uniform skin tone. Hyperpigmentation can also be caused by pollution, hormones, certain drugs and the skin's reaction to harsh clinical treatments like peels, intense pulsed light (IPL) and laser. I dive deep into pigmentation and treatments for it in chapter 19.

Red

Excessive redness of the face may be caused by the sun damaging our blood vessels (called capillaries) in the dermis. They are the thinnest blood vessels in our skin and are responsible for bringing nutrients to our skin cells and removing the rubbish — so we really need to look after them!

They are often referred to as 'broken capillaries', but this is incorrect — these capillaries are far from broken. They are in fact stretched and floppy rather than thin and elastic. As a result, the blood in them is more visible because they're so much wider. They mainly occur around the nose, cheeks and chin and are usually caused by the sun causing free radical damage to the blood vessels. Visible capillaries can also be caused by skin injury, or excessive damage from attacking your pimples or harsh microdermabrasion treatments if your skin is sensitive.

The best way to treat these spidery red vessels is to have laser or IPL treatments by a dermatologist or qualified therapist, and the best prevention is to avoid sun exposure and use ingredients that keep your blood vessels nice and healthy. Vitamin A is a shining star here.

Another cause of excessive redness in the face is due to a skin condition called rosacea, which is discussed in detail on page 281.

2 Changes in skin texture and how light reflects off two surfaces

By this I mean those surface changes that relate to skin ageing. I like to use the analogy of comparing an apple to a lemon. The apple looks smooth and the lemon dimply and uneven because of the way light reflects off their surfaces. It's like that with skin. If our skin texture is even and smooth, the light reflects off it evenly and it looks more luminous. But if our skin has a rough and uneven surface, the light will reflect off it in different directions and it will look uneven. Think enlarged pores, wrinkles, crepiness, dryness and flakiness. This is because our skin is losing collagen, elastin and hyaluronic acid, and our skin processes — like cell turnover — are becoming slow and lazy.

There are many skin treatments that can address uneven skin texture by triggering our skin cells to make collagen, including skin needling, laser and fractional treatments. Chemical peels are also an excellent choice for improving the surface texture of crepey skin and enlarged pores.

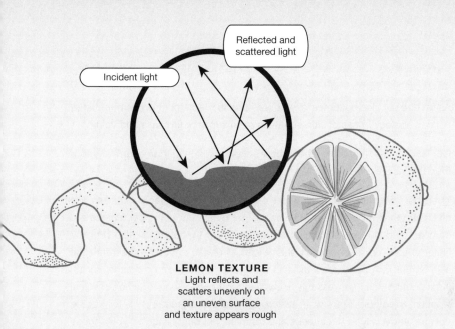

LEMON TEXTURE
Light reflects and
scatters unevenly on
an uneven surface
and texture appears rough

VS

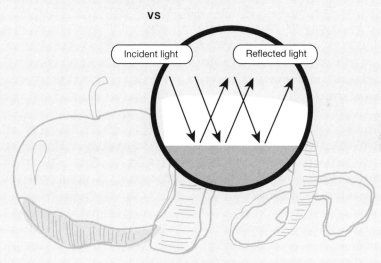

APPLE TEXTURE
Light reflects and scatters
evenly on smooth surface and
texture appears even

All cosmeceuticals that address collagen and elastin production will help improve skin texture, and alpha hydroxy acids (AHAs) and beta hydroxy acids (BHAs) are also great because they help shed the old, flaky cells that aren't reflecting light evenly. BHAs like salicylic acid will also pull oil and gunk out of those blocked pores, so if the skin around the pore is still nice and stretchy, the pore will rebound and your pores will look smaller. If the pore isn't elastic enough (through ageing or sun damage), you will need ingredients to help with your collagen and elastin production.

As we age our skin becomes lax and less elastic. Remember my semi-deflated balloon analogy? Loss of skin tightness means loss of firmness and volume.

Our skin loses firmness when there's less collagen. You might say our foundations are gradually collapsing.

The other thing that's happening as we age is that we're losing bone mass. We all know that we become shorter as we get older. Our spine becomes more compact and our bones shrink. But did you know that our skull also shrinks? Unfortunately our skin doesn't shrink with it! This is another reason that the skin on our face becomes looser as we age. Sadly, there's no cosmeceutical ingredient that can address this. However, for those looking for a non-surgical solution, injectable fillers with hyaluronic acid are a great option for adding volume, especially to the cheeks and temples. I strongly suggest you choose your injector wisely and really make sure you're both on the same page about the results you want. You also need to be realistic and not expect to peel away 20 years with a couple of syringes of filler. The aim is to restore the lost volume over time, not to alter your appearance and look like a caricature of yourself. Just as with all treatments and skincare routines, the aim is maintenance, not drastic change.

For more subtle improvements in skin tightness we can use cosmeceuticals to increase collagen and improve hyaluronic acid production. Refer to my list of collagen and hyaluronic acid boosters on page 204. When you increase collagen and hyaluronic acid, the deep dermal layer of the skin thickens and volume is added to the skin.

To see the anti-ageing skincare routine I do every day, go to page 113.

So yes, ageing is inevitable, but there are many things we can do to slow it down and, yes, even reverse the process. I want to age with as much grace (and skincare) as I can muster so I can always be the best version of me at any age.

chapter 19

Pigmentation

The biggest concern for most women, apart from wrinkles, is pigmentation. These little dark spots affect more than 80 per cent of women over 25, and cosmetic chemists like me are always looking for ingredients to lighten and brighten the skin surface. Let's take a close look at the dark side of pigmentation (pun intended).

There are three types of hyperpigmentation that are treatable with cosmeceuticals and skin treatments: sunspots, post-inflammatory hyperpigmentation (PIH) and melasma. Again, apologies for getting a bit sciency but most of us will fall into one of these three categories so it's worth discussing them.

Sunspots (aka age spots)

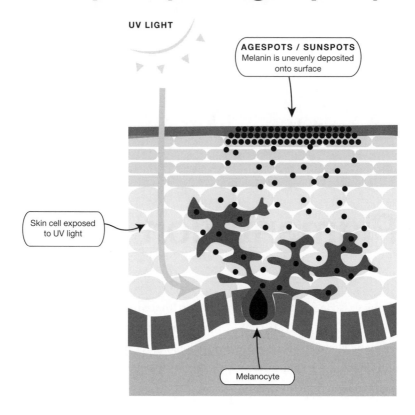

UV LIGHT

AGESPOTS / SUNSPOTS
Melanin is unevenly deposited
onto surface

Skin cell exposed
to UV light

Melanocyte

Sunspots are the most common form of hyperpigmentation; they're a non-cancerous hyperpigmented spot caused by solar damage. When the sun hits the skin surface, our little melanocytes work very hard to protect our skin cells from severe damage. They coat the cells with a protective shield of melanin, our natural dark pigment, but sometimes these melanin-producing cells go into overdrive and produce sun spots that can vary in size and colour from light brown to very dark.

What's the difference between freckles and sunspots?

Freckles are genetic and usually occur on the face and arms, and people with freckles are generally fair skinned and have had freckles since they were children. Both freckles and sunspots darken with sun exposure and sunspots tend to stay dark in winter. Sunspots develop as we age, and many of the sunspots that appear in our forties are a result of sun damage from years before.

Cosmeceutical ingredients for sunspots

If you suffer from pigmentation you often need to use a number of different cosmeceutical ingredients in your routine because they work in slightly different ways.

Sunscreen

If you protect yourself from solar radiation you're not telling the melanocyte to protect you. No tanning and burning means no new sunspots. Sunscreen is the bomb!

Peptides specific for hyperpigmentation

Tyrosinase is a chemical naturally found in our body that's the essential enzyme responsible for making protective pigment in our skin called melanin. Without melanin we're albino! However, if it becomes overactive we end up with an uneven skin tone, age spots and sun damage — yuck!

Thanks to science, a new laboratory-made peptide ingredient called oligopeptide-34 is great for fighting pigmentation. It's really clever because it calms the tyrosinase enzyme while keeping the melanocyte cells healthy, so the result is less pigmentation in the skin and a more even skin tone. Many other skin-lightening ingredients are very effective at reducing pigmentation, but unfortunately they can damage or even destroy the melanocyte. While we want to calm down the hyperactive melanocytes so they don't make too much pigment, we still need these precious cells to defend us from solar damage. It's a delicate balancing act.

Alpha hydroxy acid (AHA)

I really like lactic acid. It's my fave AHA for skin brightening because it's a built-in hydrator and less aggressive than glycolic acid. AHAs reduce the appearance of pigmentation by sloughing off the pigmented spots sitting on top of the skin that have accumulated melanin as a natural defence mechanism to sun damage. But you must be sure not to irritate the skin with too much acid. You can definitely over exfoliate. Alpha hydroxy acids like lactic acid, mandelic acid and malic acid are great at helping exfoliate dead surface cells to reveal the fresh, bright skin beneath. But beware, these fresh baby cells are very fragile and susceptible to more solar damage, so remember to use sunscreen every day.

Niacinamide

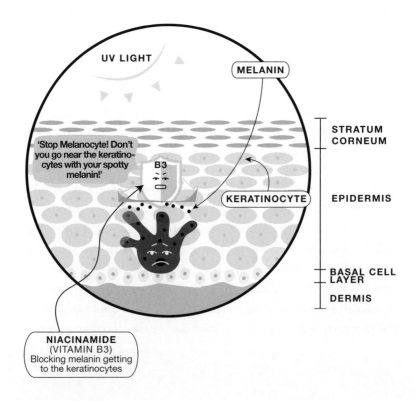

I know I keep banging on about niacinamide, but it really is an all-in-one cosmeceutical. It works by preventing the transfer of excess pigment from the cell that makes it (the melanocyte) to the cell that takes it (the keratinocyte in the epidermis).

Vitamin C (in an active and stable form)

All forms of vitamin C must be converted to the usable form (L-ascorbic acid) for it to work. L-ascorbic acid is a skin lightener and tyrosinase inhibitor, which is important because tyrosinase is a protein enzyme found in the pigment-producing cell (melanocyte), and if tyrosinase isn't in the cell melanin can't be made. If there's too much tyrosinase activity, there can be a problem with the overproduction of melanin, which will appear as sunspots or other types of pigmentation.

Vitamin A (in an active and stable form)

Active forms of vitamin A work by increasing cell turnover, so the unsightly pigmented cells are sloughed off the surface of the skin. This cosmeceutical also reduces the clumping of melanin and the activity of tyrosinase, both of which work together to lighten sunspots.

Kojic acid

This is a great tyrosinase inhibitor derived from mushrooms.

Tranexamic acid

This ingredient is great for reducing sun-induced pigmentation and brown marks following acne breakouts, and it may help reduce the appearance of melasma. It also works in synergy with vitamin C.

Saccharide isomerate

This is a marine ingredient extracted from plankton. It inhibits the production of melanin on multiple levels and prevents pigment being transferred to the epidermal cells. Measurements taken from pigmented spots showed a 61 per cent reduction in melanin content and significant lightening after using this ingredient. It looks promising.

Hydroquinone

This ingredient is issued by medical prescription only, so it's technically not a cosmeceutical — it's a drug. While hydroquinone is effective, it's banned in many countries due to side-effects and skin irritation. It's not recommended to be used long term, and you should only use this drug as prescribed by your doctor.

Post-inflammatory hyperpigmentation (PIH)

PIH is the red or brown areas that appear on the skin after excessive trauma, heat or infection. You know when you pick at a pimple and the red mark persists for weeks or even months? That's PIH. It's because you've wounded the skin and those chivalrous melanocytes really want to get in there and protect, as usual, by making more pigment. And like they often do, they overreact and the result is a red, purple or brown flat mark. Many people refer to PIH as a type of scar, but technically this isn't true because there's no tissue loss under the skin.

PIH can also occur when there's trauma to the skin from a cut, graze and even clinical treatments such as laser, IPL, treatments involving very high temperatures on the skin or strong chemical peels where the skin surface is abraded.

Some people with darker skin tones are more prone to PIH from skin trauma, which is why darker skinned individuals should avoid treatments that are too aggressive or overheat the skin. I believe the best treatments for dark-skinned and Asian people who are prone to PIH are skin needling, light chemical peels and specific lasers that are safe for dark skin.

If you're having a clinical treatment and are prone to PIH, it's recommended to use cosmeceutical ingredients that reduce melanin production for a few weeks before and after the treatment to reduce the risk of a nasty reaction to the treatment.

The same ingredients used to treat general pigmentation and sunspots (discussed above) can be used for PIH. If you're treating PIH with cosmeceuticals, my best advice is to be persistent and patient; PIH can take months to fade. Sunlight is enemy number one so it's super important to avoid the sun and protect daily, preferably with a physical sunscreen.

Melasma

This is by far the trickiest of all types of pigmentation disorders to fix.

Melasma is caused by both internal hormonal triggers and environmental triggers, and it mainly affects women (only 10 per cent of men get it — sorry ladies). Unlike small, isolated spots on the body, melasma is more patchy. The darkened areas are larger and the patches are often evenly distributed over the face, cheeks, chin, bridge of the nose and forehead. The borders of the patches are not as defined because the pigmentation is deeper in the skin, which means it's more difficult for treatments and ingredients to reach.

Melasma is often triggered by UV light and blue light, and pregnancy hormones can also cause it, which is why it's sometimes referred to as the 'mask of pregnancy'. Other hormonal changes such as menopause, HRT and contraceptives can also trigger it, and cortisol from stress can make the condition worse. So you can understand why controlling it is such a challenge!

Years ago I had a lady consult with me in my clinic and she was doing everything right: sun protection, a good skincare routine and she was trying to live a stress-reduced and healthy lifestyle. I was baffled that her melasma persisted, and then she told me about her new form of relaxation: hot yoga. Bingo! Excessive overheating excites those melanocytes and makes melasma worse. She took on a cooler form of yoga and the melasma reduced.

Melasma treatment is complex. It's controllable, but unfortunately it often returns. The cosmeceutical ingredients discussed above will help keep melasma at bay, but there's one more important element that should be considered to help control this concern: blue light. Look for mineral makeup that has iron oxides at over 3.2 per cent to protect against blue-light damage.

You need to be really careful when treating melasma. Too many times I've seen people have IPL, laser and strong chemical peels hoping to reduce the pigmentation, only to find the condition worsens. Remember, overheating the pigment can make it worse and many clinical treatments involve devices that apply direct heat to the darkened areas. The approach with melasma is gently, gently... Light chemical peels and lasers that don't cause direct overheating of the skin are the best option.

Melasma isn't a condition that can be treated and resolved forever — but, it can be controlled. You need to stay on top of it with regular treatments, lifestyle modification, staying cool and using sun protection and active cosmeceuticals.

* * *

Hyperpigmentation is one of the most common and complex skin issues. It often has a massive impact on self-confidence and is a condition I take very seriously when formulating products to combat the problem. Thankfully there are now many excellent cosmeceutical ingredients available to effectively reduce the appearance of uneven skin tone.

chapter 20

Acne, blemishes and oily skin

Acne is a condition that's very close to my heart because it affected my kids and their friends, many of whom are now my 'extra kids'! A few years ago my then teenage daughter Georgie called me and said she had a friend who was really struggling with acne. He was depressed and didn't want to leave the house; it was crushing his self-esteem. She asked me to give him a consultation and advise him on a good skincare routine. I was in full-scale manufacturing mode, not in my lab, and it had been a few years since I'd done one-on-one consults in my Camberwell clinic, but I knew I had to help Georgie's friend.

So the next day he came into my office with his mum and sister, ready to learn. He was a typical teenage boy who didn't have a handle on good nutrition, so I went through all of the lifestyle changes he needed to make and recommended the right products and ingredients to reduce his acne.

I explained to him that the products were not the only answer — he had to work with me and make some big changes to his diet and lifestyle. He took it all on and we worked as an acne-fighting team.

Fast-forward two months and I awoke one morning to an email from his mum. She was thanking me for transforming her son's skin. He was happier, more confident, and he was going out and enjoying a great social life. I was so pleased! I'm definitely not a miracle worker: this 17-year-old boy made good choices once I gave him the information and tools, and he was realistic knowing that his acne was a work in progress and we needed to work together on the occasional flare-ups.

It's these experiences that show me I'm doing what I was meant to do. I treated this boy's confidence as much as his skin, and it makes me feel really fulfilled.

Let's do a deep dive into controlling acne and blemishes. It's a complex topic so I'll do my best to keep it straightforward, but I really want you to understand it so you can be empowered to make informed choices about your products and lifestyle.

Oily skin: recap on sebum

To revisit the science, the technical word for skin oils is sebum, which is produced by the sebaceous gland. Sebum is composed of precious skin oils, or lipids, which are primarily natural squalene, waxes and oils.

Sebum helps to keep the skin waterproof and lubricated, but as we get older sebum production reduces and our skin becomes worse at keeping the water in. If our water levels aren't just right, our magic skin barrier can't work properly and we become dehydrated, which messes up our skin's natural ability to shed dead cells and have fresh new cells replace the old ones.

If you're young and have oily skin, the excess oil and dead cells produced in the oil gland live happily in the pore, so even if there's no acne and inflammation you'll notice enlarged pores and that midday oily T-zone (chin, nose and the area across the forehead) shine.

Oil and the precious acid mantle

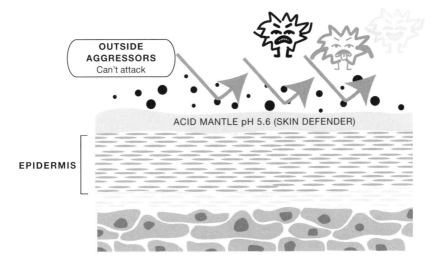

We often hear about the mysterious 'acid mantle' of the skin — it's simply the protective upper surface. The acid mantle is composed of sebum, cell debris, good and bad bacteria and sweat, which all work together in perfect synergy at a cosy pH of around 5.6. This pH creates the ideal environment for a healthy skin microbiome and enables the cells at the surface (the stratum corneum) to overlap like tiny fish scales to protect our skin barrier from water loss and external attack from things like bacteria, pollution and nasty chemicals.

A breakdown in this delicate acid mantle results in our skin barrier being compromised and this leads to sensitivity and inflammation, the basis of all skin diseases. Barrier protection is so important! This is why many skincare products are formulated around the range of pH 4 to 7 — so they don't strip the skin's mantle. Highly acidic products (around pH 2 to 3) are okay to use very occasionally if you need to create a short-term outcome with, say, a skin peel in a clinic, but you should never mess with the mantle long term.

There's a delicate balance between creating enough sebum to lubricate and help maintain the surface acid mantle, and producing excess sebum, which leads to oily skin and enlarged pores. Oily skin is simply the result of your oil glands working overtime, and excess oil and P. acne bacteria create the perfect storm for inflammation, blocked pores and acne.

A note about P. acne bacteria

P. acne bacteria is a specific species of bacteria that lives on human bodies. There are literally trillions of bacteria that use our bodies as a home — good and bad guys. P. acne bacteria is just one type that lives mainly in the pore and goes crazy if it has too much food (oil, bacteria, dirt and dead skin cells) — this is usually the case with acne.

How is excess oil triggered?

A bit of science ...

Sebum is created by receptors in the sebaceous glands binding to the testosterone hormone called dihydrotestosterone (DHT). Excess DHT, or higher sensitivity of oil glands to DHT, is usually a short-term, transient condition common in adolescence. Transient oiliness/enlarged pores can also be caused after puberty by elevated testosterone or imbalanced testosterone/oestrogen levels caused by certain drugs, contraceptives, steroids and hormone therapy.

Excess DHT can also be caused by insulin resistance and polycystic ovarian syndrome (PCOS) in women. PCOS is alarmingly becoming more common and affects women after puberty in their twenties and thirties, heralding the onset of adult acne. This is so damn unfair — acne and ageing happening at once — but the saving grace is that you're producing more natural oils so your skin is more lubricated and you're losing less moisture.

Altering your diet by quitting sugar and cutting out all high GI carbs (such as white bread, pasta and rice) can reduce the production of excess DHT. If you suspect you have PCOS, get a referral to a hormone specialist (endocrinologist) because it needs to be professionally managed.

The different types of acne

Acne is a condition that affects over 85 per cent of teens and adults up to their mid-twenties, and it also affects a small proportion of older women.

So, let's get to the 'pore of the problem'.

Acne without inflammation: whiteheads and blackheads

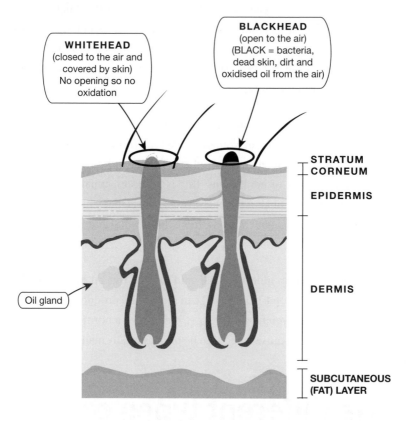

Whiteheads and blackheads are the mildest form of acne as there's no redness or inflammation involved.

In adults who don't suffer from acne, oil is produced in a normal fashion and naturally drains out of the pore opening on the skin surface. If you have acne, a stickier form of sebum is overproduced and the pore becomes blocked and acne bacteria begin to overgrow.

Whiteheads and blackheads are considered the most mild grade of acne, and we probably notice our first one around puberty. It all comes down to our hormones, which send messages to the oil glands to 'make more sebum!'

How do whiteheads form?

For whiteheads, the opening of the pore is closed to the air and covered by a thin layer of skin. The same stuff is going on here but because the oil isn't exposed to the air and getting oxidised it stays white, rather than blackening. Whiteheads are also referred to as 'closed comedones'.

How do blackheads form?

Blackheads form when the opening of the pore is packed with a blackened mass of oxidised oil, debris and bacteria, and they turn black because the blocked pore is open to the air so the 'pore gunk' has become oxidised. They become dark because normal sebum contains melanin, the dark yellowish/brown pigment that gives skin different colour tones. Melanin turns dark (oxidises) if exposed to the open air. Blackheads are also referred to as 'open comedones'.

Mythbust: blackheads

Myth 1: Blackheads are a result of dirty skin

Incorrect. The dark colour of blackheads doesn't mean the skin is unclean; it's the oxidised pigment in the oil that's exposed to air. It's really important to avoid the temptation to over-clean the skin when you have blackheads because excessive scrubbing can lead to irritation of the delicate pores. Cleansing every morning and night is ideal, and use a pH-balanced and SLS-free, foaming cleanser.

Myth 2: The best way to treat blackheads is with daily scrubs

Incorrect. Regular and harsh scrubs can irritate the skin and inflame the pores, which can cause more oil production and make the problem worse. Use a gentle scrub once or twice a week at most. Choose scrubs with less abrasive particles (like little balls) rather than rough grain or nut

(continued)

husks. I really like jojoba beads and corundum crystals because they don't tear the delicate pore lining. Remember, scrubs will remove the surface oxidised melanin on top of the blackhead but will not treat the underlying cause of it.

Myth 3: Pore strips permanently remove the blackhead

Incorrect: Pore strips and scrubs only remove blackheads for a couple of days. If the pore is still open to the air the fresh oil will oxidise and a new blackhead will appear in the same spot. The trick is to reduce oil flow and reduce the size of the pore. More on that shortly.

Myth 4: Blackheads only affect people with oily skin

Incorrect: Blackheads can also affect older individuals with dry skin. I still get them…arghhhh! Although blackheads may not be as much of an issue in older skin, enlarged pores and poor oil flow can cause small blackheads in the T-zone.

What's the best way to keep blackheads at bay?

When you're dealing with mild acne there are only a few areas to control: oil production, pore size and exfoliation.

Reduce excess oil production and pore size

With constant exposure to those flawless, airbrushed celebs it's no wonder I'm asked for advice on treating enlarged pores. Those with naturally oily skin will appear to have larger, more visible pores because of:

- clogging of dirt or oil

- blackheads

- UV rays weakening collagen that supports the tightness of the pores so they become loose and slack

- picking pimples! Trauma to the skin widens your pores permanently, like over-stretching a rubber band.

There are a number of skincare products, including simple 'toners' that claim they can miraculously shrink pores. Unfortunately, there's no magic elixir to shrink pores, but we can help them to appear smaller.

The best ingredients to reduce excess oil and pore size are:

- *vitamin A:* oil regulation and collagen production for pore tightness

- *niacinamide:* oil regulation and pore tightness

- *red clover flower extract:* this new botanical contains the active ingredient biochanin A, which reduces excess sebum and improves cell turnover and pore 'springback' to help minimise pore size. I love this ingredient!

- *barosma betulina (buchu leaves):* this ingredient contains the active molecule diosmin, which directly targets the oil gland and excess sebum.

Remove dead skin and debris from deep within the pore

Salicylic acid (BHAs) is great for this. Think of salicylic acid as a mini bottle brush. It gets deep inside the pore to clean out the build-up of dead skin, dirt and oil, like a brush cleaning the inside of a bottle. Salicylic acid is great at getting into the pores because it loves oil, which helps dislodge the blackhead plugs and clear up the whiteheads. As a bonus, salicylic acid helps to reduce redness and inflammation to keep those angry pimples at bay.

Remove the dead skin from the surface

There are a couple of ways to do this:

- *lactic acid, malic acid, mandelic acid (AHAs):* alpha hydroxy acids are stars at working on the surface of the skin to chemically exfoliate. The stuff that holds our dead skin cells together is called keratin — this is the main protein of our skin, hair and nails. The AHAs act like a 'glue dissolver' removing the dead skin covering the whiteheads and the dark oxidised oil (the blackhead) from the surface.

- *physical exfoliant scrubs (for example, jojoba beads and alumina/ aluminium oxide crystals):* physical exfoliants work differently from chemical exfoliants. Gentle scrubs physically abrade the skin surface and slough off the dead cells and the blackhead surface — they don't get deep within the pore to unplug the blackhead. This is why scrubs 'appear' to remove the blackhead, but it returns after a few days when the oil oxidises and turns black again.

Avoid comedogenic skincare and makeup

These are enemy number one of blackheads and blocked pores. Comedogenic simply means 'causes comedones' (and comedones are blackheads and whiteheads).

When the gunk is trapped by comedogenic oils, the skin can't remove toxins, and this can make blackheads and acne even worse. Comedogenic ingredients can also prevent the penetration of beneficial water-soluble ingredients to the skin by creating a waterproof barrier on the top of the skin.

Please don't be afraid of using oil on your face if you're prone to blackheads — it's all about the type of oils you use. Stick to 'non-comedogenic' oils that don't block pores.

Non-comedogenic oils include castor bean oil, sea buckthorn oil, shea butter, sunflower oil, safflower oil, jojoba oil, argan oil, rosehip oil and lanolin.

Comedogenic oils include cacao butter, peach kernel oil, coconut oil (it's fine to eat though!), soybean oil, wheatgerm oil and cotton seed oil.

There are also ingredients that aren't oil based and can still block pores.

Dimethicone and other 'silicones'

Dimethicone is a really popular additive in skincare and cosmetics. Synthetic silicone oils (aka the 'cones') lurk in many skincare products, makeup and makeup removers. They add to the emollience and 'feel' of a product and are really common in foundations, pressed powder cosmetics, moisturisers and hair products. While dimethicone is not technically comedogenic, many people with oily skin tend to break out when they use products with 'cones'.

COMMON TYPES OF COMEDOGENIC OILS

Cacao butter

Peach kernel oil

Coconut oil

Soybean oil

Wheatgerm oil

Cotton seed oil

In my opinion, it's best to avoid dimethicone in makeup and skincare products if you suffer from acne or blocked pores. There are loads of great lightweight, non-comedogenic oil alternatives.

* * *

When it comes to removing blackheads, please leave it to the professionals. I have seen many girls permanently scar their faces by over-squeezing a stubborn blackhead and causing an infection. If you have blackheads that won't budge from using a good homecare regimen, make an appointment with a qualified skin therapist.

TERRI'S BLACKHEAD-BUSTING SKIN ROUTINE

Morning

1. Gentle SLS-free cleanser
2. AHA/BHA serum to exfoliate and unclog pores
3. Lightweight gel moisturiser or light non-comedogenic moisturiser
4. Sunscreen or sun-protective mineral makeup (dimethicone free)

Evening

1. Gentle SLS-free cleanser
2. Vitamin A serum
3. Vitamin B serum
4. Lightweight gel moisturiser or light non-comedogenic moisturiser

Once or twice weekly

1. Gentle physical scrub focusing on T-zone and blackheads
2. Purifying detox mask to draw out impurities (look for ones with bentonite, zeolite or charcoal)

Acne with inflammation

Unlike blackheads and whiteheads, which are not linked to redness and infection, inflammatory acne is based on an overgrowth of the main bacterial culprit of acne, P. acne bacteria.

Acne is characterised by four major processes all going on at once in the pore:

1. Excess oil (sebum) is produced because of imbalanced hormones sending messages to the oil gland to dump more sebum into the pore.

2. Overproduction of new skin cells is common in acne sufferers. A pore is basically a hole in the skin surface that dips deep into the skin. If you have acne, you're producing more skin cells on the surface, so the pores are still part of the skin surface even though they look like they're inside the skin. If you have excess cells on the surface of the skin it follows that you'll have excess dead skin cells shedding inside the pore too, but the pore pokes inside the skin so these new skin cells have more trouble escaping because they're trapped by the excess oil and debris.

3. Overproduction of P. acne bacteria. These nasty little microbes are always present in our skin, but when you have acne they go into overdrive. When they encounter all the yummy oil and dead cells, they have a party and set up a bacterial feeding frenzy, and even more bad bacteria are made.

4. When acne feeds on debris, skin cells and oil, it produces a substance to help with its digestion, but this substance causes irritation in the pores so our body gets a message to fight the invaders, and inflammation results.

So, with the combination of dead skin cells, sebum, bacteria, inflammation and white blood cells, plus an escape valve to the surface of the skin that's blocked, you have the perfect storm for a big red zit, aka pimple!

Grades of acne

Acne is categorised into four grades according to how severe it is. If you suspect your acne is getting worse, read this section closely.

Grade 1: comedonal acne

This is the non-inflammatory type of acne that only has blackheads, whiteheads and small non-inflamed pimples on the T-zone (especially the nose).

Grade 2: papular/pustular acne

As well as blackheads and whiteheads you now have inflammation added to the mix. There are two more types of zits that accompany grade 2 acne. They are:

- *papules:* these are the first type of actual 'pimple'; they're raised, tender, red lumps.

- *pustules:* these are red, raised and swollen, with a white or yellow pus-filled centre. This is because infection has set in and our body is bringing the white blood cell army to fight at the infection site in the pore, and pus production is the gross by-product.

Grade 3: nodular acne

This form appears as more severe papules, pustules and possibly the appearance of severe nodules. A nodule feels hard, painful and there's no pus because the infection is much deeper. If nodules are squeezed or ruptured, the infection can spread further into the dermis and scars can occur. I'd recommend professional treatment for this more severe form of acne.

Grade 4: cystic acne

This is the most severe form of acne … please see a dermatologist!

Grade 4 acne is the most challenging to treat because of the likelihood of deep dermal scarring. At this progressive stage, the first painful acne cysts appear. A cyst looks like a nodule, but it's softer to the touch because it's filled with pus. The body is really trying to fight the infection in cysts.

An acne cyst occurs when the infection advances from a pimple and the pore ruptures from the pressure and inflammation like a balloon that's become filled with too much oil, debris, bacteria and by-products of inflammation.

The infection from a cyst spreads much deeper and extends well beyond the pore into the dermis. If cystic nodules aren't treated, deep and permanent scarring can occur. (I discuss scarring in chapter 21.)

The bad news is that there's no magical cure for acne, but the good news is that it doesn't last forever. Eventually the body puts itself into balance, usually because our hormones return to normal. This is called 'hormonal burnout' and heralds the end of your acne condition. Yay!

If you believe your acne is getting worse, and as soon as you think there's a risk of deep scarring, see a dermatologist because you may need short-term acne medication with oral retinoids. This medication has side-effects, so weigh these up against the risk of long-term scarring.

Tackling acne head-on

Here are my top 10 tips to help address your acne.

1 Clean your face twice daily

Warm water and an SLS-free cleanser will remove the excess oil and daily grime that may cause blocked pores. You need to add water to rinse off the cleanser — you don't want a film of makeup goop left sitting on your face to clog you up! Be careful not to scrub your face too hard; excess heat and friction on the skin can increase oil flow and irritation and cause further inflammation. I also recommend you wash your face as soon as you come home from work or school because this is when your skin will need a good clean! And avoid makeup wipes if you have acne or blocked pores.

2 Exfoliate

AHAs (lactic, malic, mandelic and glycolic acid) and BHAs (salicylic acid) are recommended to unblock pores and remove dead skin build-up. If you have severe skin congestion, clogged pores or acne, use an exfoliating serum at least three times a week, or daily if your skin can tolerate it.

3 Remember your As and Bs

Vitamins A and B applied in the evening are super important for controlling your acne. Vitamin B will reduce inflammation (the root cause of the pimple!) and help reduce excess oil while keeping your skin hydrated and glowy. And our hero, vitamin A, will slow down that overproduction of pore-clogging skin cells, regulate oil flow and help keep pores nice and tight.

4 Use a spot-treating acne serum without benzoyl peroxide

Benzoyl peroxide is definitely *not* one of my faves. This ingredient kills the bacteria, but it doesn't address the other factors that contribute to acne. Peroxide is just a band-aid on the problem and the harsh ingredients set up oxidation in the skin, and also strip our natural acid mantle and the good bacteria on our skin. Look for acne spot treatment serums that help treat all the underlying problems happening in your pores: skin cell overproduction, excess oil, P. acne bacteria and inflammation.

5 Moisturise

While too much oil and the wrong type of comedogenic oils found in many moisturisers aren't recommended for acne, your skin still needs hydration. Your skin can be high in oil but low in water. This is where water-based hydrators are really important. Gel moisturisers with a low oil content and hydrators like glycerin, sodium PCA, sodium lactate and sodium hyaluronate are all great at drawing water into the skin like a sponge, without contributing to oiliness.

6 Avoid comedonal makeup: choose minerals

Just think about it. You use all the right skincare, you eat well and you're trying to manage your stress levels. You're doing everything right to keep your pimples at bay...and every morning you apply that super trendy heavy makeup that covers any evidence of imperfections but also suffocates your skin! Read your labels and make sure the ingredients in your makeup won't clog your pores. You can undo all that good work by slapping on comedogenic makeup — sometimes staying on your face for over 14 hours a day. It's like wrapping cling wrap over your face! Avoid using heavy foundations containing comedogenic oils or pore-blocking ingredients.

Loose mineral makeup is hands down the best choice. Check that it's formulated with high levels of zinc oxide, which not only protects from solar damage but also calms the inflammation and redness that go hand in hand with acne.

The other great thing about mineral makeup is that you can layer it with a kabuki brush on areas of your face that need more coverage — but remember to keep a kabuki brush clean by washing it every week to remove the oil and bacteria build-up (always clean your brushes with gentle soap or shampoo).

I've seen many acne sufferers hugely improve their skin by only changing one thing in their skincare routine: they ditched their old makeup and switched to a zinc oxide-based mineral makeup.

7 Hair products can affect your skin

When you use comedogenic hair products you may be clogging your skin around the hairline and fringe. Products you use on your hair every day can creep onto your skin and clog your pores. Try to use products with gentle non-comedogenic ingredients because these will not only make your hair look great, they will also make sure your skin remains healthy and zit free.

8 Eat well

Every organ in your body needs food to function. The skin is our largest organ and it responds directly to what we put in our mouths. A study on Micronesian natives found there was almost zero incidence of adolescent acne in the group. Then teenagers from the tribes were taken out of their environment and given a typical 'Western' diet and acne began to develop. Food is often the trigger for skin conditions and a good diet can definitely help control acne.

An acne-friendly diet is basically an anti-inflammatory diet. Try to avoid fructose, glucose and other 'white' sugar, highly processed foods (white rice, white bread, pasta), sugary dried fruits and juices. Try and reduce your dairy intake, but more about that later. Eat foods rich in antioxidants, such as berries and apples, and eat at least six handfuls of different coloured vegetables every day. And don't forget to drink at least six large glasses of water every day!

9 Don't stress

I know, I know … it drives me mad when I'm told to relax and just breathe! You know how breakouts flare up when you're stressed and anxious? There's real science here. When we stress out, we create the hormonal steroid cortisol. Steroids interact directly with our oil glands and disrupt our natural oil balance, making acne worse. Try meditation or yoga classes (not hot yoga!) to reduce stress levels and keep cortisol under control.

10 Don't pick!

I know it's hard to look at the bumps on your face and resist picking, but this has to stop! Every time you burst that bubble, the bacteria spread deeper into the skin and may lead to a more serious infection and even permanent scarring. Suffering a few more days with a pimple that hasn't been picked is much better than permanent scarring.

This is the eating plan I gave my daughter's friend. Addressing diet, coupled with a well-managed skincare regimen, made a massive difference to his acne.

Research based on scientific studies, not celebrity infomercials, concludes that dairy and sugar can both cause spikes in acne-producing hormones. Western culture is addicted to junk food, thanks to the food industry. Consumption of refined sugar and dairy has skyrocketed over the past 50 years... and so has the number of teenagers and adults with acne. I believe it's now more important than ever to educate acne sufferers on the importance of an anti-acne eating plan. I don't believe in the word 'diet' — this is a long-term plan for great skin health until natural hormone levels rebalance.

Cut out the 'bad' fats

Our typical Western diet is full of inflammatory fats. These are saturated fats, trans fats, excess omega-6 fats and processed vegetable oils (soy and corn oils). These fats can irritate cells in pores and this has been linked to acne.

Stick to a low GI plan

The typical Western diet contains foods that contribute to imbalancing sex hormones such as testosterone, IGF-1 and insulin, and this imbalance triggers acne. The biggest factor in a diet that affects hormones is a high glycaemic index (GI). Clinical trials found that individuals consuming a high-GI diet (bread, rice, cereal, pasta, sugar and flour products) had significantly more acne.

The truth about dairy

Traditional dietary guidelines suggesting we drink at least three glasses of milk a day for good nutrition have been questioned by many nutritional experts. The lactose (milk sugar) in a glass of milk can spike insulin levels by up to 300 per cent and has the equivalent sugar content of a can of soft drink.

Let's look at some biology logic. Milk is evolutionarily designed to provide nutrition to offspring from a mother of the same species. Cow's milk naturally contains anabolic steroid hormones, which are very similar to the steroids that bodybuilders use for muscle growth, and the same hormones can also cause acne or make it worse. Unfortunately, there's no such thing as

100 per cent hormone-free milk. In 2009, a review of 21 medical studies and six independent clinical trials found clear links between acne and dairy products. Two controlled trials found that cow's milk increased both the number of people who suffered from acne and the severity.

The nutritional regimen

The best approach is to avoid white sugar, lactose, fructose, cane sugar, refined carbs and dairy, and consume an antioxidant-rich, plant-based diet with lean animal protein.

Here are some simple dietary steps to help prevent and treat acne.

1 Stay away from animal-based milks and other dairy products. Substitute with rice, hemp, coconut and almond milk, and there are some great dairy-free yoghurt substitutes. Read the labels and avoid any products with added sugar.

2 Eat a low glycaemic index (GI), low sugar diet by opting for whole wheat bread, pasta, quinoa and brown rice.

3 Eat chocolate! Yay! Studies show that dark chocolate doesn't increase the severity of acne — so treat yourself (but avoid added sugar). There are some great brands of sugar-free, stevia-based dark chocolate.

4 Make sure you eat your vegetables:

- eat six to nine servings of vegetables a day
- eat the rainbow with an emphasis on leafy greens and red/orange/yellow vegetables.

5 Consume omega-3 and omega-6 'good fats'. These fats have anti-inflammatory properties, but be sure to consume these fats in the correct proportion. Fish oil and flaxseed oil (for vegans) are excellent sources of balanced omegas. Supplements are also recommended.

6 Nuts and seeds are acne friendly and packed with those good fats. Avoid smoked or salted types; raw and activated nuts and seeds are best.

7 Spices and teas such as turmeric, ginger and green tea are excellent anti-inflammatories. Cinnamon is also great as it helps to naturally balance blood sugar.

8 Consider over-the-counter supplements. As a general guide, the following supplements are recommended, but please consult with a nutritionist or naturopath who specialises in acne management:

- vitamin A: 25 000 IU/day for three months (don't take if pregnant or lactating)

- vitamin E: 400 IU/day

- green tea supplements: 5000 mg/day

- evening primrose oil: 2000 mg/day

- zinc citrate: 30 mg/day

- prebiotics and probiotics as directed for improving gut flora

- omega fats if your dietary intake is inadequate.

TERRI'S ANTI-ACNE SKINCARE ROUTINE

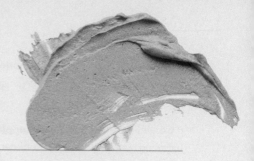

Day

1. Gentle SLS-free facial cleanser
2. AHA/BHA exfoliating serum
3. Spot treatment (peroxide free) acne and blemish serum for targeting pimples
4. Non-comedogenic low-oil moisturiser with zinc oxide (anti-inflammatory and solar protective)
5. Mineral makeup with zinc oxide. This is recommended for girls, but many guys are now turning to mineral makeup for additional skin benefits. I like to call it 'dry sunscreen for men' if the product contains high levels of zinc oxide.

Night

1. Gentle SLS-free facial cleanser
2. Vitamin A serum
3. Vitamin B essential niacinamide (B3) serum
4. Moisturiser: light hydrating gel or non-comedogenic low-oil moisturiser

Once or twice weekly

1. Gentle facial scrub focusing only on problem areas
2. Purifying detoxifying mask with zeolite, bentonite, clays or charcoal

Optional

- *Prebiotics and probiotics:* there are some excellent skin-balancing serums containing prebiotics and probiotics designed to balance the good bacteria on the skin, reduce inflammation (the core of acne) and reduce overgrowth of the bad guys.
- *Pore-refining/oil-control serums:* these serums contain ingredients which can reduce excess oil and that dreaded midday shine. When the oil flow is reduced the pore size will also appear more refined. Bonus!

Remember, acne is controllable but not curable. I know acne can really impact your confidence, but I promise you that it's not a permanent condition. You'll need loads of patience to wait until your body re-balances itself. Combining a good skincare routine with diet and lifestyle changes can successfully control acne and significantly improve the appearance of your skin.

chapter 21

Scarring

A scar is our evolutionary and natural response for quickly healing a wound before infection sets in. Today we have a complete armoury of antibiotics to ward off infection, but cavemen and women had to heal quickly and get on with hunting, gathering and caring for the tribe.

Scars are created when there's trauma and damage to the deeper dermal layer of the skin, and as a response our clever body sends out a message to the fibroblast cells in the dermis to make more collagen to heal the wound. This wound healing response creates slightly different tissue from our normal skin tissue, which is the 'not so pretty' scar.

Scarring is so much more than just a physical skin concern; it can erode self-esteem. I've seen it prevent people from leaving their homes, severely affect people's social lives and some have even needed medication for depression. Over many years of working with clients suffering from disfiguring scars from acne, burns and following surgery, I've been continually researching effective scar treatments and creating products to address scarring.

4 STAGES OF WOUND HEALING

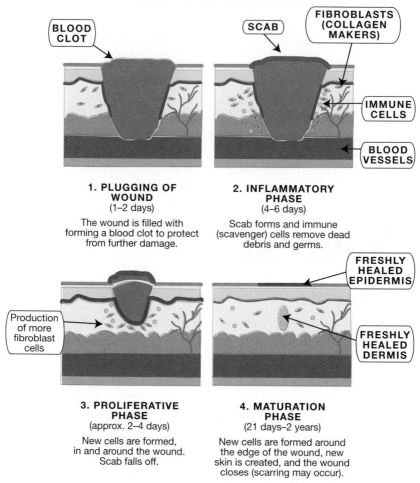

1. PLUGGING OF WOUND
(1–2 days)

The wound is filled with forming a blood clot to protect from further damage.

2. INFLAMMATORY PHASE
(4–6 days)

Scab forms and immune (scavenger) cells remove dead debris and germs.

3. PROLIFERATIVE PHASE
(approx. 2–4 days)

New cells are formed, in and around the wound. Scab falls off.

4. MATURATION PHASE
(21 days–2 years)

New cells are formed around the edge of the wound, new skin is created, and the wound closes (scarring may occur).

I'm going to focus on acne scarring in particular because it's the most common type of scarring affecting men and women in adolescence and beyond, and many of the scar types and therapies discussed in this section are also relevant to other types of scars. Unfortunately, scientists and doctors aren't miracle workers. A scar can't be completely removed, but we can, with the right treatment and client commitment, significantly improve their appearance.

Acne scars

Acne is transient, but the marks it leaves behind aren't. I'm so passionate about helping people with scarring because one small change on the outside can make a dramatic difference on the inside — and that's why I love being a cosmetic chemist!

The good news is that although severe acne scarring is challenging to treat, major improvements can be achieved with the correct treatments and active cosmeceuticals.

Scarring should be prevented above all other symptoms of acne, and by successfully treating and controlling acne until hormonal regulation is achieved you'll minimise the occurrence of scars. Some people are more prone to scarring than others, in particular those with darker skin tones. If your acne is becoming more aggressive, see the section on acne on page 223, and see a dermatologist for treatment to prevent infections and scarring.

Levels of scarring

There are four levels of scar severity:

1. low-level

2. mild

3. moderate

4. severe.

Low-level flat scarring

Low-level flat scarring is that red or brown pigmented mark that lingers on your skin for weeks after the skin has been irritated or after a nasty zit. I don't actually term this level as scarring because there's no long-term change in skin texture; it's more of a change in skin tone. It's relatively straightforward to treat. These scars are really common in darker skinned individuals, who are more prone to PIH (post-inflammatory hyperpigmentation) and generalised pigmentation.

Red or pigmented 'scarring' will generally heal over time with good topical skincare, low-level chemical peels, IPL, LED therapy and lasers designed to treat redness and pigmentation. But again, beware of performing aggressive treatments if you have darker skin because excessive trauma heat from strong peels, lasers and IPL can make the pigmentation flare up. All treatments must be performed by an experienced skin specialist you trust.

Mild scarring

This form of scarring appears as shallow sunken scars that are only visible when closer than arm's length. This mild textural scarring can be successfully treated with skin needling, fractional laser, radiofrequency (RF) therapy and dermal fillers. Good daily, topical skincare will also optimise collagen production, which will improve the end result.

Moderate scarring

This is a more severe form of scarring and can be seen from further than arm's length. Moderate scars can often be camouflaged effectively with high coverage makeup, and if the skin is stretched the scar can be flattened.

These scars need more aggressive therapy. They can be treated by ablative CO_2 lasers (which completely remove the top layer of the skin), fractional laser (which partially removes the top layer of the skin), skin needling, radiofrequency treatments and dermal fillers combined with topical skincare.

Severe scarring

This is the most difficult scarring to address. It's very difficult to camouflage and doesn't flatten out if the skin is stretched.

Severe scarring can be treated with CROSS (Chemical Reconstruction Of Skin Scars) therapy. This treatment uses a concentrated solution of an acid called trichloroacetic acid (TCA). The TCA is placed directly on the scar to create a controlled acid burn, avoiding the surrounding healthy skin. The new collagen production to heal the TCA burn creates a flatter scar that's easier to camouflage and will appear white over time.

Severe scarring is also treated using the punch graft technique, which is usually performed by a specialist surgeon who surgically cuts out the area of the scar and replaces it with a skin graft of the same size. Afterwards, the treated area should heal and appear flatter and less obvious.

Other less-invasive treatments for severe scarring involve fat transfer and short-term dermal filler, which are explained on page 255.

Types of scars

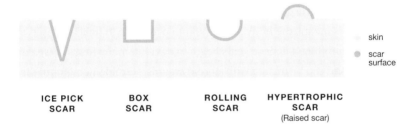

| | | | skin |
| | | | scar surface |

ICE PICK SCAR   **BOX SCAR**   **ROLLING SCAR**   **HYPERTROPHIC SCAR** (Raised scar)

Scars can be classified according to their appearance, and are often associated with severe acne scarring.

Ice pick scars

Ice pick scars are under 2 mm wide and have defined edges, usually due to healing from acne. They're narrow, deep and V-shaped and appear as large, empty pores. These scars are very difficult to camouflage.

Rolling scars

Rolling scars are generally over 5 mm wide and have rounded, sloping edges giving the skin a rippling texture. They're usually not as deep as ice pick scars and many box scars.

Box scars

Box scars can appear like rolling scars but they have clearly defined margins with a box-shaped profile in cross-section. Box scars can be shallow or deep, and can vary in width from 1 to 4 mm. They can resemble chicken pox scars.

Raised scars: keloid and hypertrophic

Unlike ice pick, rolling and box scars, which are depressed on the skin surface, raised scars sit above the skin surface. This category of thick, raised scarring has two sub-categories: keloid and hypertrophic. Both types of scar are often the result of injury, burns or surgery rather than acne, and result from the overproduction of collagen in an abnormal response to healing. This means the body has gone into overdrive to heal and excess collagen is produced. Raised scars begin to develop in the first few weeks of healing and can be treated with steroid creams, steroid injections of the scar and/or specialised laser therapy.

Keloid and hypertrophic scars are very similar in appearance. They're both raised, smooth and are usually pink or purple. Keloid scars spread beyond the original wound site and hypertrophic scars are raised on the site of the injury only. Hypertrophic scars are more likely to shrink over time, whereas keloids tend to stick around.

Clinical scar treatments

Please don't mess about here. Consult with a dermatologist or plastic surgeon to arrange clinical scar improvement.

Our industry is constantly evolving and there are new treatments being developed to improve the appearance of scars, but here are a few of the most popular scar treatments.

Skin needling

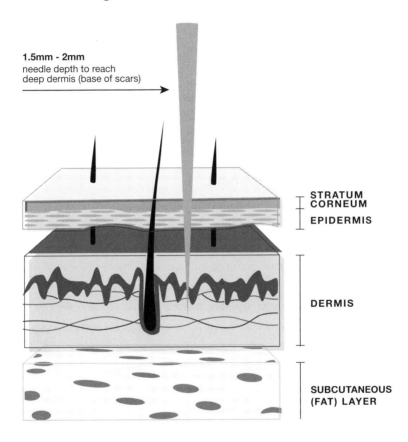

1.5mm - 2mm
needle depth to reach
deep dermis (base of scars)

STRATUM
CORNEUM

EPIDERMIS

DERMIS

SUBCUTANEOUS
(FAT) LAYER

Skin needling, often referred to as Collagen Induction Therapy (CIT), should be performed by qualified skin specialists. It creates a controlled injury to the deeper dermis, and though only a fraction of the skin is injured, a significant healing response is triggered that produces collagen production and textural improvement. Basically, the skin is tricked into thinking it's had a massive injury when only a small fraction of skin has been pierced with a surgical needle. In response healthy collagen is produced and the skin makes the scar look better over time.

All skin types, even darker skin, can be treated. There's little social downtime and the side-effects are minimal.

It's recommended to have a series of eight to ten fortnightly to monthly treatments for optimal results, which will be achieved after 12 months. The one-year mark is when the new collagen created by the treatment has matured. Skin needling will reduce the surface depressions and is recommended for ice pick, rolling and box scars.

Fractional laser treatment

This is a non-invasive treatment that leaves the skin surface relatively intact with only a small fraction of the skin damaged. It's a bit like skin needling, but hot laser columns are shot into the skin instead of needles. These fine, targeted lasers cause channels of heat injury to the epidermis and dermis that result in new collagen production. This is great news for those pesky wrinkles too! The skin surface will be red and swollen for around five days, and the final result for scars will be seen after about one year. Ice pick scars are successfully treated with approximately five fractional laser treatments, usually performed monthly.

Ablative (CO_2) laser resurfacing

Ablative laser resurfacing involves the entire skin surface being removed by creating a controlled injury. This is an aggressive but effective treatment with significant social downtime of around two weeks. The CO_2 laser causes tissue vaporisation and can improve acne scarring by up to 80 per cent due to the new collagen production the laser stimulates.

It's important to closely follow post-care instructions after CO_2 laser resurfacing. Complications of this treatment can include infection, milia formation and post-inflammatory hyperpigmentation (PIH) in darker skinned patients.

Steroid injections

Steroid injections are recommended for those red, raised and itchy scars (keloid and hypertrophic). A steroid injection will usually flatten and soften these scars over time, but must only be administered by a qualified physician because high doses of steroids may cause unwanted side-effects such as alterations in skin tone and texture, and the scar may even become inverted.

Dermal filler injections

This is a good option if the scar is sunken because the filler can raise the scar level to the surrounding normal skin. Most fillers, such as hyaluronic acid fillers, are only temporary so the treatment will need to be repeated every few months. There are some permanent fillers available, but these are more likely to cause complications.

Fat transfer, using your own fat from other body areas, is a more permanent and safe option, but it's a fiddly and non-precise procedure. The injected fat is often reabsorbed by the body and multiple small treatments may be needed to permanently raise the scar.

Cosmeceutical treatment

Clinical scar therapy must be coupled with topical skincare to achieve optimal results. The cosmeceutical ingredients you apply should target collagen production, reduce inflammation and promote barrier repair.

Scar therapy pre-treatment skincare regimen

Prior to scar treatment, follow this regimen for a minimum of two weeks.

- vitamin C to set up high levels of antioxidant protection:
  - pure L-ascorbic acid crystals mixed with 80 per cent serum or water

  or

  - vitamin C serum with a stable and effective form of vitamin C (for example, ethyl ascorbic acid)
- vitamin B3 serum to strengthen the skin barrier prior to treatment
- vitamin A serum to regulate the production of new, healthy skin cells and create new, healthy blood vessels to provide nutrients to the healing scar site. It will also help reduce the possibility of developing hyperpigmentation at the treatment site, which can often occur in darker skin types.
- mineral sun protection — you know the drill …

Scar therapy post-treatment skincare regimen

Commence scar therapy only with the consent of your surgeon. Use occlusive ointment immediately after treatment.

Initially you'll need to keep the wound site protected, and you may be required to apply an occlusive barrier over the treated area until the new skin surface has regenerated. This occlusive will provide a moist protective cover to the treated area and prevent excessive water loss from the skin (which is vital for a good healing outcome). The occlusive should ideally contain anti-inflammatory and antibacterial ingredients. Petroleum jelly is often used as an occlusive, but this crude-oil derived product is pretty basic and doesn't contain ingredients that promote rapid healing nor reduce inflammation.

Once the dressings and stitches have been removed and there's no evidence of the skin weeping, topical skin therapy can commence.

These ingredients will promote healing:

- Vitamin C supports the production of normal collagen while the new scar is forming, and reduces excessive inflammation at the treatment site. It can be in the form of:
  - pure L-ascorbic acid crystals mixed with 80 per cent serum or water

  or

  - vitamin C serum with a stable and effective form of vitamin C (e.g. ethyl ascorbic acid).
- Vitamin B3 serum provides barrier support and repair, promotes new collagen production and promotes healthy skin immunity during healing.
- Vitamin A serum regulates the production of new, healthy skin cells, creates new healthy blood vessels to provide nutrients to the healing scar site, promotes collagen production and reduces the incidence of post-inflammatory hyperpigmentation (PIH) at the treatment site. Ensure you use a gentle form of vitamin A, such as encapsulated retinol, as prescription strength retinoic acid may cause irritation and inflammation at the treatment site.
- Mineral sun protection: solar radiation can undo all of your good work, so make sure you're protected from the sun!

A normal skincare routine may be resumed when all signs of skin redness and inflammation are resolved.

Terri's top picks for scar therapy

- *Vitamin B serum* — for barrier strengthening and healing. Vitamin B stimulates the production of the major skin barrier proteins to promote healing and protect the skin surface from inflammation. It also promotes collagen regeneration for the remodelling of scars, and reduces hyperpigmentation, which can be a side-effect of scarring or scar treatment.

- *Vitamin A serum* — for collagen production and the formation of healthy blood vessels. Vitamin A promotes the production of collagen and new surface cells, which is important in the healing process. Vitamin A also helps with the production of healthy blood vessels in the dermis to enable the vital supply of skin nutrients and remove toxins during scar healing and treatment.

- *Vitamin C/L-ascorbic acid* — for wound healing. L-ascorbic acid is essential for wound healing due to its ability to stimulate collagen, reduce redness and lighten pigmentation. It's also an excellent ingredient for reducing the inflammation associated with creating a scar. Vitamin C is often recommended immediately after surgery that may create a scar, and it's the perfect partner for clinical scar therapy following fractional and ablative laser (which may produce significant inflammation).

- *Physical sunscreen* — for sun protection. The sun's UV, infrared and blue-light rays are a scar's worst enemy. They basically reverse the natural healing process. Furthermore, if the skin is healing during scarring or following scar treatment it's more susceptible to solar damage and exposure increases the chance of the development of skin cancer. It's vital to protect the skin, preferably with mineral zinc oxide, which provides natural UVA/UVB and infrared protection. Zinc oxide is also a natural anti-inflammatory that aids the healing process. Mineral makeup containing high levels of zinc oxide and iron oxide pigments can be applied once the skin surface has commenced healing.

Thankfully, scar treatment has really progressed in the past decade and we have more effective ways of significantly improving the appearance of scars. Although scarring can be challenging to eradicate completely, there's good news — they nearly always fade and become less noticeable over time.

chapter 22

Enlarged pores

Our skin type can be a tricky thing to get a handle on and master. In our teens and early twenties we battle acne, oily skin, big pores and that dreaded breakthrough shine. Enlarged pores and excess oil go hand in hand, but as our hormones balance, the oil slick clears up and we bid farewell to acne, big pores can still persist. Then, as we age, our skin often needs more oil, but large pores can still bug us. At this stage we need to look at ingredients to reduce pore size and balance (not reduce) oil for a smoother texture.

The pore-refining solution

Here are my ingredient recommendations for refining pores:

- *retinoids:* I recommend stabilised retinol or the new retinoid ester hydroxypinacolone retinoate. This will help to shrink pores by boosting collagen production and helping the skin at the edge of the pore to become firmer.

- *niacinamide:* this also helps boost collagen and make the outer barrier stronger so our pores look more refined.

- *red clover extract:* this is a botanical ingredient that's high in the natural chemical biochanin A. It has pore-minimising effects through removing clogging dead cells from the pore entrance. Clogged pores are not just a curse of youth — they can still be an issue as we get older. Red clover can also improve the firmness around the pore wall to help prevent large 'floppy pore syndrome'. (Yes, this is a thing!)

- *salicylic acid:* this good-old BHA exfoliates deep within the pores, drawing out trapped oil and impurities.

- *mandelic acid:* this AHA is very clever because it's able to target the areas with more and less oil at the same time. It selectively increases sebum in the cheeks and chin of ageing skin where oil is low, and targets the nose and forehead to reduce oil if it's being overproduced there. The result is less T-zone shine and reduced pore size in older skin.

Pore size is a huge concern for young and older people alike. And while 'porefection' isn't always achievable, there are some excellent ingredients that can reduce the appearance of enlarged pores, from teen acne to post-menopausal skin.

chapter 23

Skin sensitivity

When I was consulting in my Melbourne skin clinic I would always ask my clients how they described their skin. Over half said their skin was sensitive. I asked myself, is skin sensitivity really this common or are they misdiagnosing their condition?

Sensitive skin envelopes so many skin concerns, both minor and chronic, so this chapter is a bit meaty and technical — apologies in advance! It's really important to understand exactly which type of skin sensitivity you have so you know how to best deal with it. Knowledge is power, and I want to empower you to make informed decisions.

Sensitive skin is a broad lay term rather than a medical diagnosis. It's generally used to describe skin with reduced tolerance to ingredients or changes in the environment like excessive heat or cold, hot water, humidity, sunlight (photosensitivity) and pollution. When your skin is irritated you may feel itching, burning, stinging or dryness and see visible redness, lumps and bumps. There are literally hundreds of ingredients in contact with our body each day, so if you suddenly develop lumps and bumps it's often difficult to determine exactly which ingredient is causing the irritation.

If you think you're sensitive to an ingredient in one of your skincare products, it's best to do a skin sensitivity elimination detox. This is a skin irritant test, not an allergy test:

- Stop using all skincare products.

- Use just glycerin and water to wash your face and castor oil as a moisturiser (you can buy these from your supermarket or pharmacy).

- Wait until the skin irritation has cleared (a few days to weeks).

- Gradually introduce one product at a time for at least five days per product until you discover exactly what's causing contact irritation.

If the irritation was severe, apply the suspect irritant to a small area of the skin, such as the side of the neck, and check for irritation.

Dealing with sensitive skin

I receive more questions about sensitive skin than any other skin concern, so here are a few FAQs that may resonate with you.

Can you use wheat in skincare if you have a gluten intolerance or coeliac disease?

For those who have a gluten intolerance or are coeliac, know that these conditions are dietary — they're not related to the products you apply to your skin. In fact, the gluten protein in wheat products present in skincare products is far too big to penetrate the skin barrier and get into your system, so it's totally okay to apply products containing these ingredients to your skin. The only time you shouldn't is if they're in a lip product and could be eaten, though even then the dose ingested would most likely be too small to cause any reaction.

What are the best ingredients for sensitive skin?

Products that have a low irritancy ingredient list are best for sensitive skin. The word 'hypoallergenic' is overused and often added to labels for marketing purposes, so take that claim with a grain of salt and read labels closely, looking out for specific calming and anti-inflammatory ingredients.

Here's a list of my hero ingredients for soothing, calming and repairing sensitive skin:

- niacinamide (vitamin B3)
- aloe vera
- bisabolol
- allantoin
- colloidal oatmeal
- calendula
- blackcurrant seed oil
- beta glucan

- Canadian willowherb
- certain essential oils in low levels (particularly chamomile and lavender)
- shea butter
- olive squalene
- sea buckthorn oil
- marula oil

- meadowfoam oil
- probiotic: bifidobacteria lysate
- prebiotic: inulin
- zinc oxide sun protection
- salicylic acid (low dose, under 2 per cent)
- peptides (acetyl hexapeptide-49 and acetyl tetrapeptide-40).

What ingredients should you avoid if you have sensitive skin?

This list could be a mini book in itself, but here are the top ones to look out for:

- SLS- and sulphate-based cleansing ingredients (SLS and SLES)
- all soap has a very alkaline pH and strips our precious acid mantle
- artificial fragrance: this is the number one cause of common skin irritation
- artificial colour (FD&C or D&C dyes)
- propylene glycol: this ingredient is found in so many products!
- certain essential oils: dosage is crucial. When I formulate with essential oils I use less than 0.4 per cent dosage in a finished facial product.
- certain citrus oils and mint: *never* apply undiluted essential oils directly to the skin
- highly acidic products with a pH of 3.5 or less: sometimes small amounts of acid are added to formulas to balance the pH. What I'm talking about here is big doses of acid designed to exfoliate.
- abrasive scrubs
- many chemically based (aka organic) sunscreens, especially PABA, benzophenone, avobenzone, butyl methoxycinnamate
- alcohol-based products. Products with a high alcohol content dry the skin surface, strip the acid mantle and make the barrier more susceptible to irritation from other ingredients. If the alcohol is very low down on the ingredient list it's usually okay because it means the amount in the product is very low.
- paraben preservatives
- methylisothiazolinone preservative
- bismuth oxychloride: this is an ingredient used to add 'sparkle' and is found in loads of mineral makeup products, so watch out!

TERRI'S SKINCARE ROUTINE FOR SENSITIVE SKIN

Keep your routine as simple as possible. If you're highly sensitive to many ingredients in skincare, I suggest you introduce one product at a time to your skin by testing each on the side of your neck, waiting 24 hours to ensure you can tolerate it, and only then use it on your entire face.

Morning

1. SLS-free cleanser

2. Prebiotic/probiotic serum

3. Irritant-free/calming moisturiser

4. Zinc oxide-based sun protection moisturiser, or zinc oxide-based mineral makeup

Evening

1. SLS-free cleanser

2. Prebiotic/probiotic serum

3. Acid-free chemical exfoliant. This is a new cosmeceutical ingredient based on a combination of yeast extract, hydrolysed soy protein and soy amino acids that's able to promote skin exfoliation without acids and low pH products that aren't suited to sensitive skin. This is a revolutionary, acid-free exfoliant that works on luminosity, pigmentation and fine lines and is a great alternative to AHAs, BHAs and scrubs.

4. Vitamin B serum. Niacinamide (B3) is an essential ingredient to help repair the skin barrier and reduce irritation.

5. Anti-irritant facial oil (look for sea buckthorn oil, squalene or shea butter)

There's no doubt that treating sensitive skin is challenging and complex. My best advice is to keep your daily skincare routine simple, and keep the pH of products as close as possible to the natural pH of your skin, which is about 5.6.

Food and sensitive skin

It's true, what we eat shows in our skin. Studies have proven there's a significant link between diet and inflammation of the skin.

These are the foods to avoid if you have sensitive skin:

- sugar — particularly refined sugar, cane sugar, fructose, lactose and glucose
- refined carbohydrates (particularly white bread, rice and pasta)
- alcohol
- trans fats, hydrogenated fats and animal fats that are solid at room temperature
- spicy foods
- caffeinated drinks
- excessive consumption of dairy products
- excessive wheat
- an imbalance between omega-6 and omega-3 fatty acids
  - more omega-3s are needed in your diet to balance the omega-6s (which can be inflammatory)
  - fatty fish and walnuts are great sources of omega-3 fatty acids
- many artificial food additives
  - MSG flavour enhancer
  - sulphites
  - benzoates
  - FD&C artificial colours.

Nut and seed allergies

Some allergies, such as soy, tree nut and seed allergies can be life-threatening for some people, even if you're exposed to the allergen in small doses. These individuals are advised to always carry emergency medication to treat anaphylaxis.

The nut or seed allergen is a protein, and this component is usually removed in the processing of the oil so the risk of life-threatening reactions to the processed oils used in good-quality skincare and makeup is minimal. However, you should avoid products containing seed and nut oils that you're allergic to just in case. Reputable skincare companies (and I stress 'reputable' because there are some dodgy 'back-yarders' out there!) will always list all ingredients on the package, or have the ingredients available at point of sale. Products containing nut oils such as macadamia, argan or almond oil may contain the nut allergen in the product, so avoid them if you're allergic to those specific nuts. Although the incidence of anaphylaxis in nut allergy sufferers is rare, when nut-containing products are present in skincare there have been cases of an allergic reaction on the area where the product was applied. My recommendation is to avoid the ingredient if you're suspicious it may be present in your product.

Below is a list of known allergens. It's often a challenge to decipher a common allergen like apricot oil from an ingredient list because manufacturers are required to list ingredients by the INCI name, which usually has a Latin basis. To make your life a little easier, refer to table 23.1, (overleaf) which is from the Non-food Allergens Factsheet (August 2014) compiled by Anaphylaxis Campaign.

For information on nutrition, I highly recommend a book by Karen Fischer called *The Healthy Skin Diet*. This book outlines foods that trigger inflammation and the best diet for reducing skin sensitivity.

Table 23.1: some known common allergens that may be in your skincare

Ingredient	Latin name (INCI)	Variations
Almond (sweet)	Prunus dulcis	Prunus amygdalus dulcis
Almond (bitter)	Prunus amara	Prunus amygdalus amara
Apricot	Prunus armeniaca	N/A
Avocado	Persea gratissima	N/A
Banana	Musa sapientum	Musa paradisiaca, Musa acuminata, Musa balbisiana, Musa basjoo or Musa nana
Brazil	Bertholletia excelsa	N/A
Cashew	Anacardium occidentale	N/A
Celery	Apium graveolens	N/A
Chestnut	Castanea satvia	Castanea sylva or Castanea crenata
Chickpea	Cicer arietinum	N/A
Coconut	Cocos nucifera	N/A
Corn (maize)	Zea mays	N/A
Egg	Ovum	N/A
Fish liver oil	Piscum lecur	N/A
Hazelnut	Corylus avellana	Corylus americana
Kiwi fruit	Actinidia chinensis	Actinidia deliciosa
Lupin	Lupinus albus	Lupinus luteus, Lupines texensis or Lupines subcarnosus
Macadamia	Macadamia ternifolia	Macadamia integrifolia
Milk	Lac	N/A
Mustard	Brassica alba	Brassica nigra or Brassica juncea
Oat	Avena sativa	N/A
Peach	Prunus persica	N/A
Peanut	Arachis hypogaea	N/A
Pistachio	Pistacia vera	Pistacia manshurica
Rice	Oryza sativa	N/A
Rye	Secale cereale	N/A
Sesame	Sesamum indicum	N/A
Soya	Glycine soja	Glycine max
Sunflower	Helianthus annuus	N/A
Walnut	Juglans regia	Juglans nigra
Wheat	Triticum vulgare	N/A

Note: An allergic reaction is specific to the individual. Please consult your doctor if you believe you have an allergy to a specific ingredient.

Types of sensitivity and inflammatory skin conditions

In this section, I'll be focusing on common inflammatory skin conditions that are underpinned by sensitivity and inflammation: dermatitis and rosacea

After seeing so many of my friends and clients go through pain, lack of confidence and frustration with these conditions, I feel it's definitely worth discussing each in detail.

- Dermatitis
    - Contact dermatitis which can be either:
        - Irritant contact dermatitis
        - Allergic contact dermatitis
    - Atopic dermatitis (eczema)
    - Seborrheic dermatitis
- Rosacea

Dermatitis

Dermatitis is a very broad term describing irritation and inflammation of the skin, and there are many types of dermatitis. It's a common skin condition and people with dermatitis often have skin that's sensitive to several triggers. It's another condition that really affects self-esteem during flare-ups because the irritation can often affect visible parts of the body and the face.

Dermatitis sufferers have sensitive skin, so they should follow the sensitive skin nutrition, skincare and lifestyle routine outlined on page 263. If you're having a bad flare-up of dermatitis and your skin is open, weeping, hot or infected, seek medical help because prescription medication may be needed.

Contact dermatitis

This dermatitis rash occurs on areas of the body that have come into contact with substances, and can be either of the following:

1. *Irritant contact dermatitis:* this isn't allergy related. It involves irritation on the area of direct contact with the irritant. An example would be someone constantly coming in contact with liquids on their hands such as cleaning products, soap, handwash, hand sanitiser or alcohol. Irritant contact dermatitis can be burning and itchy and the skin will look red and very dry.

2. *Allergic contact dermatitis:* this involves inflammation being present in the area where the substance you're allergic to touches you. Common ones include metals (e.g. nickel) and poison ivy. The rash from an allergen is usually a very itchy rash with blisters and borders around the inflamed areas.

Irritant contact dermatitis

Skin irritation can sometimes be referred to as 'irritant contact dermatitis', which results from contact with a substance or surface, known as 'the irritant'. Contact irritant dermatitis (skin irritation) doesn't involve a direct overactive immune response with the release of antibodies, as is the case with allergies. Rather, it causes inflammation and damage to the skin surface at a greater rate than the body's own natural repair mechanisms. The irritation persists until our body naturally repairs the skin or we intervene with medication.

Harsh chemicals in shampoos and body cleansers — such as SLS, phthalates found in artificial fragrance, some acidic products, hair dyes, household cleaning products, pollutants and paints — frequently cause skin irritation. Irritation can also happen when there's excessive friction or rubbing of a material against the skin. Some individuals are more sensitive than others and can be irritated by a substance that doesn't bother others.

Symptoms of skin irritation

Redness, swelling, itching, burning and even blistering are irritation symptoms, but confusingly they can also look like an allergy. Remember, allergic reactions can cause these symptoms to appear in different areas of the body, but skin irritation is usually limited to the specific site of direct contact. This is why it's often called *contact* irritant dermatitis.

You may develop irritation immediately after contact with the skin irritant, but generally your skin will slowly become more and more irritated after repeated exposure. If you've ever worked in a restaurant washing dishes you may have developed contact dermatitis from constant exposure to the harsh SLS in detergents.

Finding the irritating culprit

If you know that allergy is not the cause, you can test skin sensitivity by following the elimination skin detox on page 262. This will enable you to narrow down the culprit of contact irritation.

Treatment of contact irritation

If the contact irritation is severe and mild anti-irritant ingredients (discussed on page 262) aren't helping, you may need to pull out the big guns and look at short-term steroid creams. It's not recommended to use steroids long term because they can damage the skin.

Allergic contact dermatitis

Skin irritation and skin allergy: yes, there's a difference!

The visible symptoms of an allergic reaction and a contact irritation reaction often look the same: itchy, red, swollen skin. If a product has caused an irritant reaction, the symptoms of skin irritation are usually limited to the specific area where the substance had direct contact with the body. If you're allergic, your body sets up an internal attack (because it thinks the allergen substance is an invader) and the allergic reaction is present beyond the site of contact and can occur all over the body, and can lead to a life-threatening situation.

Allergy explained

I majored in immunology in my science degree so allergy and inflammation are areas that have always piqued my interest. Allergy is essentially an abnormal reaction by the immune system to a substance (the allergen) that normally doesn't cause a reaction in most people. Typical allergens that cause allergic contact dermatitis can be found in plants, fragrances, preservatives, cosmetics, metals (such as nickel, chrome or silver in jewellery), detergents, latex and clothing.

If you're allergic to something and are exposed to the allergen, your immune system reacts and releases special defence fighter cells in the body which migrate to the place where the allergen had first skin contact, and causes these defender cell soldiers to release inflammatory chemicals called histamines. This cascade of events results in symptoms of allergy appearing, such as redness, irritation and itch.

Allergy symptoms

Symptoms of a skin allergy include red, itchy, swollen, raised skin which may result in blistering, and may not always appear on the direct area of allergen contact. It's sneaky because a delayed onset of symptoms can also occur. You may have contact with a potential allergen for months or years before your body suddenly reacts against it because the body can take time to make antibodies and mount an attack. Every time the body is exposed to the allergen, more antibodies are made. Generally, the symptoms of allergies get worse with each subsequent exposure to the substance, so once you know the culprit you *must* avoid contact with it. Once your body has mounted a full-blown immune response to the particular allergen, you'll develop symptoms a few hours after every contact. The worst-case scenario might be breathing difficulties or an anaphylactic shock. So don't mess about!

Treating allergies

If you think you have an allergy, don't play detective yourself— make an appointment with an allergist or dermatologist and have a patch test. Once you know exactly what to avoid you have the power to control it.

The medical treatment of allergies involves the short-term use of steroids and/or antihistamine in tablets or creams, which will reduce the immune system's response of inflammation and address the itch, burning and other symptoms.

Atopic dermatitis (eczema)

The cause of eczema is based on the inability of the body to naturally repair a damaged skin barrier. Scientists have figured out that eczema sufferers have a mutation in the gene that produces a main skin barrier protein called filaggrin.

A compromised skin barrier means that moisture leaves the skin too fast and the skin becomes dry and scaly. Environmental allergens (irritants from the person's surrounds) can also enter the skin and activate the immune system, producing inflammation, which makes the skin red and itchy.

Eczema is a chronic skin condition where the skin develops red, scaly itchy patches, particularly in the creases of the body. This condition is debilitating, and it breaks my heart to see anyone struggling with eczema. If you or your child suffer from eczema, I hope this section helps to clarify your condition and give you some strategies.

Eczema usually starts in childhood and affects about 20 per cent of babies under the age of two. Infant eczema usually improves between the ages of two and five. Adult eczema is less common and thankfully is usually less severe in middle age.

Certain triggering foods and environmental factors can cause flare-ups. As with other types of dermatitis, eczema sufferers have sensitive skin, and eczema has been linked with other diseases such as food allergies, hay fever and asthma. In fact, people with a family history of eczema, allergies, hay fever and asthma are more likely to have eczema, and children with eczema have a higher risk of developing food allergies, asthma and hay fever later in childhood.

(A note on eczema flare-ups)

If you experience flaking, painful flare-ups you should also look for a thicker occlusive ointment that really holds the moisture in with added non-steroid anti-inflammatories. Look for ingredients such as castor bean oil, shea butter and other soothing butters, and lavender essential oil (if you're not sensitive to it).

If the skin is scratched and over irritated fluid may appear, and the rash can crust over. Infection of the irritated areas is common and must be treated. Using rich, hydrating moisturisers and cortisone-based ointments can help ease the symptoms, and it's also important to avoid skin irritants such as soap, hot water and synthetic fabrics. I discuss this in more detail on page 282.

Because people with eczema aren't very good at holding water in their skin, it appears dry and flaky. One of the most important factors in an eczema skincare routine is to make sure the skin is well hydrated with non-irritating moisturisers and oils to help prevent water loss from the skin. Eczema not only affects confidence, it can also affect a person's quality of life as sufferers can often spend much of the night awake and scratching.

With eczema, the skin barrier has been broken, providing the perfect opportunity for eczema to flourish. A healthy protected barrier is the best defence against outside attack from microbes, irritants and any environmental bad guys. If you have eczema you're vulnerable to a nasty bug called *Staphylococcus aureus*, and if these bacteria take hold you need to take serious action with antibiotics.

The main triggers of eczema directly affect the protective skin barrier function. Eczema triggers include:

- specific foods that cause intolerance
- FD&C dyes (artificial colours)
- many irritating preservatives
- perfumes, especially artificial fragrances
- soap (the pH is very alkaline and not compatible to the pH of our skin)
- certain fabrics (both synthetics and wool)
- excessive heating and air conditioning (humidifiers are recommended)
- stress (can cause flare-ups)
- animals
- dust mites
- constant exposure to water and/or soap

- sanitisers

- allowing the skin to dry out

- scratching (if you have a baby with eczema, use night mittens and make sure their nails are clipped)

- minor skin infections

- chlorine in pools or spas

- contact with allergens in the environment such as grass, bark, pollens, seeds, trees and airborne irritants.

Symptoms of eczema include:

- dryness

- severe itchiness

- red and scaly areas, especially on skin creases like the elbows, back of the knees and groin

- watery fluid weeping from affected skin

- weeping sores that may become infected by bacteria or viruses.

Controlling eczema

- *Itch:* If you can control the itch, you can help stop barrier damage and reduce infection. Cold compresses are a great idea—always have ice packs or frozen peas on the go. Non-drowsy antihistamines can also help, but these should be recommended by a specialist because long-term use of any medication isn't ideal unless absolutely necessary.

- *Infection:* To prevent opportunistic bugs growing in the broken skin it's recommended to apply prebiotic and probiotic skincare, which helps balance the good bacteria and prevents overgrowth of the bad bugs. During a flare-up it's good to take a daily bath with a mild antibacterial bath product. If you're not sensitive to essential oils, a bath with a few drops of lavender is excellent at calming the skin and mildly controlling bad bacteria.

- *Dryness:* The use of emollient moisturisers is vital to stop the skin drying out, and the best time to apply your rich lotion is straight after showering and before bed. Choose your brand wisely and read your labels so you avoid the common eczema irritants. In general, the simpler the formula, the better. Avoid artificial fragrance as a priority and choose a moisturiser with a higher oil or butter content because this will help prevent water loss from the skin.

General tips for controlling eczema

- Gently towel dry your skin (with a soft towel) and don't rub too hard.
- Add pure bath oils to a daily bath or massage oils or moisturisers directly after bathing or showering.
- Avoid harsh cleansing products or soap.
- Avoid hard water as the alkalinity can aggravate eczema—if you know you live in a hard water area, install a water softener in your shower head.
- Use a non-irritating cream cleanser on irritated areas of the body.
- Keep cool in bed: use lightweight blankets and doonas with natural fibres—cotton and bamboo are great.

- Keep your nails short so scratching won't damage the skin surface too much because this can cause infection.

- Use cotton gloves inside rubber gloves for household cleaning, and add a low-irritant hand cream underneath.

- Avoid fabrics on your skin that make you itchy, e.g. some acrylics and wool can make the skin scratchy. Cotton, cotton-synthetic mix and bamboo fabrics are great. Before you buy an item, read the label and rub the fabric against your neck as a spot test. The slightest amount of sensitivity is a warning sign.

- Remember, hypoallergenic is not a medical term and it doesn't guarantee you'll not react. If you're using a product for the first time, try a patch test on a hidden part of your body.

- I know this goes against everything I say, but in the case of eczema a little bit of sunlight is helpful and can soothe symptoms. Some dermatologists recommend controlled UV therapy for eczema. Never get burned and don't go out in the hottest part of the day; short bursts of gentle sunlight are best.

- If you think your eczema is triggered by an allergen like dust mites, cat dander or grasses, a skin prick test will help you determine what triggers to avoid.

- Avoid extremes of temperature and humidity. Changes in body temperature—even sweaty workouts—can cause flare-ups.

- Avoid air conditioning—this can really dry out your skin.

- Choose to swim in the ocean rather than chlorinated pools. Ocean water is eczema friendly.

- Some foods are eczema friendly and are great for all types of sensitive skin (a nutritionist will give you the best advice). I strongly recommend the book by Karen Fischer called *The Eczema Diet*. She explains that certain foods rich in salicylates like tomatoes, oranges, avocado, almonds and broccoli can make eczema worse. Karen has been personally touched by eczema with her child's and her own dermatitis, and has made it her life's passion to help others with eczema and dermatitis.

TERRI'S ECZEMA SKINCARE ROUTINE

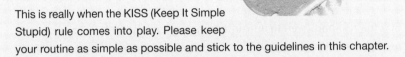

This is really when the KISS (Keep It Simple Stupid) rule comes into play. Please keep your routine as simple as possible and stick to the guidelines in this chapter.

One of my favourite ingredients that should be added to your anti-eczema routine is niacinamide: vitamin B3 is the best ingredient for rebuilding your skin barrier and holding in moisture.

Morning

1 Cleanser: pH balanced; free of artificial fragrance and SLSs/SLESs

2 Prebiotic/probiotic balancer: this will keep a balance between the good and bad bacteria

3 Vitamin B3 serum

4 Emollient moisturiser with added anti-inflammatories and minimal irritants

5 Mineral makeup: must be high in zinc oxide (anti-inflammatory and solar protection) and iron oxides (blue-light protection). No FD&C dyes, talc or bismuth oxychloride.

Evening

Repeat the morning routine, but leave out step 5.

Eczema is a medically diagnosed condition and often needs prescription medication. While there are excellent non-prescription serums and moisturisers formulated to address eczema, I strongly recommend you work with your dermatologist to control this condition.

Eczema responds well to anti-inflammatory creams and ointments, and topical steroids (corticosteroids) are the most common treatment and can be prescribed by a doctor. I don't recommend long-term use of high-strength topical steroids because they have a negative impact on the skin, causing dermal thinning, crepiness and premature ageing. Low-dose steroids are best: only apply in a thin layer no more than twice daily.

There's a new prescription-only anti-inflammatory ingredient called pimecrolimus which I think is a good alternative to cortisone creams and doesn't cause thinning of the skin. This is a drug so consult a skin specialist before use.

Finally, if the skin is infected, antibiotic intervention is necessary and this must be supervised by your doctor, but please try to keep your eczema controlled to avoid skin infections because incorrect or long-term use of antibiotics can cause serious health concerns with future infections.

Australian researchers are leading the way with a new monthly injectable treatment to help those suffering from this chronic condition— and the results look very promising. This is a 'biologic' drug made from proteins derived from human DNA and 'grown' in a lab. It works by blocking factors called interleukins (ILs), which help our immune system fight invaders. In eczema and severe dermatitis the immune system goes haywire and ILs are overproduced, making the body attack itself. This new drug calms down the immune system and reduces the severity of eczema.

Seborrheic dermatitis

This is a less common type of dermatitis that causes scaly, flaking patches and red skin and is often accompanied by stubborn dandruff. It also affects the nose, chin, forehead and other oily areas of the skin. In adults it can occur at any time, and is often a long-term condition. Babies commonly have this condition (called 'cradle cap') on their heads, but thankfully it's a short-term condition in infants. If your baby has cradle cap, don't pick at it — use gentle oils to help lift it off naturally.

If you have an ongoing sensitive skin condition that involves constant skin irritation, itchiness, redness, flakiness or a rash that won't go away, you need to consult with a dermatologist because many forms of dermatitis need medical intervention.

Rosacea

Rosacea is a complex condition that can really affect self-confidence. The exact cause isn't yet known but it's thought to be a combination of genes, environment, *Demodex* mites and an overly active immune system.

There's an urban myth that rosacea is caused by alcohol consumption, but this is false — although alcohol does make rosacea worse. It occurs when there's an abnormal increase of blood flow to the face due to chronic inflammation of the blood vessels and skin.

Rosacea is an extremely common condition affecting a huge sector of our population. It's most common in women over 25; however, men who suffer from rosacea usually have more aggressive forms of it. Rosacea typically occurs in fair-skinned, blue-eyed women of Irish or English descent, and for this reason it's often referred to as 'the curse of the Celts'. However, after numerous trips to Hong Kong over many years I've consulted with many Asian clients who have this condition.

Rosacea can vary from person to person: some people will have constant symptoms, whereas others may have occasional flare-ups. It can be stable in some people, whereas others experience gradual worsening over time.

The stages of rosacea

There are four progressive stages of rosacea:

1. In the early stages the individual will notice frequent blushing, which often occurs as a child. The blushing then becomes more common and may become permanent. The face may show general redness or there may be distinct visible blood vessels (telangiectasia) present. Princess Diana had this type of rosacea. The redness is usually symmetrical and gives a 'butterfly' effect on the face.

2. Red bumps or fluid-filled lumps (like acne but without blackheads or whiteheads) can occur with or without the persistent blushing.

3. If untreated the rosacea can progress and rhinophyma of the nose can develop. This involves a gradual enlargement of the oil glands and thickening of the skin on the nose. This is more common in men and is often confused with alcoholism. Former US President Bill Clinton has this condition.

4. In advanced cases rosacea may also affect the eyes — this is called ocular rosacea. The eyes may experience a burning, gritty sensation, and the eyes and eyelids may begin to redden and become sore.

Typical rosacea symptoms can include:

- persistently red flushed face (cheeks, forehead, chin and nose)
- small, visible facial blood vessels
- small red spots/bumps on the face, sometimes fluid filled
- sensitive skin that's often dry and flaky
- a red, bulbous nose with thickened skin and an uneven texture (when advanced)
- a burning sensation in the eyes, irritated eyelids or an uncomfortable, 'gritty' feeling in the eyes (when advanced).

Factors that can contribute to the condition worsening include:

- hot drinks

- spicy foods

- excess sunlight (especially without sun protection)

- alcohol

- intense exercise

- high weather temperatures

- hot baths/saunas

- emotional stress

- irritating skincare ingredients

- using corticosteroid creams.

What to avoid if you have rosacea

It's best to avoid any foods or liquids that cause blood-vessel dilation or internal inflammation.

Inflammatory foods include:

- sugar (refined sugar, fructose, cane sugar, corn syrup)

- refined carbohydrates (particularly white bread, rice and pasta)

- alcohol

- trans fats, hydrogenated fats and animal fats that are solid at room temperature

- spicy foods

- caffeinated drinks

- over-consumption of dairy products

- excessive intake of wheat

- imbalance between omega-6 and omega-3 fatty acids: more omega-3s are needed in your diet to balance the omega-6s (which can be inflammatory) — fatty fish and walnuts are great sources of omega-3 fatty acids

- many artificial food additives, such as:
  - MSG flavour enhancer
  - sulphites
  - benzoates
  - FD&C artificial colours.

The ingredients in skincare to avoid if you suffer from rosacea are:

- SLS- and sulphate-based cleansing ingredients: these are more irritating than other foaming and cleansing ingredients

- artificial fragrance: this is the number one cause of skin irritation

- propylene glycol: a common skincare ingredient

- certain essential oils: *never* apply undiluted essential oils directly to the skin

- acidic products: these are often not tolerated by clients with sensitive skin, so it's best to avoid AHAs (particularly glycolic) and L-ascorbic acid

- abrasive scrubs

- artificial colours: irritation is due to the small particle size, which may penetrate the skin surface

- chemically based sunscreens: a common skin irritant

- alcohol-based products: these dry the skin surface and make the barrier more susceptible to irritation from other ingredients.

TERRI'S IDEAL SKINCARE REGIMEN FOR ROSACEA

Treat your skin as though it's sensitive and inflamed and ensure you always use pH balanced products.

Morning

1. SLS-free cleanser

2. Prebiotic/probiotic serum

3. Irritant-free/calming moisturiser

4. Zinc oxide-based sun protection moisturiser or zinc oxide-based mineral makeup

Evening

1. SLS-free cleanser

2. Prebiotic/Probiotic serum

3. Acid-free chemical exfoliant. (See 'Terri's skincare routine for sensitive skin' on page 265 for more on this new cosmeceutical ingredient.)

4. Vitamin B serum. Niacinamide (B3) is an essential ingredient to help repair the skin barrier and reduce irritation.

5. Vitamin A serum: be careful! Some forms of vitamin A can be irritating if you have rosacea. I recommend a retinol that's encapsulated in a liposome because this will be the gentlest on sensitive skin. Some companies will state this on the label but it's not always easy to find—sorry.

6. Anti-irritant facial oil (look for sea buckthorn oil, squalene, shea butter).

If you suffer from rosacea I strongly urge you to find a great skin therapist. This condition is something you really need to stay on top of, and a good therapist will be able to perform gentle treatments to support your skin care routine and lifestyle.

The best clinical treatments for rosacea management are:

- IPL or laser targeting abnormal blood vessels to diffuse redness
- LED (light emitting diode) cold light therapy. This is a very gentle treatment recommended for chronically inflamed skin — yellow and red light are excellent for calming rosacea.

Antibiotic creams or capsules can also help the condition. However, I don't recommend long-term use of antibiotics because this can breed antibiotic resistance and imbalance in the gut and skin microbes.

Because there's no cure, rosacea needs to be managed over a long time and you really need to commit to a management plan as part of your lifestyle. But don't be disheartened — with the right products, lifestyle choices and treatments, the appearance of rosacea can be greatly controlled.

*   *   *

This chapter was a bit complicated, I know, but as you can see, sensitivity can wear many hats. I hope I've enlightened you on this very broad and most common skin concern and helped you understand the different types of skin sensitivities and how best to address them.

chapter 24

Dryness and dehydration

Dry skin is another misunderstood skin condition. Two things form the basis of skin dryness: lack of water and lack of oil. It therefore follows that there are two types of skin dryness: water dryness (dehydration) and oil (aka lipid) dryness. Your skin can suffer from either or both types of dryness at the same time, so it's important to know what you're dealing with to achieve balance.

LIPID (DRY) SKIN	**DEHYDRATED SKIN** (most common)	**BOTH**

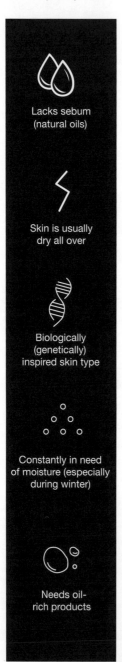

LIPID (DRY) SKIN

Lacks sebum (natural oils)

Skin is usually dry all over

Biologically (genetically) inspired skin type

Constantly in need of moisture (especially during winter)

Needs oil-rich products

DEHYDRATED SKIN

Skin lacks water

Can be experienced by all skin types

Skin can be oily and dry simultaneously

Triggered by environment factors/diet/incorrect use of product

May experience breakouts

Needs water-rich products

BOTH

Dull

Itchy

Sensitive

Tight

Flaky

Water dryness (dehydration)

HEALTHY 'NORMAL' SKIN

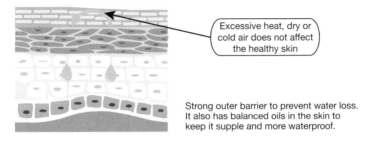

Excessive heat, dry or cold air does not affect the healthy skin

Strong outer barrier to prevent water loss. It also has balanced oils in the skin to keep it supple and more waterproof.

DEHYDRATED SKIN (WATER-POOR)

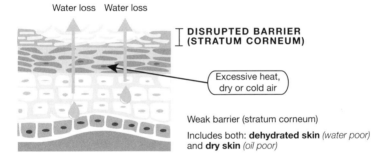

Water loss   Water loss

⊺ DISRUPTED BARRIER
⊥ (STRATUM CORNEUM)

Excessive heat, dry or cold air

Weak barrier (stratum corneum)

Includes both: **dehydrated skin** *(water poor)* and **dry skin** *(oil poor)*

OIL-POOR SKIN (LIPID DRYNESS)

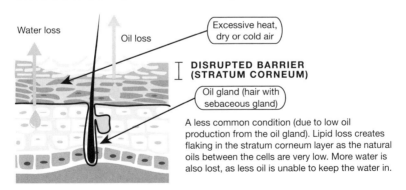

Water loss

Oil loss

Excessive heat, dry or cold air

⊺ DISRUPTED BARRIER
⊥ (STRATUM CORNEUM)

Oil gland (hair with sebaceous gland)

A less common condition (due to low oil production from the oil gland). Lipid loss creates flaking in the stratum corneum layer as the natural oils between the cells are very low. More water is also lost, as less oil is unable to keep the water in.

Dehydrated skin is usually a result of environmental conditions. Water can be lost from the skin in a dry climate or other environmental conditions such as air conditioning or aeroplane cabins, or if you don't drink enough fluids. Dehydration is easily addressed with good skincare and an adequate fluid intake. And FYI, you can have acne and still have dehydrated skin.

Some people experience water dryness periodically — my skin feels like a giant cornflake after long-haul flights, but a few days of skin kindness soon gets me back to my old self!

Oil dryness/lipid dryness

If your skin starts to appear dull, rough and worn out, it's a sign of lipid dryness. Lipid dry skin can often have a matte appearance that lacks sheen, is no longer supple and lacks natural 'slip'. Oil dryness tends to be a chronic condition, and those who have it often experience premature ageing and skin sensitivity because the skin barrier may be compromised.

The delicate barrier of lipid dry skin constantly needs to be supplemented with nurturing oils that should behave like the skin's own sebum, so products should contain ingredients to lubricate the skin and stop it from losing too much of its own water through TEWL. (TEWL is a techie term for transepidermal water loss, and simply means the loss of the skin's own water supply to the air.)

The science of dryness

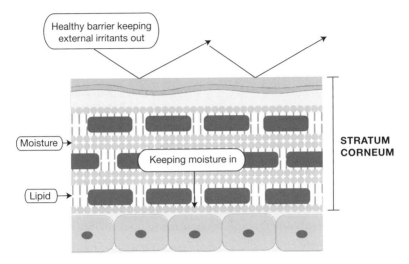

Healthy barrier keeping external irritants out

Moisture

Lipid

Keeping moisture in

STRATUM CORNEUM

Water is the most important molecule for the human body — and our skin! That outermost protective layer of our skin, the stratum corneum, has a primary function of acting as a giant tarpaulin to keep water from leaving our skin. Maintaining the water levels in our skin depends on a few factors, such as our skin's natural moisturising ability, the general health of the outer barrier, and the oil molecules between the dead cells that make up the stratum corneum.

A type of natural oil found in the spaces between our dead skin cells is called ceramide. These magic molecules act like a natural raincoat, preventing water loss and keeping our barrier strong. Low or altered levels of ceramides have been linked to the skin conditions eczema, psoriasis and dermatitis when the barrier isn't working efficiently.

Ceramides and other oil molecules in the stratum corneum join forces with the protein (keratin) that holds the dead skin cells of the stratum corneum together. Think of the dead skin cells in the barrier as the bricks and the keratin and natural skin oils as the mortar — together they form a mini army to stop water escaping, or TEWL.

That dry, flaky skin we see when we've spent too long on a plane is a result of too much TEWL because of the low humidity in the cabin. Any time there's more water in our skin than in the outside air, our skin will take water from the deep dermal layer of the skin to supply the rapidly dehydrating surface layers. And this doesn't only happen on planes: any time the air is really dry we lose water if our barrier isn't tip-top. TEWL also highlights all those fine, crepey lines, which is the last thing we need when we step off a plane wanting to look our best for a work event or to greet family and friends!

Also, if our natural skin water levels aren't just right, our magic barrier can't work properly and this affects our skin's natural ability to shed dead cells and have new cells replace the old ones, so we lose more water! It's a vicious cycle.

Is dryness a short-term or chronic condition?

My skin always feels drier in Melbourne winters; central heating, cold wind and constant changes in temperature wreak havoc with my skin's hydration. Of course I know I need to drink more water, but I often turn to coffee or a high-caffeine chai latte instead during my busy workday. There's a big difference between having dry skin as a long-term condition (chronic dryness) and occasionally suffering from dryness because of dehydration, a change in environment, skincare products or diet.

People with chronic dry skin usually suffer with naturally low oil and ceramide levels, and it's no surprise that chronic dryness is usually accompanied by sensitivity, because the outer skin barrier is so weak. As a result, people with chronic dryness are more susceptible to inflammation, redness and dermatitis, and will react more to ingredient 'nasties' and climate changes than those with oily, combination or normal skin.

Cosmeceuticals for dry skin

So how do you deal with dry skin? There are a number of options depending on your skin concern and the level of dryness.

Everyone needs vitamin B3, and from there you can choose the type of moisturiser that's best for you.

Niacinamide/vitamin B3

Yes, B is for Barrier! Vitamin B3 is clearly the best ingredient for keeping the barrier really strong. This multitasking cosmeceutical rebuilds the protective outer barrier and helps to make the 'mortar' (keratin) that glues the outer skin cells together. It also increases the natural ceramide levels of the skin to keep us hydrated and luminous. What's not to love about vitamin B3?...seriously!

Moisturisers

Moisturisers are divided into three categories:

1. humectants (for attracting water in dehydrated skin)

2. emollients (for reducing water loss, and keeping the skin moist, smooth and flexible)

3. occlusives (a thick sealing skin cover for holding in the water in very dry or barrier-damaged skin).

Humectants

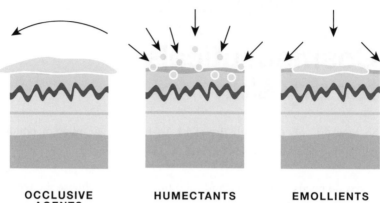

OCCLUSIVES / HUMECTANTS / EMOLLIENTS — WHAT'S THE DIFFERENCE?

OCCLUSIVE AGENTS

Reduce water loss by forming barrier

HUMECTANTS

Attract moisture from environment and within the skin like a water magnet

EMOLLIENTS

(usually oils and waxes)

Fill in the rough, dry patches to soften, soothe and reduce water loss from the skin

Humectants are clever little molecules that act like microscopic sponges or water magnets. They're naturally occurring molecules in the epidermis and in the deeper dermis that hold many times their own weight in water.

Humectants are really important when I'm formulating my products — almost everything I create will have at least one humectant. These little 'water lovers' are important to ensure the skin doesn't become 'water dry' or dehydrated. Hyaluronic acid, for example, can hold up to 1000 times its weight in water and in the skin. That's one heck of a sponge! This ingredient mostly keeps the skin surface hydrated (the molecules are usually too big to penetrate deeper into the skin), but this is still important visually because it helps to stop crepiness. In skincare products the ingredient used is actually a derivative of hyaluronic acid called sodium hyaluronate, so check your labels.

Other skin-hydrating humectants I use in my formulating bag of tricks include glycerin, sorbitol, betaine, lactic acid (which also helps with ceramide production), sodium lactate and sodium PCA.

As a cosmetic chemist I know how important it is to combine humectants with quality oils to further lock in the moisture that the humectants trap, which is why I always recommend a moisturiser as the final step in a skincare routine. The exception is people with very oily skin, who can apply an oil-free moisturiser with humectants only.

Emollients (oils)

Oils act as emollients to soothe and soften dry, rough skin and help lock in moisture. They do this by filling in the rough, dry patches on the surface, making your skin feel smooth and reducing water loss. Emollients make the skin feel moisturised and lubricated without the thick feel of heavy occlusives.

I love formulating with oils! There's such a variety of textures and skin benefits and I have so many choices in my formulating lab. Some oils can also act as anti-inflammatories and are great for calming sensitive skin, while essential fatty acids found in ingredients such as olive squalene (one of my faves) can help reinforce our skin barrier and fight free radical damage.

Many of the oils I love are very similar in molecular structure to our own sebum, making them very compatible with our skin. Look for great oils such as jojoba oil (fun fact: it's technically a wax), sea buckthorn oil, marula oil, meadowfoam oil, grapeseed oil, blackcurrant seed oil, shea butter, castor oil and argan oil.

Avoid comedogenic oils even if you don't have oily skin. Comedogenic oils can clog your skin even if you have dry or more 'mature' skin (I don't like the word 'older' — sorry).

Occlusives (usually heavier oils and waxes)

Like emollients, occlusives help reduce water loss but they're much heavier and actually form a protective layer on the skin surface to physically block water loss. Occlusives are best applied to dampened skin so there's water on the surface to lock in. Ideal occlusives are hydrogenated (thickened) castor bean oil and non-comedogenic waxes, which are a gentle alternative to petroleum jelly. Be aware, some occlusives (especially those containing comedogenic oils and waxes) are very heavy and greasy and are only recommended for excessively dry, flaky skin. They're often used after clinical treatments, and aren't recommended for oily skin or acne sufferers because some occlusives can trap the oil and bacteria and cause blocked pores and hair follicles.

Examples of occlusives are:

- *petroleum jelly:* I'm not a huge fan of this ingredient. It provides a barrier but offers no cosmeceutical benefit to the skin.

- *thickened castor bean oil:* this is a good one! Castor oil contains built-in anti-inflammatories from ricinoleic acid so it's great for sensitive and irritated skin.

- *lanolin:* pharmaceutical grade lanolin is best because all of the impurities and pesticide residues have been removed. Lanolin allergy is rare, but more common in those with eczema and skin sensitivities. It's often the chemicals that have been sprayed on wool that cause skin irritation or allergy from this ingredient.

- *seed or nut butters:* shea butter is one of the best occlusive butters because it has added anti-inflammatory benefits.

TERRI'S DRY SKIN HOME CARE ROUTINE

Morning

1. Gentle SLS-free cleanser or lotion-based cleanser

2. Prebiotic/probiotic: pre-serum balancer for barrier protection

3. Vitamin B serum: everyone's essential niacinamide (B3) serum

4. Hydrating eye serum: the eyes are one of the first parts of the face to show dryness, especially after a big night out!

5. Rich moisturiser: intense hydrating moisturiser rich in emollients and humectants

6. Crème-based mineral makeup: must offer UV protection, coverage and barrier protection without comedogenic oils or waxes

Evening

1. Gentle SLS-free cleanser or lotion-based cleanser

2. Prebiotic/probiotic: pre-serum balancer for barrier protection

3. Vitamin B serum: everyone's essential niacinamide (B3) serum

4. Vitamin A serum: this will improve new cell production for a healthier and more even barrier. Opt for a gentle, retinol-based serum that won't cause dryness.

5. Eye cream: a richer, more emollient formula is better for night. Avoid occlusives or heavy waxes because they may cause milia, those hard, tiny, white bumps around the eyes.

6. Rich moisturiser: intense hydrating moisturiser rich in emollients and humectants

   or

   Oil moisturiser: for intensely dry skin (must contain non-comedogenic oils that penetrate the skin without being too greasy).

Note: If the skin is flaking and excessively dry, an occlusive moisturiser will be needed at night until the barrier is restored. Apply over vitamin B serum.

Addressing skin dryness

Here are my tips for dealing with dry skin.

1. *Avoid dry interior conditions:* temperature extremes wreak havoc with your skin and constant heating in winter or air conditioning in summer will dry out the skin and emphasise fine lines. If this is unavoidable in your workplace, invest in an air humidifier to prevent your skin from drying out. I have a massive humidifier by my desk all day and it makes a huge difference!

2. *Avoid cold, dry and windy climates:* this can be challenging if you live in a harsh winter climate, but know that these three factors create the perfect environment for dry skin.

3. *Avoid hard water:* high levels of minerals and traces of heavy metals in tap and shower water can lead to skin dryness, and some metals can also cause skin sensitivities and barrier disruption. A home filtration system is a great solution and you can easily screw them into the shower head. Look for shower filters that remove skin irritants such as chlorine (they're also great for preventing blond hair from turning that pretty shade of green 😊).

4. *Cleanse with warm water:* use warm water and avoid hot or cold temperatures.

5. *Apply moisturisers immediately after washing:* your skin is really hydrated immediately after showering, so this is the best time to moisturise and lock in water. That goes for the body as well as the face, so moisturise straight after your shower. Keep in mind that order matters when it comes to your facial routine: cleanser, serum, then moisturiser — in this order — to lock in hydration.

6. *Use topical prebiotics and probiotics:* maintaining a balanced skin microbiome is crucial for skin health, and it's clear that every skin type will benefit from reducing inflammation and improving barrier function. Prebiotic/probiotic combination products are essential for all skin types, but especially for dry skin where the barrier may be broken.

7. *Know your skin type:* there are two types of dryness — lacking oil or lacking water (or both)—and it's important to know what you're dealing

with. If you're unsure of whether your skin is oily dry or water dry, ask your dermatologist for a skin hydration test. Most dryness is caused by dehydration from the environment or lack of water, but as we get older we produce less oil, so unless you have a chronic dry skin condition needing special attention, always use humectants on your skin at every age regardless of skin type, and add more emollient oils as you get older.

8. *Remember the sunscreen:* here I go again about sunscreen…dehydrated, flaking skin is even more susceptible to solar damage, so use a high-quality mineral sunscreen or mineral makeup which contains zinc oxide and iron oxide pigments to protect your delicate skin barrier.

9. *Drink plenty of water:* water hydrates the entire body, and your skin cells are no exception. Good hydration levels are almost as important as oxygen for our cells to function properly! When our cells are hydrated they're plump and firm, and our skin looks luminous with light evenly reflecting off our smooth, hydrated skin surface. Hydrated skin simply appears dewy. It's like comparing the surface of a perfectly round pearl to a rough rock for natural luminosity. I know what I'd rather have my skin compared to!

10. *Avoid irritating ingredients:* these common ingredients can cause excessive moisture loss, barrier breakdown and flaking, so avoid them:

   – toners and other products containing over 5 per cent alcohol
   – SLSs and SLESs (found in many cleansers and body washes)
   – soap with a barrier-stripping alkaline pH
   – artificial fragrance and phthalates
   – harsh preservatives
   – propylene glycol
   – overuse of products with highly acidic pH (AHAs and BHAs). It's okay to exfoliate weekly, but don't be too aggressive.
   – excessive use of harsh scrubs. Again, don't aggravate flaking, sensitive skin — you're just removing the dead stuff to expose fresh, vulnerable skin.

Weekly home treatment

There are some excellent home treatment masks. Opt for ones specifically created for dry skin and leave them on for as long as possible. Overnight masks are excellent, provided the base is not comedogenic.

* * *

Dry skin is a common skin concern that has two common underlying factors — lack of water or lack of oil — and when these happen, the skin barrier loses its ability to hold water. While there is a clear difference between humectants, emollients and occlusives, all three are designed to address skin dryness either on their own or in combination in a formulation.

chapter 25

Cellulite: the facts

Cellulite, aka 'orange peel syndrome', is a curse that plagues so many of us — from teenagers to mature women. It's one of the most common skin conditions, affecting over 90 per cent of us. Cellulite appears as uneven, lumpy and dimpled skin, particularly on the back of the thighs. It affects women of all sizes and isn't dependent on body weight. Cellulite may affect some men but is more common in females, which is thought to be due to hormonal influences and the type of fatty tissue present in female skin.

What is cellulite?

THE BIOLOGY OF CELLULITE

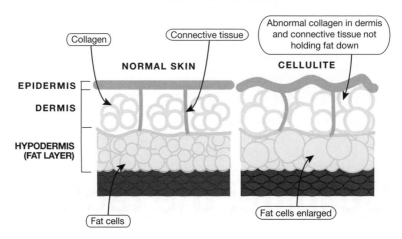

Cellulite is abnormally 'trapped' fatty tissue. When the supportive collagen fibres in the deeper dermis are disorganised, the fatty tissue literally pokes up from the fat layer in between the gaps in the collagen and into the dermis. This is a little bit like the way your inner thigh skin would bulge out from a hole in your stocking, if you compare the stocking to our supportive collagen fibres. Contrary to the common cellulite myth, this condition is not caused by toxins.

What factors influence cellulite?

Several factors can cause cellulite:

- *Hormonal:* studies suggest that oestrogen, insulin and thyroid hormones may play a role in the expression of cellulite by reducing collagen production and therefore the ability of the body to naturally destroy rogue fat cells.

- *Genetics:* some women are predisposed to cellulite, with it being passed from female to female through generations. Cellulite can also be influenced by:
  - race (it's more common in Caucasians than Asians and dark-skinned women)
  - metabolic rate
  - fat distribution in the body
  - having good circulation of blood and the lymphatic system.
- *Lifestyle and lack of exercise:* individuals who are sedentary or smoke are more likely to have cellulite because the connective tissue trapping the fat will not be uniform or function well if you're not healthy and active.
- *Diet:* individuals on diets high in fat, salt, refined carbs and sugar are more likely to have higher grades of cellulite because the fat 'lumps' between the connective tissue are larger.
- *Poor circulation:* lack of adequate blood supply or poor lymphatic drainage can significantly influence the appearance of cellulite.

How can cellulite be treated clinically?

Sorry, I'm just the messenger, but cellulite is an extremely difficult condition to treat effectively. Results are often temporary. A course of treatments is required to visibly reduce the appearance of cellulite, and additional treatments are usually necessary to maintain results. Below is a list of current treatments available, but please consult your skin specialist:

- endermology
- radiofrequency (RF)

- ultrasound

- laser

- deep tissue massage

- vibrational training to improve vascular and lymphatic drainage and help break down connective tissue — this actually improved the cellulite I had on my thighs!

Cosmeceutical ingredients for treating cellulite

The big issue with topicals for cellulite is getting them to the target cells, which are in the dermis and deep fat layer beneath it. My experience shows that the following cosmeceuticals may help treat cellulite and reduce its appearance. However, cosmeceuticals aren't a permanent solution to cellulite and they often need to be combined with clinical treatments for optimal results.

1 Vitamin A

This 'queen of cosmeceuticals' doesn't directly act on the fat cells, but thickens the dermis by stimulating collagen. When the mattress (collagen support) is thicker, the lumps (cellulite) don't poke out so much.

2 Caffeine

This often-criticised ingredient may be a cellulite-fighting hero. Caffeine has been shown to:

- reduce the activity of the enzyme phosphodiesterase, which increases fat production and storage in the body

- increase the release of sodium from fat cells, causing the cells to reduce in size

- reduce cell damage from environmental toxins because of its antioxidant ability

- enhance blood circulation and the ability to remove excess fluid and fat cell remnants from the skin.

The challenge, of course, is to get the caffeine molecules to the very deep layers of the skin. There are some treatments that can optimise delivery of this ingredient to the fat layer. These include sonophoresis, skin needling and directly injecting caffeine solution into the fat layer with mesotherapy. Unfortunately, simply rubbing caffeine scrubs into your thighs simply won't cut it. The massaging may temporarily make your cellulite appear smoother but this certainly isn't the miracle cure many companies tout it to be.

*   *   *

Unfortunately, cellulite is a complex and challenging condition to treat because there are so many things going on in the blood, skin and fat layer that cause it. The bad news is that there's no magical cure for cellulite, but the good news is that it can be reduced using effective clinical treatments combined with effective cosmeceutical ingredients.

chapter 26

Stretch marks

It's taken me a long time to become more comfortable with my body. Today I look back on my old bikini photos and yearn to have the body of that young girl in her early twenties! I'm certainly not comfortable to parade around in a bikini today, but the confidence I have now in my whole self is worth so much more than the confidence I had back when my tummy was flat and stretch-mark free.

I admit, I did everything during my pregnancy to prevent stretch marks. I rubbed oil into my tummy daily, but only three weeks before my son James was born my tummy started to itch and long, red strips started appearing. The stretch marks arrived and I was powerless to stop their progression.

After James was born I totally forgot about them. Hell, I was far too busy looking after this precious new life and just trying to fit in a shower every morning! But as I settled into the new rhythm of motherhood, I looked in the bathroom mirror every morning and saw a flesh-coloured road map on my tummy! I became fixated on getting rid of those unsightly stretch marks so I could proudly wear my bikini to our family beach holiday in Merimbula. After months of massage, oils, creams, chemical peels, scrubs — you name it — my dreams were shattered. Alas, the stretch marks were unchanged. All that remained was a bathroom cabinet full of promises in jars!

But as the years progressed those stretch marks turned from angry red slashes to silvery white ribbons and I realised they were and always will be a part of me. Stretch marks are my medal of motherhood. They remind me of the two miracles I produced, and while I'll never be a pina colada-sipping beach babe hanging out with hot 20-something-year-old cuties any more, I wouldn't swap my life now for anything!

I'm telling you this because I need you to know that I'll always be honest with you about what I can and can't do with skincare in today's cosmeceutical environment. There's no magic bullet for stretch marks, I'm afraid, but while we can never remove them entirely, there are new treatments that can definitely improve their appearance. If you want to reduce the look of your stretch marks, I just ask one thing of you: do it for you, not for your partner. It's all about feeling good in *your* skin, gorgeous lady.

Stretch marks: Q&A

Let's learn some more about stretch marks by answering a few questions.

What are stretch marks?

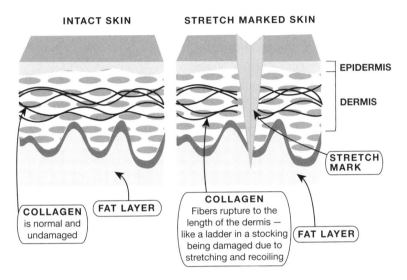

Did you know that a stretch mark is actually a type of scar? I was going to add it to my chapter on scars (chapter 21), but I think it deserves its own chapter because it affects over 50 per cent of us and has such an impact on our body confidence.

Stretch marks occur when the skin stretches and recoils too fast and a deep type of dermal 'injury' results. The rapid stretching causes inflammation with the collagen and elastin and creates a deep tear in the skin, kind of like when a rubber band has been overstretched and won't go back to the way it was.

Compare a stretch mark to a ladder in a stocking: the ladder is the stretch mark where the fibres of the stocking have been pulled abnormally. In the skin, this is the ripping of the collagen and elastin fibres in the dermis, and once this rip occurs it's very difficult to repair.

What causes stretch marks?

Changes in hormone levels during growth spurts in puberty and pregnancy pose a higher risk of developing stretch marks, and they can also develop with rapid weight loss or gain, or if you begin an intense exercise regimen with weights that causes a sudden change in body size. Also, oral or topical corticosteroids can cause stretch marks because they interfere with the collagen and elastin network in the deeper dermis. Plus there's a genetic component to stretch marks — you're more likely to get them if your mum had them.

What do they look like?

Stretch marks initially feel itchy and are red, purple or pink in colour. They can also feel slightly raised. Over time, the stretch marks fade to a silvery white and they may become slightly sunken into the skin.

Can stretch marks be prevented?

If you're genetically predisposed to stretch marks there's very little you can do to prevent them. I tell you this from firsthand experience! Natural oils, even if you massage twice daily, unfortunately don't prevent or reduce stretch marks.

Can you completely remove stretch marks?

The short answer is no, and believe me I've done my research. Like the dreaded cellulite, you can reduce their appearance but you can't remove them completely. Following are some of the most popular clinical treatments for stretch marks. Some have mixed results but there are others that are really making a difference.

- *Chemical peels:* These need to be medium to deep level peels to cause a retexturing of the skin surface. Phenol or TCA peels are the most popular peels for stretch marks because they can penetrate more deeply than AHA or BHA peels. This treatment can be extremely uncomfortable, especially if performed on a large area of the body like the stomach. The results are not significant (I've tried it!), and it's a less desirable option for extensive stretch marks.

- *Fractional laser and fractional radiofrequency:*
  - *Fractional laser* uses deep laser columns to reawaken collagen production. This will eventually make the stretch mark thinner as the new collagen plumps up the fibres around the ripped collagen of the stretch mark. What remains should be finer, silver, thread-like marks. Generally six to eight treatments are needed.
  - *Fractional radiofrequency* uses a grid of fine needles that penetrate the skin using heat generated from radiofrequency energy. This treatment will produce similar results to fractional laser, but the type of energy to create the wound is different. These 'microwounds' encourage new collagen and healing occurs in less than a fortnight. Six to eight treatments are needed for best results.
- *Skin needling (Collagen Induction Therapy/CIT):* This treatment uses fine surgical-grade needles to pierce the skin to the dermis (where the stretch mark is centred). The needles trick the skin into thinking it's had a massive injury when in fact it has only had hundreds of pin pricks. The natural response of the body is to set up a collagen-making factory which makes the stretch marks look finer, thinner and lighter in appearance. Up to eight monthly treatments are needed and optimal results will be achieved after a year. This is my recommendation for stretch mark reduction treatment due to the higher safety profile and lower discomfort.
- *Dermabrasion:* This treatment should not be confused with microdermabrasion. Microdermabrasion is an exfoliation treatment and is not designed to exfoliate deeper than the epidermis. Dermabrasion is a medical-grade treatment that removes the entire epidermis to set up a healing response and new collagen production. This is an extremely aggressive and uncomfortable treatment, and recovery time is much longer than with needling or fractional laser.

My vote goes to fractional radiofrequency, needling and fractional laser. These treatments offer the best long-term results with the least down time and highest safety profile. Again, I want to remind you to have realistic expectations here. Your stretch marks will fade and become thinner with time, but they will never totally disappear. But I'm confident that that technology is still ahead!

Can skincare help at all?

Topical skincare may help reduce the appearance of stretch marks, but there's a catch — they must be treated early for best results. The best time to start is as soon as you first notice them, and you need to be vigilant and apply topical treatments twice daily for at least three months. I recommend you try a home needling device, or other home devices such as cold plasma or sonophoresis, which are proven to increase the penetration of active ingredients when you're applying your topical treatments morning and night.

Topical ingredients that can help are:

- *L-ascorbic acid (vitamin C):* L-ascorbic acid is able to improve the appearance of new stretch marks by increasing collagen production and reducing collagen breakdown around the affected area. A clinical study showed a significant reduction in the width of stretch marks and a lightening of the red colour after skin needling (CIT), with topical L-ascorbic acid applied simultaneously.

- *vitamin A:* prescription retinoic acid or stronger non-prescription derivatives like HPR and retinol are good ways to apply vitamin A to your stretch marks. Apply to early stretch marks and try and incorporate them with clinical treatments like skin needling to really drive the cosmeceutical to the damaged collagen. Our aim here is to create new collagen and 'put the stuffing back in that mattress' because it's impossible to repair the ruptured collagen that makes up a stretch mark.

(A note for pregnant women) ——————————

Don't use vitamin A on stretch marks. We know that taking vitamin A tablets in large doses can be harmful for the developing foetus, and even though there's no direct evidence that topical vitamin A (in skincare) can harm the unborn baby (because there's been no testing performed on pregnant women), as a scientist I always err on the side of caution.

Yes, my stretch marks used to affect my body confidence but now I wear them with pride, content with the constant reminder of how amazing my body is at growing two wonderful humans and bringing them both safely into the world!

chapter 27

Hormonal changes: smart choices for pregnancy and menopause

Pregnancy, breastfeeding and menopause represent significant fork-in-the-road moments for us gals when it comes to hormonal changes, and these changes require us to look more closely at our choices of skincare ingredients and lifestyle.

Pregnancy

My most popular FAQs are about safe skincare during pregnancy. Because you're ultimately responsible for the safety of your imminent bundle of love, this is the time when the quality of the products you use on your face and body is more important than ever.

A few members of my team are currently 'blooming' with new life and they're concerned about ingredients they're passing on to their unborn baby. My general manager recently asked me to decode a baby wash she bought online that was touted to be gentle on baby's skin with added 'organic' ingredients, and when I dived into the ingredient list I discovered the presence of phenoxyethanol, a potentially irritating preservative.

The skin is a highly absorbent surface — remember, the average woman absorbs more than *2 kilograms* of questionable and potentially toxic ingredients through her skin *each year*. It's therefore essential to cut through the media myths and understand the truth behind safe skincare during pregnancy.

If it's not safe for a non-pregnant woman, it's not safe for a pregnant one. Many studies have been performed on various skincare ingredients that may be potentially harmful if applied in large enough doses, and while I don't want to incite panic and fear, I personally choose to *not* formulate with them. Refer to my list of questionable ingredients on page 97.

On the other hand, it's important to note that while many ingredients aren't recommended during pregnancy, this is often a purely precautionary measure because many women are more sensitive to skin irritation during pregnancy, so it's wise to avoid ingredients that may be potentially irritating or drying such as alcohol-based and highly perfumed products.

As a cosmetic scientist I'm not ethically permitted to test ingredients on the skin of pregnant women — and rightfully so! Many of the findings and recommendations of ingredients which are safe during pregnancy are based on anecdotal evidence, assumption and animal studies (animal testing for cosmetics and skincare is now thankfully banned in many countries, including Australia). When manufacturing products for mums to be, I always err on the side of caution.

What to avoid if you're pregnant

Let's dive into what you need to avoid when pregnant.

Phthalates

Phthalates are solvents and fragrance additives, and they're often not listed on labels because in many countries companies are only required to list 'fragrance' or 'parfum' and not the individual constituents of the fragrance. I'm so sorry, but this ingredient is hard to avoid if it's not even listed! Overall, try to avoid products with 'fragrance' or 'parfum' because these are almost always artificial fragrances.

Phthalates are added to artificial fragrances to make the scent last longer, and also to hairsprays to make the hair bouncier and less 'stiff'. Formulators using essential oils instead of artificial fragrance are less likely to add phthalates to their products. There have been findings that excess exposure to phthalates during pregnancy may contribute to male infertility and ADHD in children.

Retinoids (vitamin A derivatives)

Because I always proceed with caution when formulating for pregnant ladies, I recommend putting a hold on using products containing vitamin A. Retinoids are one of the most popular active ingredient categories and are known for regulating cell renewal and oil flow, addressing visible ageing and reducing sun damage. However, some scientific studies have concluded that high doses of vitamin A taken orally (not topically) during pregnancy can be harmful to an unborn child. There's no data to suggest that these ingredients used on the skin during pregnancy are harmful, so please *don't* panic if you discover you're pregnant and you've been using retinoid-based skincare. This is simply a precaution because no tests have been performed using topical retinoids on pregnant women.

Here are some commonly used vitamin A ingredients:

- Medical (prescription only) retinoids:
  - Differin/Adapalene
  - Retin-A/Renova/tretinoin (medical prescription only)
  - Tazorac/tazarotene (medical prescription only)
  - Retinoic acid (medical prescription only)
- Non-prescription retinoids:
  - Retinol
  - Hydroxypinacolone retinoate (HPR, the most powerful non-prescription retinoid if in a stabilised form)
  - Retinyl palmitate
  - Retinaldehyde.

High levels of certain essential oils

Essential oils are extremely powerful botanical concentrates that have been used in traditional medicine for thousands of years. Despite being natural and often therapeutic, these oils must be treated with respect and it's best to avoid using high levels of essential oils over large areas of the body during pregnancy.

I always ensure I formulate with low concentrations of essential oils to enable pregnant women to safely use them. For facial skincare products it's considered safe to apply low concentrations (less than 0.3 per cent) in leave-on and rinse-off products. Whether pregnant or not, you should never apply undiluted essential oils directly to the skin.

For information on essential oils that are and aren't safe to use during pregnancy, see appendix D.

BHAs and AHAs are safe

Many pregnant women believe they can't use BHAs during pregnancy, but this is a myth that's been disproven. Salicylic acid is an exfoliating BHA and is excellent for unblocking pores in acne and addressing skin redness and inflammation. There's currently no evidence to suggest that products containing salicylic acid applied topically can harm a developing foetus. Any concerns with salicylic acid during pregnancy are based on high-dose oral ingestion of the drug aspirin, and the use of topical salicylic wouldn't translate to high levels in the bloodstream. In addition, even aspirin taken internally is considered safe at low doses, and is prescribed to help prevent pre-eclampsia.

It is, therefore, safe to use salicylic products on the skin during pregnancy and breastfeeding. However, if an individual is allergic to salicylates (aspirin) they're advised *not* to use skin products containing salicylic acid, whether pregnant or not.

AHAs such as lactic, malic and mandelic acids are perfectly safe during pregnancy.

While using home care with AHA and BHA acids is considered safe, it's wise to avoid deep chemical peels because the acids used in clinical treatments are delivered deeper into the skin.

Soy, melasma and pregnancy

Soy is an oestrogenic ingredient that can influence female hormonal levels. Though soy is not dangerous to the unborn child, if you're prone to melasma (large, dark pigmented patches on the face) or experience it during pregnancy (which is common), soy products may worsen it and should be avoided.

It's therefore wise to avoid:

- soy-based skincare

- textured vegetable protein

- lecithin.

Mineral makeup and pregnancy

The ideal makeup for mums-to-be is quality mineral makeup. Choose brands which are free of artificial colours, bismuth and parabens. The natural zinc oxide and iron oxide pigments will act as a broad spectrum (UVA and UVB), blue light and IR sun protector, which is essential during pregnancy (particularly if you're prone to melasma).

Minerals sit on top of the skin and don't contain ingredients that penetrate the dermis or enter the bloodstream, which is why they're not potentially damaging to cells.

Sunscreen and pregnancy

There's some concern regarding chemical sunscreens being absorbed into the skin of pregnant women, as tests have shown these chemicals are present in the bloodstream a few hours following application. Furthermore, many chemical sunscreens have been shown to produce irritant skin reactions, which isn't good news because pregnant women often exhibit higher levels of skin sensitivity.

It's therefore wise to opt for zinc oxide, titanium dioxide and iron oxide (mineral) sunscreens, which protect from UVA, UVB, infrared and blue-light rays. Apply this daily.

Common chemical-absorbing ingredients to watch out for in sunscreens are:

- Dioxybenzone

- Octyl benzophenone

- Para-aminobenzoic acid/PABA (this has been banned in many sunscreens due to irritation)

- Octocrylene

- Oxybenzone

- Avobenzone/Parsol

- Octyl methoxycinnamate (OMC).

Your skin is often more vulnerable during pregnancy and it requires nurturing, hydration and sun protection. Naturally derived oils, vitamin B, vitamin C, lactic acid and hyaluronic acid are all recommended to replenish and renew your skin during pregnancy. There are many excellent products available for pregnant women — just avoid ingredients that are 'questionable' and use natural mineral-based sunscreens. Most importantly, relax and enjoy this magical period of your life!

Breastfeeding

As a rule of thumb, if you avoid something during pregnancy you should avoid it during breastfeeding. This is because many of the ingredients absorbed into Mum's bloodstream end up in her breast milk.

Also be aware of the body lotion and fragrance you're using because this may come into contact with your baby's delicate skin while feeding.

Pregnancy and breastfeeding is a special time for you and your baby, and you don't need to neglect your skincare routine — simply be more aware of the ingredients you're applying and the ability for them to penetrate your skin.

Menopause

Menopause is officially marked as one year after your final period and can happen from your mid-forties to your mid-fifties. The period before menopause (perimenopause) can last for months to years, and perimenopause may be accompanied by symptoms such as irregular periods, hot flushes, mood swings and significant skin changes. Your skin goes through some gradual but dramatic changes during menopause because of the significant dip in your oestrogen, progesterone and even testosterone levels.

Many women opt for hormone replacement therapy to reduce the symptoms of menopause and the changes in their skin. This can be controversial because of the link to breast cancer, but it's a personal choice and should be considered with your trusted physician. Bioidentical hormone replacement therapy (BHRT) is considered a safer option than traditional hormone replacement because BHRT is chemically identical to human female hormones. Despite 'natural' claims, BHRT can be synthetically created. If you're experiencing severe menopausal symptoms, I suggest you discuss options with a medical specialist such as an endocrinologist.

So, what changes actually happen to our skin during menopause, and what can we do to address them?

Addressing menopausal changes

Just when we're thinking 'yay ... no more periods or having to worry about contraception!', mother nature gets us back with menopausal acne, and telltale signs of accelerated ageing. Change is inevitable, but there are ways to address this type of ageing related to hormonal changes.

Collagen loss

Oestrogen decline causes a significant decline in collagen, which leads to more fine lines and wrinkles. Women lose up to 30 per cent of their collagen in the first five years of menopause and then 2 per cent every year thereafter, so we need to protect our precious collagen reserves and stimulate our fibroblast cells to make more.

What can be done?

You need to increase your use of ingredients that work on collagen production and collagen protection. These include retinoids (vitamin A), vitamin B, vitamin C, specific collagen-stimulating peptides and collagen-protecting broad spectrum sunscreen, particularly mineral sunscreen and mineral makeup, which protect from UVA, UVB and infrared light. Refer to my section on anti-ageing skincare (on page 197) to read about ingredients for counteracting collagen loss.

Sagging skin and jowls

This is partly due to collagen loss and partly to bone loss, which occurs more rapidly after menopause. Bone loss makes our entire skull smaller so our face begins to lose volume (think of a slightly deflated balloon).

What can be done?

Unfortunately, there are no skincare ingredients that can significantly increase the volume of the face to counteract bone loss. The best option for adding volume is injecting dermal fillers. In terms of skin tightening, I'd suggest fractional laser, skin needling or radiofrequency clinical

(continued)

treatments, which can tighten the skin and reduce the appearance of sagging over a period of months. These treatments should only be performed by qualified skin specialists and are best coupled with collagen-stimulating cosmeceuticals.

Menopausal acne

This is so unfair. You'd think that by now you've kissed acne well and truly goodbye, but unfortunately this isn't always the case. The fluctuations and dips in hormones can lead to acne blemishes, particularly around the jawline.

What can be done?

Menopausal skin is much drier and thinner than adolescent skin so the treatment should be gentle. Stay away from drying ingredients like benzoyl peroxide. Low-level salicylic acid peels (around 5 per cent) performed in a clinic will help to unblock pores and reduce acne inflammation, and a home exfoliant with salicylic acid, lactic acid and mandelic acid is recommended on alternate days. Vitamin B3 and vitamin A serums are also excellent for balancing excess oil.

Redness

The skin can become more reactive and flushing can cause redness in the face, so look for ingredients that target facial redness.

What can be done?

I love sea buckthorn oil, and there are some great peptides that target redness, such as acetyl tetrapeptide-40. In terms of lifestyle, it's best to reduce alcohol consumption and avoid overheating and spicy foods, which may make the flushing and redness worse.

Increase in facial and body hair

The changes in testosterone and oestrogen can lead to increased hormonal hair growth.

What can be done?

This can be addressed with IPL treatments (provided the hair is dark enough — not grey or blonde) and electrolysis treatments.

Increased skin sensitivity

During menopause our skin pH shifts from the sweet spot of pH 5.6 and becomes slightly more alkaline, which makes our barrier more prone to skin sensitivity because there are lower levels of natural skin lipids (ceramides) and the bacterial balance on the surface is out of whack.

What can be done?

It's vital to keep the skin barrier strong, and this means using vitamin B3 serum along with emollient moisturisers to lock in the hydration. Stay away from potential irritants, especially artificial fragrance and products that are drying or high in alcohol.

Uneven skin tone

This is the time when our precious melanocytes (those cells that make our melanin pigment) aren't working as efficiently as they once did. You may notice you're getting more sun damage on your hands, chest, face and other sun-exposed areas.

What can be done?

Stay out of the sun, cover up and use a high-quality mineral-based sunscreen. Do have a little sunlight in the early morning or late afternoon though so you get your vital vitamin D!

Cosmeceuticals such as vitamin B, vitamin A and certain peptides are excellent at addressing pigmentation and uneven skin tone (see my section on hyperpigmentation on page 215).

Lifestyle

If you lead a healthy lifestyle and apply pre-emptive strategies to reduce the symptoms, menopause can be much easier to deal with. Trust me, I've been there. ☺

These lifestyle choices include:

- regular exercise (including weight bearing) to maintain bone density and to optimise your insulin levels

- increasing your levels of macronutrients (naturally or via quality supplements) and avoiding processed foods

- ensuring your vitamin D levels are sufficient: don't avoid sunlight entirely and take supplements if your levels are low

- keeping up your good oils and ensuring you're having omega fatty acids in the right ratio.

*   *   *

Being a woman is truly wonderful. Let's celebrate all these wonderful stages of life but still focus on looking and feeling our best at any age.

For my part, I feel I now have a new zest for living. Life has shown me a kaleidoscope of highs and lows: all have given me the gift of learning valuable life lessons. But in the second half of my life, I'm in a fantastic place: my work is still fulfilling and challenging, I enjoy my relationship with my adult kids and my life partner, and I truly feel I'm doing what I was put on this earth to do: to help make you feel amazing in your skin.

Now it's over to you ☺

Appendix A

What are the most popular ingredients found in serums?

The list of active ingredients found in serums is growing as fast as the beauty industry. Peptide technology and biotechnology are certainly a growing trend for active ingredients, but the tried and tested cosmeceuticals still stand the test of time.

Here's a list of ingredients recommended for specific skin types that you may find in serums. I've only mentioned a few as the list is exhaustive! But remember, stability and correct dosage are critical.

Fine-line reduction:

- Vitamin A

    - stabilised retinol

    - hydroxypinacolone retinoate

    - retinoic acid

- Niacinamide (vitamin B3)

- Vitamin C

  - L-ascorbic acid

  - ethyl ascorbic acid

- Collagen-stimulating peptides — there are too many to list them all, but some examples include:

  - acetyl octapeptide-3

  - acetyl hexapetide-51 amide

- Marine exopolysaccharides

Congested, acne-prone skin:

- AHAs

  - lactic acid

  - malic acid

  - mandelic acid

- BHAs

  - salicylic acid

- Vitamin A

- Niacinamide

Pigmented, sun-damaged skin:

- Vitamin A
- Vitamin B3
- Vitamin C
- Saccharide isomerate (marine ingredient)
- Oligopeptide-34 (this is a great peptide for hyperpigmentation!)
- Dipotassium glycyrrhizinate (from liquorice)
- Tranexamic acid

Dehydrated, dry skin:

- Hyaluronic acid
- Betaine
- Glycerin
- Sodium PCA
- Sodium lactate

Appendix B

'Moisturiser-off'

I've created two imaginary moisturisers and listed the ingredients as you would most likely find them on a typical label (overleaf).

Both of these products are very basic and don't contain active ingredients. To keep things really simple, both products contain only the basic ingredients so you can draw your own comparison.

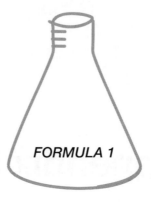

FORMULA 1

Formula 1 is a moisturiser that I would never create in my lab due to my 'clean science' philosophy.

Formula 1 ingredient list

- water
- propylene glycol (hydrator humectant, penetration enhancer)
- mineral oil (emollient)
- dimethicone (emollient)
- cetearyl alcohol (emulsifier and thickener — this ingredient is fine but is often combined with other less desirable emulsifiers)
- ceteareth-20 (emulsifier)
- PEG-100 stearate (emulsifier)
- methylparaben (preservative)
- imidazolidinyl urea (preservative)
- propylparaben (preservative)
- tocopherol acetate/vitamin E (antioxidant to stop oils going rancid — this ingredient is fine as there are virtually no questionable antioxidants that I'm aware of)
- fragrance (this will be artificial)
- diethyl phthalate
- D&C RED #40 (FD&C artificial colour)

FORMULA 2

Formula 2 is a much 'cleaner' formula, and I'd be happy to add active ingredients to this basic formula.

Formula 2 ingredient list

- water
- glycerin (solubiliser/humectant hydrator)
- carbomer (thickener)
- caprylic/capric triglyceride (emollient)
- jojoba oil (emollient)
- macadamia oil (emollient)
- glyceryl stearate (emulsifier)
- cetearyl alcohol (emulsifier)
- sodium stearoyl lactate (emulsifier)
- tocopherol acetate (vitamin E — antioxidant to stop oil rancidity)
- lavandula angustifolia (lavender) oil (natural essential oil scent)
- caprylyl glycol (preservative)
- phenyl propanol (preservative)
- methylpropanediol (preservative)
- red iron oxide (mineral colour)

Appendix C

Terri's 'great skin' recipes

GREEN DETOX SMOOTHIE

This recipe is full of antioxidants, avocado oil and nature's skin builder: chlorophyll. This green detox smoothie will help you glow in a few days and because it's very low in fruit sugar it's great for congested skin.

Ingredients:

- 2 handfuls baby spinach (don't be talked into using kale — yuck! In my opinion it's not the superfood it's cracked up to be)
- ¼ avocado
- ½ cup green honeydew melon
- ½ Lebanese cucumber
- Juice of 1 large lemon
- ¼ small knob of ginger (thumbnail size)
- ½ tsp chlorella
- 1 sachet Natvia for added sweetness (available at major supermarkets)
- 5 ice cubes
- Water for texture

Method:

Add ingredients in order to a large Nutribullet or Ninja cup. Pulverise on maximum speed for 45 seconds or until all ingredients are homogenised. Enjoy!

GREAT SKIN SALAD DRESSING

The ingredients in this salad dressing are great for general health, and specifically for reducing inflammation and body acid levels. Plus, we all know that flaxseed oil is great for providing vital omega fatty acids.

Ensure you use this dressing within a week as it's best eaten fresh. Enjoy!

Ingredients:

- 100 mL flaxseed oil (Melrose Organic is a good brand — look in the fridge at the health food store)
- 50 mL extra virgin olive oil
- 50 mL grapeseed oil
- 70 mL freshly squeezed lemon juice (or apple cider vinegar)
- 1 heaped tbsp wholegrain mustard
- 1 clove garlic (crushed)
- 1 sachet Natvia natural sweetener (available at major supermarkets)
- dash of pepper

Method:

Combine all ingredients in a jar. Put the lid on and shake well. Keep refrigerated. To use, drizzle liberally on salad or steamed vegetables. I recommend 2–3 tablespoons a day.

Hint: Add fresh superfood ginger and turmeric for some added spice!

TERRI'S MEGA-HEALTHY SEED AND NUT LOAF

I invested in a Panasonic bread maker (I have model SD 2501) a while ago so I could make healthy bread alternatives without the harmful additives. I've been perfecting my nut loaf ever since, and due to the influx of requests I'm excited to finally share the recipe with you. It's filling, tasty and best of all there are absolutely no nasty preservatives — just clean science! It's the perfect treat when hosting friends and family. I love to whip it up right before they arrive because it leaves the house smelling sensational. Enjoy!

Ingredients:

- 1¼ tsp dry yeast
- 500 g whole wheat bread flour
- 2 tbsp chia seeds
- 1¼ tsp salt
- 2 tbsp skim milk powder (can use coconut milk powder)
- 2 tbsp coconut oil
- 1 tsp Natvia natural sweetener (eryth/stevia mix)
- ¼ tsp bread improver

- 360 mL lukewarm water
- Seeds:
  - ¼ cup pepitas
  - ¼ cup sunflower seeds
  - 1 tbsp chia seeds
- Nuts:
  - ¼ cup activated almonds
  - ¼ cup organic walnuts

Method:

1 For a large loaf add all the ingredients except for the nuts in order to the bread pan.

2 Set bread machine to the following:

- Rapid bake setting (Menu 02 on the Panasonic machine): approximately 2-hour bake
- Large loaf setting
- Medium or dark colour setting (depending on preference)

3 Start the bread machine and set the timer to 16 minutes.

4 At 16 minutes into the breadmaking cycle, open the lid and add the nuts (this enables the nuts to cook whole in the loaf without crushing).

5 Close the lid and allow the cycle to complete for the remaining time.

6 When the cycle is complete, remove the loaf after a couple of hours leaving it in the warm machine. This makes slicing easier.

7 Serve with a cheese platter, some fresh ricotta and raspberry chia seed jam or avocado and Vegemite — yum! Store in an airtight container and eat within 24 hours (no yucky preservatives here so eat it fast!) or slice up to freeze in individual snap-lock bags.

Enjoy!

SUGAR-FREE COCONUT CACAO BALLS

Ingredients:

- 110 g mixed raw seeds and nuts (pepitas, sunflower seeds, almonds)
- 110 g pitted organic dates
- 45 g organic coconut oil
- 30 g raw organic cacao powder
- 1 tbsp chia seeds
- 55 g desiccated coconut

Method:

1 Place nuts and seeds into a high-speed mixer until pulverised (a Thermomix or Vitamix is ideal).

2 Place all other ingredients (only 35 g of desiccated coconut) into the mixer on high speed until evenly blended.

3 Scrape sides and mix further until mixture comes together.

4 Roll into bite-sized balls and cover in remaining 20 g of desiccated coconut.

5 Refrigerate and serve.

VEGETARIAN ROASTED VEGGIE AND QUORN LASAGNE

Ingredients:

- 1 300 g packet of **Quorn mince** (This is the closest mince meat substitute I have found. It's really high in protein and it's made from a type of fungus called mycoprotein. It also makes a great vego version of spag bol!)
- 1 eggplant (cut into 2 cm slices)
- 2 zucchinis (thickly cut lengthwise)
- 10 medium mushrooms (halved)
- 1 large sweet potato (thickly sliced)
- 250 g baby spinach leaves
- 750 mL organic tomato passata sauce (thick variety if possible)
- 1 clove garlic
- 1 tsp Natvia
- 1 vegetable stock cube (low salt)
- 10 medium wholemeal lasagne sheets
- 200 g smooth ricotta cheese
- 100 g smooth cottage cheese
- Milk (enough to make the ricotta/cottage mixture into a thick sauce consistency)
- 1 tsp dried chives
- 1 tbsp extra virgin olive oil
- Himalayan pink salt

Method:

1 Lightly brush veggies with olive oil and a little Himalayan salt.

2 Line a large sandwich press with baking paper and roast the veggies in batches between the paper. This is a fast, no mess way to get that yummy roast veg flavour. Set aside the veggies.

3 Sauté garlic in a large saucepan with extra virgin olive oil.

4 **Add Quorn, Natvia, stock cube, spinach leaves and tomato passata and simmer for 10 minutes.** Allow the sauce to thicken and reduce slightly so it's not too runny.

5 **Mix ricotta and cottage cheese and chives with a little milk until smooth and the consistency of thick yoghurt.**

6 **Brush olive oil over a large, deep loaf pan.**

7 **Assemble the lasagne: start with Quorn sauce followed by lasagne sheets and veggies and alternate, finishing with ricotta/cottage cheese sauce on top.**

8 **Cover top with foil and bake at 180° Celsius for 35 minutes.**

9 **Remove foil and allow cheese sauce (ricotta/cottage/milk mixture) to slightly brown under the grill.**

Serve with salad and 'Great Skin' salad dressing.

Appendix D

Essential oils and pregnancy

Essential oils that can be used safely—in low concentrations (<0.3 per cent)—during pregnancy include:

- Cypress
- Eucalyptus
- Geranium
- German chamomile
- Lavender
- Manuka
- Neroli
- Orange

- Patchouli
- Peppermint
- Rose
- Rosemary
- Rose Geranium
- Sandalwood
- Tea tree
- Ylang Ylang

Avoid the following essential oils during pregnancy:

- Bitter almond
- Angelica
- Aniseed
- Basil
- Black pepper
- Camphor
- Cedarwood
- Cinnamon
- Clary sage
- Clove
- Fennel
- Ginger
- Horseradish
- Hyssop
- Jasmine
- Juniper
- Lemon
- Marjoram
- Melissa
- Mugwort
- Myrrh
- Nutmeg
- Oregano
- Pennyroyal
- Pine
- Sage
- Stinging nettle
- Tansy
- Thyme
- Wintergreen
- Wormwood

Index

formaldehyde 97, 153

FOXO3A 210

fractional laser treatment *see* laser treatment

fragrance 44, 52, 55, 70, 102–103, 119, 129, 264, 269, 276, 281, 292, 294, 299, 317, 322, 325

free radicals *see also* antioxidants
— damage by 28, 30, 38, 39, 88, 89, 146, 152–153, 202, 205–206
— dealing with 90
— definition 89

frown lines *see* wrinkles

function of skin 3–11; *see also* acid mantle; barrier, skin

GAGs (glycosaminoglycans) 9–10

garlic 138, 182

genes and skincare 171–184
— epigenetics 171–175, 198

genetic (DNA) repair and ageing 197, 198, 209–210, 303

ginger 138, 162, 243

glitter 166, 169

gluten intolerance 263

glycation 31, 129, 132, 135, 148, 201–202

glycolic acid 27, 32, 60, 61, 62, 181, 218, 238

glycotoxins 135

grapeseed oil 86, 87, 295

green tea and green tea extract 40, 90, 91, 103, 110, 129, 134, 138, 159, 160, 202, 207, 243

growth factors in skincare 177–179

hair products 44, 147, 232, 239, 240, 269

healing and repair of skin 141, 177, 247, 256–257, 258, 277, 284, 297, 311; *see also* barrier, skin; scarring; wounds, skin

healthy skin 145–153

Healthy Skin Diet, The (Fisher) 267

HGH (human growth hormone) 132

hormonal changes 44, 102, 221, 237, 240, 249, 301, 302–303, 316; *see also* steroids
— acne 227, 228
— breastfeeding 191, 321–322
— menopause 191, 322–326
— pregnancy 191, 316–321

humectants 103–104, 293, 294–295, 297, 299, 300

hyaluronic acid (HA) 80–83, 214, 255
— function 81–83
— loss 121, 213
— use 82–83, 103, 294, 321

hydration 103, 218; *see also* dehydration; dry skin and dryness
— facial 116, 118, 119, 120, 191, 205, 224, 239, 321, 325
— internal 116, 118, 128

hydroquinone 220, 221

hyperpigmentation *see also* melanin; melanocytes; melisma; pigmentation
— causes 39, 63, 211–212
— management 40, 140
— post-inflammatory (PIH) 63, 215, 220–221, 250, 255, 257
— sunspots (age spots) 21, 215, 216–220
— treatment 22, 26, 60, 63, 140, 211, 215

hypoallergenic 97–98, 263, 283

immune system 14, 26, 150, 151, 182, 183, 201, 206, 271, 272, 279, 285

infections, skin 5, 26, 96, 151, 220, 233, 235–237, 240, 247, 249, 255, 278, 280, 281, 282, 283, 285